PRAISE FOR

GROWN MAN NOW

●

GROWN MAN NOW IS A POIGNANT AND EXHILARATING STORY of how a family member with special needs strengthened and promoted the human capacity for love in his parents, brothers, and sister.

Grown Man Now is a book for all readers because it is a story about universal human values: love, courage, persistence, resilience, hope, family, and yes, humor. It is a demonstration of how tenacious the human spirit can be when the welfare of a family member is at stake and of how powerful a compensating force nurture can be in combating the unfairness of nature.

Above all, *Grown Man Now* is a story of the difference a mother's unconditional love, a love guided by knowledge and wisdom, made in the life of her special needs child. If only all Down syndrome bearers were so lucky.

It is a beautiful, valuable story, well written, and extraordinarily interesting.

—Gurney Chambers, PhD, Dean Emeritus
College of Education and Allied Professions, Western Carolina University, Cullowhee, NC

WHILE MANY BOOKS ARE AVAILABLE ABOUT THE LIFE STORIES OF CHILDREN, youth, and even young adults with intellectual disabilities, where else but in *Grown Man Now* can we learn about a 50-year life story? Through this compelling family story, we learn from Jane and Billy what we all crave in our personal and family lives—loving family bonds that truly withstand the test of time.

—Ann Turnbull, EdD, Co-Director, Beach Center on Disability,
The University of Kansas, Lawrence, KS

THIS IS A STORY THAT SHOULD BE READ BY ALL PARENTS who want their children to have stable, happy lives, whether their children have disabilities or do not.

The best life for a person with intellectual disabilities is the same as for anyone else: to be loved and supported by family and friends. The family does not have to be super-human, and the friends do not have to be perfect, they all simply need to care. This is the lesson that Jane Schulz teaches us in *Grown Man Now*. Billy was born with Down syndrome, but Jane and her family, with a strong sense of fairness and morality, knew that what would be best for Billy would be the same as for everyone else. Now, with a half a century of experience, the results are as we might expect. Billy's life is full and has meaning. What more could anyone want for their child?

—David L. Westling, Adelaide Worth Daniels Distinguished Professor of Special Education, Department of Human Services, Western Carolina University, Cullowhee NC.

BILLY HAS BEEN STIMULATED TO LIVE TO THE UTMOST OF HIS CAPACITY! It has been a privilege to be a part of his life in person and now to revisit the wonder of his achievements described here in Jane's penetrating, authentic narrative of love, courage, and vision.   —Beverly Jackson, M.D., Family Friend, Sylva, NC

JANE SCHULZ OFFERS MUCH INSIGHT, LOVE AND COMPASSION in this detailed account of how her family welcomed and celebrated a child with a disability, not only from her experiences as a parent, but also as a professional in the field of special education. Like my sister Margaret, Billy's life is an inspiration to everyone who knows him.

—Embry Burrus, author, *Mama and Margaret*
Assistant Clinical Professor, Department of Communication Disorders,
Auburn University, Auburn, AL

Jane B. Schulz, EdD

GROWN MAN NOW

A graduate of Auburn University, Dr. Schulz taught elementary and special education in public schools for five years and at Western Carolina University for more than twenty years. She received a number of awards for teaching and was granted the Distinguished Service Award by the Exceptional Children's Division of the North Carolina Department of Public Instruction.

She is the author of *Parents and Professionals in Special Education,* co-author of *Mainstreaming Exceptional Students* (4 editions), and co-editor of *Bridging the Family-Professional Gap.*

In her writing and presentations, Dr. Schulz's focus is on inclusion, parent-professional collaboration, and celebrating diversity. Her son Billy is frequently her partner in the presentations.

GROWN MAN NOW

For Charlie

Celebrate life!

Jane Schultz
Billy Schultz

GROWN MAN NOW

Jane B. Schulz

™

in2wit™ LLC
Post Office Box 6458
Kingsport TN 37663 USA
info@in2wit.com

ISBN 1-978-1-935095-05-7 (Pbk.)

LIBRARY OF CONGRESS CONTROL NUMBER:
2008928068

in2Wit and colophon are trademarks of in2Wit Publishing, LLC.

Printed in the United States of America

10 9 8 7 6 5 4 3 2 1

For devoted teachers
and
community advocates
who offer hope
and opportunity

Where there is great love there are always miracles.

—Willa Cather

Contents

I AM A LONG-TIME VETERAN IN THE DISABILITY FIELD. Forty seems to be my magic number. My son JT, who experiences significant disabilities is 40 years old, and I have worked in the disability field, primarily at the university level, for 40 years. I have also known Jane and Billy Schulz for that same number—yes, 40 years. During this time, I have read more family stories than I can even count. So I ask myself, why should reading this book surprise me? Didn't I know all about Billy's and Jane's life already? Haven't I read what sometimes seems as if every variation on every family story that presents itself in the disability field? The answer is a resounding "no"! In a nutshell, *Grown Man Now* blew me away!

There were many "ahas", but for me the major ones centered around Billy's incredible positive contributions to his family—especially around the role of care-taking. I was awed by Billy's critical role in his family in lifting the spirits of his grandmother, parents, and siblings, as well as offering real help—especially in the caretaking of his father and grandmother—probably nothing short of truly life-saving for his mother. Many books are available about the life stories of children, youth, and even young adults with intellectual disabilities. Where else can we learn about a 50-year life story? Where else can we gain insight into the family experiences of older adults with disabilities, even those approaching senior citizen years, in terms of the reversals—when the children with disabilities grow up and become the caretakers for their parents and grandparents.

More than anything this powerful book by Jane Schulz, about her amazing son, Billy, reminds me of the infinity symbol. Truly, "what goes around comes around." Through this compelling family story, we learn from Jane and Billy what we all crave in our personal and family lives—loving family bonds that truly withstand the test of time.

The Schulz family—every single one of them—provides keen insights about what it means to be family and how we all, regardless of our different circumstances, have the choice and opportunity to live life to the fullest. In the paraphrased words of William Faulkner, the Schulz family, through their family story of Billy's life, is a testament to the fact that families who confront the unexpected experience of disability can not only survive, but, indeed, prevail.

—Ann Turnbull, EdD, Co-Director, Beach Center on Disability,
The University of Kansas, Lawrence, KS

WITH THE REMOTE CONTROL of the projector, he shows slides of his home, his workplace, his church, and his family: he comments on each picture. The audience alternates between tears and laughter; he knows how to play them—pauses for laughs, times his punch lines.

"This is me at Weight Watchers. An' I loss 30 pounds!"

The audience cheers. Lowering his gaze and his voice, Billy adds:

"An' then I gain it *all back*."

The crowd laughs uproariously, identifying with his struggle.

"An' I got a good life," he says, ending his presentation. The audience stands and applauds.

Hi, I'm Billy. These my slides bout my life and my family.

He smiles broadly, making his way toward me. "How I do?" he asks, seeking my approval. As he envelops me in his huge hug, I reply, "You did a great job. I'm so proud of you!"

I watched my son, a grown man now, as he told his story with poise and confidence. I scanned the audience for their reactions. With his distinctive appearance and unique language, he commanded the attention of hundreds of parents, teachers, and other professionals.

During his presentation I drifted back to the delayed diagnosis of Down syndrome, when I had anxiously wondered what his future would be, remembering the uncertainty, the struggles in rearing Billy and the times I had said from the depths of my despair, "I can't do this!" Now, observing him and his poise, I thought "Who would have dreamed that we could be in this place, speaking to all these people?"

Many times, I hadn't known what to do *with* Billy; now, at this point in my life, I would be lost *without* him. Regardless of my frame of mind, I am uplifted and energized by his morning greeting: the ritual begins with his exuberant "Happy Tuesday!" He hugs me, checks out my grubby workout sweats, and sincerely declares, "You are so pretty, Mom."

Billy is a man of influence. He walks into a group of strangers, some of whom look at him in curiosity, some with disdain, and some with only a fleeting glance before they turn away. He greets them expansively: "Hi, I'm Billy," and soon they are talking with him about television, movies, or music. When he speaks to parents who have children with disabilities, they frequently tell me that seeing Billy and hearing about his life encourages them about their own children. One father wrote to me, "Now I'm not so afraid of the future."

A tremendous influence on me and the entire family, Billy inspires sensitivity and determination in his siblings. The desire to obtain the best life possible for him sent me back to college to learn and to teach. Billy enhanced my career at every step.

Billy is not all sunshine and light. He has fears and anxieties that present him with overwhelming challenges; he has many weird and puzzling behaviors. But far outweighing those behaviors are his goodness, his generosity, and his talent for loving unconditionally.

Billy and I are like beans and corn planted together in an open field: one supplying the nutrient, the other providing the support. We believe that if you want to bring about change, you have to *be* that change.

COMPARED TO MOVING from our home in Sanford, North Carolina—leaving the best friends I had ever had, and dealing with financial disaster and an uncertain future—having a baby seemed the most normal thing I could be doing. We had left town with our tails between our legs, desperate for a fresh beginning.

Driving east into Jacksonville for the first time, I noticed a number of pawn shops, bars, and pool halls, with military policemen stationed prominently at several corners. It was a sharp contrast to the sleepy, refined southern town we had left. Jacksonville was a small, unsophisticated coastal town on the fringe of Camp LeJeune Marine Corps Base; it had not kept up with the demands of its growing population. But I could not have cared less about the appearance of the town: different was wonderful. Having escaped our business fiasco in Sanford, we were free! Free from angry voices on the telephone, threatening letters, and sleepless nights spent

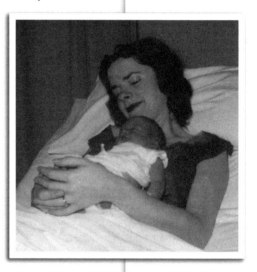

looking at the ceiling and wondering what would happen next.

My husband Bill had found an apartment in a complex where most of the residents were civilians connected with the base. We found good neighbors, another struggling mission Lutheran church, and a school nearby for John. Tom and I were happy being at home with our first television, watching *Captain Kangaroo* and getting ready for the baby.

Bill seemed to have found his niche. He was working night and day, selling a spectacular amount of life insurance to the marines. With renewed confidence in

> Mom, tell me bout when I born an you and Dad got lost.

Bill, I was sure that our problems would soon be solved and that we could build a comfortable, secure life for our family.

Our vision of security was shaken when labor progressed more swiftly than we expected for our third baby. Bill negotiated what he intended as a short cut to the hospital, but we were lost on a slippery country road, struggling against the unforeseen freezing rain, and frightened. We barely arrived in time. The delivery was short and much easier than I had experienced with John and Tom. When the nurse placed my tiny baby in my arms I fell in love with him, so cuddly, so sweet. The doctor pronounced him fine and sent us home.

Little Billy and I were getting along so well, both of us sleeping through the night, that all of us went to church a week after leaving the hospital. While standing for a hymn, I felt a rush of blood and began hemorrhaging profusely. I signaled to Bill and the two boys and, holding the baby in my arms, ran from the church.

At home the hemorrhaging persisted with added force, a veritable flood. When I lay on the bed, blood spurted onto the walls, the door, the floor. Bill was in a state of panic, but managed to call the doctor and help me change my saturated clothes. He took me to the hospital where the obstetrician, driving his pink Cadillac, met us. After examining me, he said calmly, "I guess this is your first period." That sounded ridiculously understated, but what did we know? We later learned, from Mother's queries at the hospital where she worked, that it was the doctor's negligence in not delivering the placenta which had caused the hemorrhaging.

Because Billy was breast feeding, he stayed in the hospital with me while I recovered. I could only imagine the task Bill faced when he returned to the apartment—cleaning my clothing, even my best high-heeled shoes, and the whole room where I had been. He never mentioned it; he was just concerned about me and taking care of the two boys at home. The total carelessness of that doctor and that hospital was revealed when I later wrote for Billy's birth certificate and was advised, "Our records indicate that this child was born dead."

JOHN AND TOM were thrilled with their new little brother; they took turns holding him and letting his little fingers curl around their larger ones. Bill and I sought simple names since we knew our children would have a lifetime of spelling Schulz. We named him William for his dad and Robert for his uncle. He was "Billy" from the start.

Billy was such a contented and responsive baby that the entire family enjoyed him thoroughly. My mother, who came to help each time I had a baby, declared that Billy was the prettiest of our babies, and small enough for her to handle.

Billy had difficulty nursing and did not gain weight as he should have. In his baby book I fudged a few ounces each time to make the record look better—my first attempt at denial of a problem. The only complication mentioned by the doctor was Billy's yellow coloring—jaundice, a sign of possible liver problems. The doctor told us that sunlight (Vitamin D) would help, so I began taking him out on the back steps where I sat, pulling his blanket back to expose his little bare body to the sun's rays. It was fun to just sit and look at him, smiling and talking, establishing the close bond between us, a bond that would grow stronger with each day of our lives.

Although I had a feeling that this child was distinctive in some way, I tried to push away all thoughts of a problem. However, Billy was our third child; we were familiar with normal development. Billy did not turn over on schedule, did not sit up when he should have, and had difficulty managing baby food.

This me and my brothers. I ask my mom was I a pretty baby an she said I was beautiful. An everybody love me.

Recognizing that Billy's development was slow, Bill and I took him to a pediatrician, who said, "Give him time—he'll catch up." Though we were worried, there were no further medical resources in that small town. Since Billy had all the physical characteristics of Down syndrome, it is amazing that the physicians were unable to form a diagnosis. Later I asked myself these questions:

Were they out to lunch the day chromosomal abnormalities were discussed in medical school? Or did they ever discuss it? Or were these particular physicians too cowardly to reveal the nature of the problem?

Any answer seemed inconceivable and cruel.

John and Tom joined us in working with Billy, trying to get him to sit on his own, to eat more food, wanting him to follow normal patterns. His slower development did not prevent their having fun with him; in particular, they loved to make him laugh. They noticed things that were different, like his ability to put his toes into his mouth and to spread his legs horizontally from the hips. Tom called him a "nunkhead" and, when asked what that was, replied, "Nunkheads is people what plays with they feet."

As Bill's career continued to flourish, we moved into a nice house, became active in our church and John's school, and made many friends. A number of marines and their families lived in the new neighborhood. We enjoyed one couple in particular, playing bridge with them and sharing meals. One night Chuck phoned Bill to say, "You and Jane need to hurry over, we have an emergency!"

Leaving John in charge, we rushed to Chuck's home, expecting a sick child or some tragedy. Chuck opened the front door just a crack, whispering: "Come on in, I have a batch of home brew ready to explode and no empty bottles!" Our work was cut out for us. We were relaxed, living a peaceful, stress-free life again.

We particularly enjoyed living near the beach. During the summer we frequently spent days playing in the water and the sand. According to our routine, John preceded me and the younger boys and set up the playpen for Billy, to be covered with a protecting sheet. In the winter we took our little black cocker spaniel for walks, watching him splash in the ocean.

A year later, as we were feeling at home in Jacksonville, my brother John—who was Bill's supervisor in the insurance company—announced that a new regulation had been issued by the Marine Corps stating that salesmen were no longer permitted to work on the base. Since many of the marines lived on the base, this regulation would greatly restrict Bill's sales. Thus, Bill was transferred to Fort Benning in Columbus, Georgia, to sell insurance to members of the army stationed there.

Although this announcement came as a surprise, it appeared to be a blessing. Fort Benning was much larger than Camp Lejeune, and Columbus was a small city with cultural, educational, and professional advantages not available in Jacksonville. We looked forward to the move.

If the towns in North Carolina were considered Southern, Columbus was the superlative example. The older part of town was patterned with wide streets and sidewalks outlined with magnificent trees. Stately antebellum homes had been restored to their original elegance, lending an air of grandeur to the neighborhood. There was a historic opera house, a large coliseum, and many churches with ornate steeples dotting the skies. There were also areas of poverty and neglect, areas less readily visible.

South Columbus was the section closest to Ft. Benning, where Bill would work, the locality best suited to our needs. We found a rental house near several schools, in a neighborhood of modest well-kept homes. Columbus, we felt, could offer us the permanence we were seeking; we hoped, too, that a larger place would offer help in dealing with Billy's slow development.

Our first order of business was to make an appointment with a pediatrician. Bill and I took Billy, then eighteen months old, to see Dr. Rhea, who had been recommended highly by mothers with whom we had talked. We met him with fear of what we might learn about Billy and hope for direction in rearing him. Dr. Rhea examined Billy thoroughly, checking his palms, spreading his legs out from his hips, looking at his tongue, his eyes, his ears. After a long time, he called in his associate, who went through the same motions. Following consultation with his partner, Dr. Rhea looked at us with empathetic tears streaming down his face and softly informed us, "Your little boy is Mongoloid. You can tell from the slant of his eyes, the shape of his palms, and the over-flexibility of his limbs."

Our suspicion that Billy was not normal now confirmed, we received the label used prior to the 1960s. Facing the reality, we asked, "What can we expect?"

"He will be retarded and sickly, but he will love music."

"What can we do to help him?"

"Take him home and love him."

This advice constituted our early childhood training program.

The diagnosis was far from good news, yet both of us were relieved to have a name for Billy's condition. Still we had no idea what the label Mongoloid really meant. We stopped at a department store on the way back, bought a humidifier and a record player, and went home to do the best we could.

Close family members who knew Billy were not surprised at the diagnosis; they had also observed him. The reaction of family members was varied and interesting. Mother, who had also moved to Columbus, said, "Don't call him mentally retarded; just call him retarded."

Even years later, Bill's brother—who had lost his son in a tragic automobile accident—said to us, "I know just how you feel."

Bill asked, "What do you mean?"

He replied with empathy, "Well, I lost a child, too."

Billy, at eighteen months of age, was already well integrated into the family, our church, and our neighborhood. By then I was six months pregnant with our fourth child and somewhat concerned about her welfare, although Bill and I did not dwell on it. We were too busy.

Soon we bought our own home in a pretty neighborhood, not too far from the army post where Bill would be working, and moved in only three days before Mary's arrival. Then we were really busy. With four children we had little time to grieve or to worry. Frequently, however, in the still of the night, I cried softly in desperation, knowing that Billy was a child who would need out-of-the-ordinary care and attention—skills I did not have. I wondered how I could help him, what I could do to help him, where I could turn.

BILL was a doting father when the children were young, slipping into the stern role his father had modeled as the children grew older. Intensely proud of his family, he yearned to be a good provider and worked hard toward that goal.

Bill and I were in complete accord in accepting Billy's disability and in seeking services for him. While I was more concerned with Billy's development and education, Bill became active in the Association for Retarded Children and later in seeking benefits to which Billy was entitled.

In our family, Bill was the one who took the children to the doctor, to track meets, to school, and to work. Many years later, after we moved to the North Carolina mountains, Bill was the one who drove his Jeep in the snow to bring Mary home from her school in Boone for holidays. In Billy's case, transportation required a complex schedule; Bill's willingness to accept it as his task allowed me the freedom to develop my career.

This my mom
an my dad
but
my dad died
an I miss him.

As each child reached adolescence, Bill had difficulty in adjusting to his loss of control. He still expected compliance and was reluctant to recognize their quest for independence. This conflict resulted in serious battles and misunderstandings, leaving some scars that never completely healed.

Bill's primary expectation was obedience. Therefore, when Billy showed signs of rebellion, he and his dad had many loud and disturbing confrontations. Billy eventually learned to "play the game," feigning acquiescence and then doing his own thing.

Research consistently shows that the presence of a child with a disability contributes to divorce in many families. Our experience was the opposite: Billy's need for both of us was a strong and binding force. Our concern for his development and welfare and the search for opportunities for him helped to keep us together.

An this my brothers an my sister an I love them.

Most parents think that their children are remarkable; in my case it's true. I think you will agree and will understand that to know Billy and me, you must also know our family.

This my brother John come from Rome Georgia.

John, my first born, my solace and companion, was born while Bill was in the Navy. Living in a small suburb of Chicago, I had to travel by train to Evanston to see the obstetrician, who saw me only two times before my delivery. The night John was born I woke up with a tummy ache; Bill reminded me of the shrimp we had had for dinner, reconsidered and called a taxi for the ride to the hospital. I was embarrassed because I was wearing his Navy shorts, held up with blue ribbons because, just following World War II, elastic was in short supply and no one had ever heard of maternity underwear.

After Bill's discharge from the Navy, we moved to Milwaukee, Wisconsin. Johnny, as we called him for years, kept me company during the dreary winter days. We snuggled under quilts and read for hours, developing a bond of love for the written word. When we moved to a new place where we had no friends or family, he was my companion. Since there were eight years between him and Tom, John was, for a long time, our only child and composed a family picture much different from that of our eventual family with four children.

John got into a great deal of trouble in school, starting with kindergarten, when he slid down the coal chute in his teacher's home-turned-school. When he entered public school, I never had to introduce myself—he looked so much like me. He easily made friends but had trouble with some teachers. One day he came home with his hands covering his ears because his teacher had yelled at him.

High school was a bumpy ride for John. Bright, an avid reader, he did not fit into the academic mold and his grades fluctuated from A to F, depending on the teacher and the semester. When it was time for him to go to college, Bill decided that a military school would "straighten him out." With three little ones, John was the one I could talk with; when he went away to college, I went into his room, picked up his guitar, and cried with loneliness for him.

I knew military school was wrong for him, and when he came home at Christmas, I suggested to him that he leave. He said, "No, Mom, I have to finish the year. I can't let it beat me."

Push-ups were the primary punishment at John's college; he came home with shoulders much broader than when he entered. The next year he continued his education at Columbus College, where he met Barbara. After they were married, they went on to finish college at the University of Georgia, both majoring in English and embarking on teaching careers.

Working with junior high school students identified as "potential drop-outs," John designed excellent modules for vocational training, one of which was building and operating a greenhouse. This venture ultimately led to his landscaping career. His pride and joy became riding his tractor, moving earth and creatively designing flower beds, gardens, and waterfalls. When he disclaimed his role as an artist, I pointed out that he just uses a very large paintbrush to make the world more beautiful. Full of fun and laughter, outgoing and friendly, he is both observant and non-traditional.

John and Barbara blessed me with two remarkable grandsons: Paul and John Robert. When John's family visited us in North Carolina, the boys spent part of their summer vacations with us. One story we tell reflects Paul's reluctance to leave. My habit is to buy whole-wheat bread, but when Paul visited, I would buy his preferred white bread, too. One summer, at the end of Paul's vacation, I reminded him that it was time for me to take him back to Georgia. He tearfully exploded, "But Grandma, my white bread's not all gone!"

Several years later, when Paul had graduated from high school, I took him to San Francisco, where I was doing a presentation at a conference. After my first day's meetings, we got back together and discussed our experiences. He reported a surprising encounter, "Grandma, a prostitute stopped me today with a proposition."

"Whoa! What did you tell her? "

"I told her no thank you, I didn't care for any."

One of my most cherished times with John Robert, whom we call J.R., was a trip we took to visit my brother Fred and his wife Marie at their farm in Maryland. We flew to Washington and on the return trip took a train to the Metro and a taxi to their apartment where we spent the night. We had such fun on the farm riding horseback, swimming, and relaxing. J.R. and I prepared a Mexican dinner for Fred and Marie, surprisingly a new cuisine for them. On the flight back to North Carolina, J.R. remarked that he had experienced five modes of transportation that were new to him: plane, train, subway, taxi, and horse.

As my first grandchildren, Paul and J.R. introduced me to the utter delights of savoring childhood.

Because John was ten years old when Billy was born, they did not grow up together as Tom, Billy, and Mary did. John was always the "older brother" and frequently the babysitter. He was in school when the younger three were growing up and, I'm sure, felt isolated at times. However, John has been greatly influenced by Billy in his interactions with people who require special consideration and attention.

John once brought a high school friend, Randy, home to live with us. Bill and I were playing bridge with friends when John asked to speak with us, told us of Randy's dysfunctional home situation, and asked if he could stay with us. We responded that he could if his mother agreed. Randy (who could play the guitar, harmonica, maracas, and washboard at one time) proved to be one of our most beloved guests; we were devastated when, after he joined the Navy, he went down with a submarine.

 In his landscaping work, John frequently works with Hispanic men who primarily speak Spanish. He always teaches them English while he is learning Spanish, usually becoming involved in their lives and helping them to solve problems resulting from discrimination. In his social life John has become friends with a young woman who has a disability, and who has some of the same speech patterns as Billy. He loves her and enjoys taking plants to her, admiring her home, and talking with her. Like me, he has an invisible sign on his forehead: "Tell me your problems."

Several years ago I was writing a chapter in a book entitled *Cognitive Coping, Families, & Disability*[1] and asked John, Tom, and Mary to describe the things about Billy that meant the most to them. John wrote:

> I have two brothers, Tom and Billy. I am 8 years older than Tom and 10 years older than Billy. Keep this in mind.
>
> Tom and I first developed a special relationship when he was 17. Billy and I always had a special relationship. I often feel that I neglect Billy and I am prone to impose guilt feelings on myself for this reason. I live in another town far away and don't see Billy as often as I would like.
>
> Periodically I will talk to Billy on the phone, mostly by accident. He is always glad to hear my voice. I will say, "What's happening, Billy?" He will answer, "Fine." Before the conversation is over, Billy will always get around to saying, "I have a wonderful brother."
>
> "What's his name?" I ask.
>
> "John."
>
> When Tom and I are around Billy, he will often say, "I have a wonderful brother!" Tom and I jump on this, saying, "What's his name?" This turns into a won-

---

1   Schulz, J.B. (1992) "Heroes in Disguise," in Turnbull, A.P., Patterson, J.M., Behr, S.K., Murphy, D.L., Marquis, J.G.,, Blue-Banning, M.J., *Cognitive Coping, Families, & Disability*. Baltimore: Paul H. Brookes, p. 37.

derful game with Billy being very diplomatic. Billy will usually end up telling us a poem that he wrote himself:

> I have a brother name is John
> I have a brother name is Tom
> I love my brother name is John
> I love my brother name is Tom.

Then he laughs and hugs us.
I have one thing to say for Billy: I have a wonderful brother.

As their children grew older, John and Barbara were confronted with many problems which led to their divorce. Billy couldn't understand their separateness and longed for them to reunite. While they did not reconcile, we are still in touch with Barbara and she is part of our family. On one occasion, I was buying a birthday gift for her and the salesperson, a friend of mine, exclaimed, "You're buying a present for your ex-daughter-in-law?"

A major point of conflict for their marriage was John's alcoholism. In his fifties, John conquered the monkey on his back. He doesn't like for me to say I am proud of him for his recovery, but I am. He successfully deals with an affliction that my father, my brother, and my husband were unable (or unwilling) to face. What an accomplishment, and what a marvelous answer to multitudes of prayers!

John is still my talking buddy. We share tales by phone every Sunday morning and sporadically in between. Anyplace I live becomes a showplace, filled with beautiful flowers and shrubs, designed by John to give me pleasure year round.

An this is Tom, come from Charlotte.

Tom was the answer to Bill's wishes, my longing, and John's Sunday School prayers. After waiting eight years for our second child, all three of us were ecstatic and lavished Tommy with attention. He was a picture of the contentment we all felt: he was fat, placid, and happy.

Our delight in Tom was strengthened by his success in school and his overall conformity to the rules of school and home. A story we delight in exemplifies his lack of competition with his older brother and his kindness.

It was our practice for the children to place their report cards on the kitchen counter for everyone to examine. John had put his less-than-perfect card on the counter when Tom came in with his—all A's. Tom picked up his brother's card, examined it slowly, and remarked, "Hey, Bub, you didn't miss a day!"

Determined to pursue a medical career, Tom began ordering specimens to experiment with, such as worms and mice. One day Billy was at home alone when one of Tom's shipments arrived. Curious, Billy opened the box and out jumped about forty tiny frogs. He later recalled, "They are scare me to *death!*" Although we didn't see the event, all of us could picture his amazement as the frogs scurried all about the house. In the months that followed, Tom's medical experiments increased in complexity; he ordered pig fetuses, which turned out to be unapproachable for Tom, and he rethought his career goal.

Tom is an artist. When he started doing construction work to support himself and his wife, Michelle, he always maintained, "I am an artist." He went to college episodically, but lack of finances required him to develop his skills as a builder. His projects always reflected his artistic ability and creativity.

In 1983, Tom built a house for himself, Michelle, and their children on land just above our home, giving us the opportunity to be part of his children's lives as they grew up. Adorable youngsters, Carrie and Isaac frequently ran down the hill to see us. I have a picture of Isaac riding on the lawnmower with Bill and another of both children sitting on the sofa with me, reading a book. On one such occasion, while we were reading a Christmas book, Isaac declared, "Grandma, I can read that." He took the book from me, sounding out: "The wise men came, and brought gold, and Frankenstein, and Murray."

The children's close proximity was a treasure for me, and I think it was important to them as well. From college, Carrie wrote to me:

> I run down the Locust Creek hill to your house often; my mind wraps itself around the memory of running to a place where I could be myself. I am ever thankful for that space, and conjure it up still.

Unfortunately, Tom and Michelle's marriage also ended in divorce. Tom relocated and continued his building business and his painting. Every night he came home from an exhausting day and painted. I asked him how he could find the strength to do that and he replied, "Mom, my painting energizes me." Following his calling, he moved to Asheville, set up a studio downtown, and became active in the art community there. During this time, he met and married Sheila.

I was in the hospital following back surgery when Tom visited me and announced that he was going back to college. He pointed out that he was about the age that I was when I did the same thing. I was delighted to see him pursue his education and passion. He and Sheila moved to Boston, where Tom earned a Master of Fine Arts degree. Together, they developed a unique business which merged creative vision, artistic talent and architectural enhancement. When he and Sheila moved back to the South, they brought their spiritual gifts as well to the Charlotte area.

Tom has always been a major force and influence in Billy's life, a force that is reciprocal. When teaching art classes in Boston, Tom frequently referred to Billy's influence and began those classes with "Happy Tuesday!" reflecting Billy's friendly greetings. Most of all, he has gained understanding of himself through Billy, as you can discern from his piece quoted from *Cognitive Coping*. Tom wrote:

> In my life, everything bears the seed of beauty and everyone wears the mantle of heroics. For the most part, I owe this vision to my brother Billy. Growing up in a family graced by his joy and directness has expanded my concept of what is the essence of potential: that is living life delicately balanced between the sanctity of each individual moment and the broader spectre of genetic predestination.
>
> Billy says to me, "We have twin eyes." And I wish that was true if only for a moment. Then I could see the world as he does. Truly it must go way beyond what any of us could ever imagine. Billy asks questions that none of us will allow ourselves to. He is the Vasco de Gama of feelings. He sails around uncharted emotional territory when 2 years after my marriage has ended he asks me, in front of my daughter, "Tom when you and Michelle get back together?" I know that I must tell the truth. I don't always know what to say. Sometimes he grabs my hand with his hand that is like a paw or a catcher's mitt and he says, "I love you" or "Don't worry—it will be all right" and I think, who is this guy?
>
> I can never be so tired that I do not think of Billy forcing himself to climb a set of stairs to go to a concert. I can never be shy without seeing him turn to a stranger and saying in this voice so full of melody, "Hi, my name is Billy."
>
> Billy has taught me that there exists a simpler path. When he is tired he sits down. When he is happy he says so. And when he doesn't want to do something, he is completely immovable—defying most natural laws of the universe. I often rationalize the complexity of my "normal" life by comparison: "Oh yes but he doesn't have kids to raise and tax bills due." But for every life situation that has ever arisen calling out to me, "Hey, Tom, deal with me with anxiety and fear" I picture Bill and his brick-like smooth-surfaced countenance and know there is another way.
>
> I would never pretend that Billy has no problems. For if nothing else is mine to hold it is the knowledge of his humanity. Just below his surface ripple emotions as deep as the ocean. But I do fantasize that one day I will open up to the joy of living, the boundless offerings of love available, and the graceful navigation of stormy social seas just like my brother Billy. For he is my hero. (pp. 37, 38)

When he has a problem, Billy calls Tom, who explains things better than anyone I know. (Once, I asked him to explain shooting stars to me; he thought for a moment, and said, "Mom, it's like a cosmic fart.") When they were young children, Tom led Billy about the neighborhood, conscious of his need for protection and guidance.

Growing up with Billy in their lives left its mark on Isaac and Carrie, too. In the neighborhood where we lived, close to Tom and his family, there was a young man who had been left with brain damage from an accident. His behavior was rather strange and his speech difficult to understand. He told me one day, "Tom's children are the only ones in the neighborhood who don't make fun of me."

Tom is my friend, my confidant, and my adviser. During the trials of my marriage, he was close by to listen and to understand. When I was in graduate school, he helped me with statistics, sitting up all night with me as I worked on my dissertation. When Bill had a stroke, Tom was there. If I needed him today, he would be here.

An this my sister an I love her.

While other chapters comprise the details of his birth and development, I want to emphasize how welcome Billy was. Our three boys were beautiful and compatible. However, they tell me that, after Billy's birth, I was on my way out of the delivery room and said, "I'll see you next year." And so I did.

Mary was born eighteen months after Billy's birth. My doctor, Dr. "Honey" Munn, said to me, "You have a little girl."

I responded, "But that's impossible!"

True to his name, he said, "Honey, everything's possible with the Lord."

Our family was complete.

Needless to say, I was thrilled to have a daughter. She was my doll. I had no idea how important she would become to Billy and to me.

For many months, Mary and Billy were like twins: both in diapers, both eating baby food, both fitting into one stroller. Gradually, Mary's development—physical, mental, and linguistic—passed Billy's. This was a bittersweet time for us, rejoicing in Mary's precocity while increasingly aware of Billy's delayed development.

Mary was Billy's first and best teacher. Using his mimic skills, he tried to do and say everything as she did, from eating skills to potty training. She has continued to teach him and to help him, even in adulthood, with such tasks as cooking and decorating his apartment. She was also a teacher to me as I developed lesson plans and made materials for my own classes.

Mary was so much fun for me as I wrestled with John's adolescence, Tom's frequent boyhood accidents, and Billy's crises. Her excitement over small things has always been a delight for me: "Look, Mom, at how these little flowers are made!"

Every gift, no matter how small, captured her attention and gratitude. Making dresses for her was a unique and welcome experience.

At a young age, Mary exhibited her independent nature, illustrated by an encounter with Bob Wisor, our dear and devoted neighbor. As she reached for a forbidden object, he slapped her hand, accompanied by a loud "No!" She looked at him scornfully and walked away.

Mary was an excellent student, demonstrating her writing, artistic, and musical ability. After graduating from Appalachian State University in North Carolina, majoring in commercial design, she went to Holland for two years. She had met Jos, a young man from Holland, during her senior year and declared that she wanted to go to Europe to work. Putting her on that plane was one of the hardest things Bill and I had ever done. She still recalls the look on my face as she departed and how my brave countenance crumpled when I mistakenly assumed she could no longer see me.

Mary found a job with an advertising agency in Amsterdam, moved into an apartment, and began to learn the Dutch language. In describing the difficulties of adjusting to a foreign culture and language, she identified with Billy:

> You wouldn't believe how much Billy is on my mind. I know now how it is to spend an extension of time feeling frustrated because you can't understand what people are saying, feeling dumb, guessing when you cook or wash because in the store you thought it looked like a likely label, wanting to laugh, too, when someone tells a joke and you only caught part of it and the room is full of charged guffaws, making a thousand mistakes when trying to tell someone something because you haven't a large enough vocabulary and the structure of language isn't logical in your mind, not knowing how to measure, not knowing what the street signs say so that you find yourself suddenly in a dangerous situation, not knowing how to ask for help nor what to do in an emergency nor how to do your banking or call for a doctor's appointment, not having a concept of how much money you're spending, being the butt of jokes in your ignorance and not being able to defend yourself and tired of laughing with them or shrugging it off, knowing you have to get up and go to work—jostling with crowds before you're awake, coming home to an empty house tired, knowing you have to eat and feeling no joy in it and doing it anyway, taking care of a few little things before you find you've been thinking so hard all day that all you want to do is lie down and wait until sleep gives you some peace.

When I received that letter, I just wanted to bring her home! Reading it now I am touched by the depth of her understanding of Billy and the effect he has had on her.

Within two years, Mary imported her "Dutch treat" from Holland. She and Jos were married in our church and lived with us for two years while he attended college. It was a good time for all of us, as we came to know Jos and to spend pleasant mealtimes helping him polish his English. They moved to Chapel Hill where he obtained his PhD in chemistry, enabling him to secure a position as an analytical chemist in Tennessee, not far from us.

Mary continued her education with self-acquired computer skills and has become a successful information designer. She and Jos are a strong and loving team, building a happy and enabling home for their own family.

I was present at the births of Daniel and Warren, two of my most treasured experiences. Watching them grow and being part of their lives is a true bonus in my life. While enjoying them as adolescents, I cherish memories of them as babies. I can see Daniel as a toddler at my retirement party, dressed in a little suit with a train on it, wearing sandals, and running through the crowd of adults toward me when I walked into the room. He jumped into my arms, flattening my corsage with his joyful hug.

And I can feel little Warren cuddled in my arms, in the green chair, with an illness that needed comforting. I whispered to him, "I used to hold you this way when you were a tiny baby."

He cut his eyes up to me and asked, "And did I love it?"

Living near Daniel and Warren now also contributes to Billy's further growth as an adult and has given him new and enriching experiences, as will become apparent in later chapters.

Mary is my friend, my sustainer, and my support. Except for her two years in Holland, she has been a phone call away from me, available in times of celebration, illness, and conflict. I have laughingly called her the sunshine of my twilight years; the older I get, the more I realize the truth of that designation.

Like every family, ours is unique. I consider each of our family members remarkable but not perfect. We have experienced addictions, indebtedness, bankruptcy, bad choices, and divorces. We have our strengths and our weaknesses, but we always pull together. I believe the presence of Billy in our lives is a major factor in our unity—it isn't just because we know he needs us; we also need him. We need his happiness, his concern for us, and his faith in us. Each of us has had a role in raising Billy and each of us, in return, has been influenced by him.

Someone once told Tom that our family was dysfunctional, to which he responded, "Maybe it is; I only know that I have always felt loved."

WHEN BILLY WAS BORN (1956), there were no services available for him or for our family in caring for him. I went to the Health Department to see if I could find some direction, and although none was forthcoming, I did pick up some literature. It was then that I first learned about the discovery of the chromosomal abnormality that has been linked to Billy's disability.

Bill and I decided at this time to seek a parent support group, and we joined the Association for Retarded Children (now referred to as the ARC). The negative attitude of many of the group was revealed at our first meeting, when a member led all of us in prayer, concluding with "Lord, help us to bear the burden of our retarded children."

This idea had never occurred to either of us, and when we went home, I looked down at our beautiful, sleeping child, declaring, "He is not a burden."

At that time I began to think of Billy's needs as challenges and was as aware of my own inadequacies as of his deficiencies. Bill and I became active in the ARC, however, and met interesting parents and children through the group. Bill became an officer in the association, later learning the advantages of belonging to a strong advocacy organization.

Shortly after Billy's second birthday, while Mary was still an infant, we had a major catastrophe. Bill described the event in a letter to his aunts:

> On February 15th we had one of the worst fires at the house I have seen for many a day. About 10 minutes to seven on a cold windy Saturday night, John went out

This my sister Mary. An my sister help me an my sister loves me.

the kitchen door to the carport only to come running in saying that there was a fire in the utility room. I jumped up, ran out, yelled for Jane to call the fire department, moved the car out, and turned on the hose. By that time it had a good start, and was coming out the door being driven by the wind to the carport. By the time we put it out, the kitchen door had burned out, it entered the house proper, getting the cabinets in the kitchen, floor, and ceilings in the kitchen, dining area, and living room…Now, the house was covered with insurance, but we never got around to taking out insurance on the furniture.

We moved out that night for all power was turned off, due to broken pipes and burned wires. We had to rent a house around the corner as temporary quarters until our house is repaired.

The night of the fire was, of course, filled with frenzied activity. Mother, who was having dinner with us, took John and Tom home with her; I clutched Mary and Billy in my arms and ran next door to our neighbors' house. Realizing that there was nothing I could do about the fire, I fell into our routine and bathed the two babies in the tub.

Another neighbor grabbed his hunting jacket and came to help Bill, not discovering until later that the pockets of his jacket were full of shotgun shells. Many friends came to offer their condolences, stating, "It could have been worse." I cherished the remark of one neighbor who, unlike the others, said, "It could have not happened."

Although this was a traumatic event, it afforded me some peaceful time with the children. With little housework to do in a temporary home, I focused on them. John began to babysit, Mary stopped nursing, Tom learned the Lord's Prayer, and Billy found that he could pull the toilet paper all around the house. When

we moved back to our own home, our normal routine and concerns resumed.

Billy's developmental lag became more apparent when compared with Mary's rapid progress. Both of them were in diapers, in high chairs, and in cribs. When I took them about the neighborhood together in one stroller, people frequently thought that they were twins.

Without discussing the need, the family became Billy's teachers, striving to motivate him—prodding, pushing, and pleading. He tried everything we modeled, often discouraged by his failed attempts.

Billy's frustration was painful to him and to the family. Frequently, after putting the children to bed, Bill and I went to the living room to relax, with the door to the hall and bedrooms closed. Sometimes we would hear a noise, open the door, and see Billy lying near the door. He would drag himself to the end of the hall and bang his head on the floor in obvious frustration. His inability to walk and to speak appeared as agonizing for him as it was for us. His ineffectual efforts broke our hearts.

In trying to help Billy gain the skills he needed, Bill and I established landmark targets; for example, we determined, "Once he walks he will be all right." Thus we focused on his walking. We overlooked the crawling stage; he had been dragging himself by his arms for some time.

We tried everything! We had a part-time maid who said, "Put him behind the door and brush his legs with a broom." I even tried that. Finally our neighbors, the Wisors, presented a solution. Bob, who was in the army, had been stationed in Japan; there, the babies walk at an early age with the help of a unique tool called a katakato. Bob made a katakato, a wooden device similar to a scooter in reverse. When Billy held on to the bar, rabbits popped up with each step he took. In a few weeks, when he was about two and a half, he was walking with the katakato; soon thereafter he walked without it.

Our next target became speaking. Each member of the family mouthed, repeated, and acted out words. Billy watched and imitated our actions but did not speak the words. The entire household was involved; everything we said was exaggerated. When he did not produce the sounds, I found a speech therapist who agreed to work with him. They presented quite a picture, sitting on the side of his bunk bed, the therapist holding up cards and pictures, and Billy, very attentive, trying to follow her direction. Billy was quite cooperative, and the therapist thoroughly enjoyed working with him. She finally, reluctantly, told us that he was not developmentally ready to speak and that

we were wasting our money on her lessons. All of us, terribly disappointed, realized that our hopes had been unrealistic.

I learned that speech and language are not synonymous; Billy showed pleasure, affection, and frustration in many ways. When he reached out to us, his love was overwhelming; when he had a need, he gestured until we got the message.

One example of Billy's communication methods was apparent when Uncle John (Billy called him "Punka Don") was visiting. He looked up at John with adoration (which was returned) and asked, "Pane?" John could not understand the meaning, although he tried desperately, until Billy made a whirring noise and moved his hand and arm in up and down motions. At last John said, "Oh, yes, I came on the plane."

Sometimes Billy's inability to communicate was unsettling. I always involved him in simple areas of housekeeping. He especially liked to watch me cook, to observe the electric mixer, and to lick the spoon. One day I was making a lemon cake, with Billy perched on the counter where he could see. The phone rang and I stopped the mixer, responded to the call, and returned to the cake project. I noticed, for the first time, that the Comet cleanser was close to the mixer. An alarming thought came to me: *had Billy poured cleanser into the batter?* I asked him, showing him the cleanser package, if he had done that. He just looked at me and grinned. I poured the batter out and started over.

One of the first things I learned about children with Down syndrome is that their language development is considerably slower than other areas of their growth. Thus, from an educational point of view, the goal is for communication, rather than perfect speech. Nevertheless, for a number of years we worked toward Billy's total and normal language development. It was a lot to ask of him and of those who tried to understand him. He certainly tried, and some of his efforts were funny as well as sad. One of the last sounds children learn to make is the "y" sound. I worked on it with Billy, saying "yyyyellow." For years he responded with "yyyy.... lellow!" Eventually we noticed how well Billy expressed himself and how other people picked up and borrowed much of his language. Although it is certainly important for people to understand what he is attempting to convey, it is also important for the rest of us to accept his unique expressions, indeed to cherish them and even to use them for ourselves. We call it "Billy talk."

We incorporate Billy's words and expressions because they are more than cute: they are short, pertinent, and very expressive. For example, if it looks as if it might rain I take a "rainbrella, case instead." It is a useful phrase; members of our family and close friends use this and other examples of Billy talk frequently.

When my friend David Shapiro was finishing a mammoth textbook he was writing, I stopped by his office and asked, "How's the book going, David?" He paused a moment and responded, "Jane, I'm tivedit!" He meant in Billy talk that he was more than tired of it; he was sick to death of it.

One completely rewarding area of Billy's early development was toilet training. To help a child develop this skill frustrates many parents, but for Billy it was no problem. My positive expectations and ignorance are probably what made this task totally non-threatening and even fun. We had a potty chair for Billy and Mary, which they took turns using. Billy, Mary, and I sang and read, and after the job was completed, all three of us clapped and hooted and hollered. It may seem strange that this was a happy time, but we celebrated our successes where we found them. By the time he was three years old, Billy was able to stay dry all night. Not surprisingly, this is the only developmental timeline that I documented. Nor is it surprising that I later became something of an expert in teaching toilet training to children with developmental disabilities—an interesting addition to my résumé.

Billy's social development, patterned after his siblings, was remarkable. In the absence of concrete direction for his behavior, Bill and I raised him in ways we had found successful with our other children. We took him to church, where he was fully accepted; shopping, where he was viewed with curiosity; and walking in the neighborhood, where he was received with mixed attitudes. One family in the neighborhood did not allow Billy to play with their children, evoking Mary's first awareness of social injustice. She declared, "Then I won't play with them either!" This family later had a baby who was severely disabled. Their tender care for her helped us realize their attitude toward Billy had been based on lack of understanding.

There were other families, of course, who were very kind and receptive of Billy. Mary's friend Laurie, who lived across the street, had a darling little sister, Becky, about five years old, who looked like an angel. Billy loved her and wanted her to spend the night with him, so, with some trepidation, I asked her mother if that would be possible. Without hesitating, she said, "Of course, if Becky wants to go."

Becky was delighted and so was Billy. Bill put a cot for Becky near Billy's bed, and when we looked in on them later, they were sound asleep, clasping hands across the beds, Becky's curls spread over her pillow, Billy's smiling face turned toward her. It was a moving and beautiful sight, one that brought tears to my eyes. We later learned that Becky's father had an uncle who was severely disabled, and lovingly cared for by his family. We were discovering that experience contributes to understanding.

When Tom and Billy came home from a walk one day, I could tell that there had been a problem. When I asked Tom about it, he responded, "Some of the kids were laughing at Billy and asked why he couldn't talk."

With my heart in my throat, I asked, "What did you say to them?"

He said, "Well, I told them that some children are smart and some are sweet, and Billy is one of the sweet ones."

As dear and understanding as Tom's response was, this incident brought me from my diaper retreat into the real world; my questions and my charge began. Would this child—whose appearance, development, and language were different—be accepted in our neighborhood? In the greater community? How could we, as a family, promote his acceptance? Would he have to conform to accepted patterns of language and intellect, or would his "sweetness" be enough?

On a personal level, I wondered if I were neglecting the other children in trying to meet Billy's needs. I had read about a mother who said of her mentally retarded child, "I gave her my life." Her other children retorted, "And we gave her our mother."

I didn't want that to happen, so in response to an acquaintance's remark, "I understand that you have a special child," I countered with, "Actually, I have four special children."

I felt sure that as a family we were responding to Billy's requirements for time, patience, and understanding. I did wonder if everyone else's needs were met when Mary, as a teenager, once remarked, "You know, Mom, I never got to be the baby."

There were many times when Billy demonstrated his independence, which usually lathered the family into a panic. One Sunday after church he disappeared. Since the church was located on a busy highway, everyone became alarmed and searched each room. At last we looked in the sanctuary and there saw Billy in the pulpit, the pastor's stole around his neck, shaking his finger at the imaginary congregation, and preaching with gusto "Da doo, da doo, da dah." This was an example of his marvelous imitative ability, which has served him well.

On another day when we were shopping in a mall, Billy disappeared. After a frantic search, we looked into a display window and saw him, poised and stationary among the mannequins.

When he learned to ride a tricycle, Billy had access to the neighborhood, riding around the block and stopping to chat with people that he knew. As he grew older, we got a large tricycle for him, and he continued his meanderings. Fortunately, it was a time when children were perceived to be safe in their surroundings.

Although he had, and still has, a happy disposition for the most part, Billy could pitch a fit at a moment's notice. He learned at an early age that he could get attention by crying, yelling, and writhing on the floor. He also learned that this behavior was most effective when there were onlookers. One day I took him to a store where he wanted something that he couldn't have. He fell to the floor, kicking and screaming, waiting for me to fill his wishes. By this time I knew he was being manipulative, and I walked away to another aisle. The technique was effective, although I imagine the observers were probably dismayed that anyone could walk away from that poor retarded child! Billy never tried that again.

And stubborn! There was no force in the world that could move him when he did not want to be moved. If he was sitting in a chair and someone said, "Billy, get up," he could remain sitting for an interminable time. I had heard many people describe this phenomenon as characteristic of children who have Down syndrome. A number of years later, when I came to know Julia Malloy, I understood. Julia, director of a school for children with Down syndrome, had written books about their characteristics and learning modes. She explained that children who have Down syndrome need plenty of turn-around time in changing activities.

I embraced this concept, understanding now that Billy was unable to take in a command or a request for action without knowing the consequences. He also had difficulty handling more than one process or step in a sequence. In other words, you needed say to Billy, "I want you to get out of that chair so we can [do an activity] and I will come back in five minutes." I found this method more productive and far more pleasant than some of the confrontations we had with Billy that appeared to be battles of will.

Billy learned to pout when things did not go his way, sticking his bottom lip far out and looking mournful. His siblings started mimicking him and laughing when he did that; soon he was laughing too. Always a clown and a mimic, many times after our dinner, he would stand in his chair as if to make a speech, proclaiming in dramatic gibberish his salient points. At the conclusion, the family clapped loudly; he extended his hands as if to silence us and bowed graciously. This became a ritual, with one of the family members introducing him with "Ladies and gentlemen, presenting...Billy!"

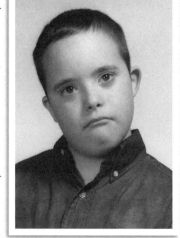

We took family trips together to visit relatives and to explore new surroundings. One of our favorite outings was to Miss Bea's cabin across the Chattahoochee River into Alabama.

Miss Bea was a dear friend of Mother's and soon adopted all of the children, showing special love for Billy. When she invited us to the cabin, there was always a "treasure chest" filled with toys suitable for each child. Picnics there included round pimento-cheese sandwiches, fried chicken, Coke in little bottles, and treats from a Columbus-based producer of peanuts. Billy loved these trips and for years to come, the cabin was Alabama—going there was "going to Alabama."

Longer trips proved Billy to be a good traveler. A memorable trip was to Florida and the home of Mother's sister, Aunt Freda, who lived near the Hialeah racetrack. While there we went to Seaquarium. Billy was fascinated by all the fish and came to get us, pointing to a fish with a protruding lower lip: "Look!" he cried, "A Billyfish!"

In our ignorance—or wisdom—we took Billy everywhere and included him in all our family activities. Wherever we went, Billy's appearance attracted attention. I was sensitive to this intrusion of our privacy and wondered how I should handle it. There were many situations and behaviors that puzzled me, including our own, and I was certain that someone, somewhere, had all the answers.

ONE OF THE YOUNG MEN who works with Billy asked me if Billy has Down syndrome. When I replied yes, he said, "You know, I like the way he looks." I wanted to hug this young man, because I too love the way Billy looks: the mystery of his features, the openness of his expressions. Every time I see someone else who has Down syndrome, I feel an instant connection.

I do my ekercise at the gym three times a week.

Years ago there was a film on TV about a mother and her son who had Down syndrome. As she was tucking him into bed one night he looked at her and said, "I'm so tired of looking like Down syndrome."

That hit me hard, and later I asked Billy how he feels about the way he looks. His instant reply? "I'm a handsome man."

He does have all the physical characteristics common in people with Down syndrome. When his good friend Steve (who also has Down syndrome) was visiting, Steve and Billy were looking at their feet and declared, "We got twin toes!"

Billy also has many physical characteristics of our family: the stocky German build of his father's family and my black hair. He also has certain familial personality traits—a good sense of humor and stubbornness in particular.

One evening Billy and I were guest speakers in an education class, and after he left, a student asked his age. I told him and he said, "My goodness, I wouldn't have thought he was nearly that old. Is looking young a characteristic of people with Down syndrome?"

In one of those inspired moments, I responded with a laugh, "No, that's a family characteristic."

Billy is not as tall as other members of our family, and is overweight. The tendency to gain weight has always been a problem. My friend Bev Jackson asks, "Why don't you just let him enjoy eating? What difference does it make?" The difference is that I am really concerned about his health and truly believe the weight plays a part in that. I also know it contributes to his sleep apnea. Perhaps because of my concern—and that of other members of the family—Billy does say from time to time, "I tired of being fat."

One of these times came when Mary and Jos were to be married and had asked Billy to be their best man. He, Bill, and I wanted to look great for the wedding, so all three of us joined Weight Watchers, with excellent results. Billy actually lost 30 pounds, bought a new suit, and looked great for the wedding. It didn't last too long, but we know that Weight Watchers works for him so we return from time to time. However, the initial motivation provided by the wedding is gone, and subsequent attempts to lose weight have not been very successful.

Exercise is important for both of us, and for several years we walked every day. There is a beautiful walking trail at Western Carolina University, and frequently Bev met us there. We walked and talked and thoroughly enjoyed and profited from the exercise. Going up the hills was difficult for Billy, however, and finally he refused to go. It may have been his fallen arches or boredom or who knows what. Seeking another solution, we joined a gym and embraced working out as a lifelong commitment. We engaged trainers who were college students and found one, Chris, who was wonderful with Billy. As long as Chris was there, Billy looked forward to his workouts and gained strength and stamina. Unfortunately, students come and go, and we had several along the way—some motivational, some unmotivated. When we no longer had trainers, Billy continued to work out sporadically on the treadmill and the cross-trainer.

Since Billy, as an adult, has been diagnosed with diabetes, exercise is critical to his well-being. Based on our prior experience, I realize that a consistent trainer is vital to his maintaining a steady program. He now works with Terrie once a week and without her twice a week. Although we go to the gym together, we use separate rooms, and Billy follows his routine independently. His trainer told me recently that working with him has been one of her most rewarding experiences.

Billy's foray into weight training actually occurred years ago, when we first moved to Auburn, Alabama. Tom was in high school and was interested in body building. With his usual resourcefulness, he made a bench press from an old coffee table, bought some weights, and set up a weight room in the garage. He and Billy worked out together, with the result that both of them today are strong and able to lift heavy objects.

Billy hasn't had as many serious physical problems as some people who have Down syndrome; we have been very fortunate on that score. I have a friend who told me that her daughter's Down syndrome is only one of her problems, citing a heart defect and attention deficits. Ironically, Billy is the only one in our family who doesn't wear glasses and has had neither a tonsillectomy nor an appendectomy. He does have hypothyroidism, which responds to medication.

The physician who told us that Billy would be sickly did prompt us to buy a humidifier, which was used so much when Billy was young that the walls in his bedroom were streaked with moisture from running the humidifier all night. While he didn't have a great many colds, he was unable to blow his nose and clear himself. Thus the humidifier ran all winter; I can still smell the eucalyptus in the air.

Early on, it was apparent that Billy's dental structure was abnormal. He had teeth growing behind other teeth into the roof of his mouth. Advised to have those teeth pulled, we took him to a pediatric oral surgeon. When the nurse told us that Billy was going in a space capsule, we were all excited, since his favorite book at the time was *Tom Corbett, A Trip to the Moon*. We had read it so many times that Billy learned to count backward before he learned to count forward! So being in a space capsule was an exciting prospect.

Unfortunately, the space capsule was a miserable, scary experience and the numbness enabled Billy to chew his inside jaws to shreds. I learned then to be honest with him and to explain every procedure in detail. When Tom read this, he added some information I did not have: Tom went with Billy to calm him and observed Billy giving the dentist a swift kick as he exited the space capsule.

As an adult, Billy had trouble with his lower front teeth being loose. Our excellent dentist and good friend explained the process to fix the teeth and stated that it would be quite expensive. He said to me, "I know Billy's life span will be short, so I wonder if you want to spend that kind of money."

"Treat him as you would treat me," I replied.

Other ongoing problems have included a persistent skin problem, with rashes on his face, neck, and under his arms. The first dermatologist we saw prescribed a tincture that burned Billy terribly. Even after we found a more knowledgeable dermatologist, the cause of the condition was elusive, with the final diagnosis being a yeast infection. We ran through a host of sprays, salves, and creams, and for years I have treated him almost every night. He says, "Mom, doc me up." Typically his skin is very dry, and he is showing wrinkles on his face and gray in his hair. When we tease him about being an old man, he says, "I like it!"

When we first moved to Sylva, North Carolina, Billy had severe stomach pains. I took him to a doctor who, after a brief examination, immediately diagnosed a hernia, and scheduled the operating room for early surgery. I had not been in town long enough to establish connections with the medical community, but I had made a friend, Shirley McMahan, who was a nurse and was familiar with the physicians in our area. When I expressed my lack of confidence in the diagnosis and concern about surgery, she suggested that I contact a pediatrician, Dr. Bobby Earnest, whom she respected. I made an appointment, and Dr. Earnest said, "Well, frequently children with Down syndrome are constipated, so let's deal with that less invasive possibility first."

He prescribed a laxative and the problem was solved. Although Billy was about fifteen at the time, the pediatrician continued to see him and I learned that all my questioning had not been in vain.

As an adult, Billy suffered with gout for several years. Episodes occurred several times a year and gradually became more frequent. During this time, Billy lived in a trailer behind our house; one morning he called to tell me that he was hurting badly. I went to check on him, and he crawled on his hands and knees to open the door. Another time he walked down to my house using a mop as a crutch. He was so brave and so pathetic it made me cry. Since those early attacks, we are blessed that appropriate medication has prevented recurrence.

Whenever he was sick, whether with a cold or something more serious, Billy stayed at my house until he was feeling better. Thus I heard his nighttime breathing, as I also do when we share a hotel room. He snores loud enough to awaken the town, and I also began to notice that he would stop breathing for periods of time. When I talked with the doctor, he suggested a sleep study to investigate the possibility of sleep apnea. We made a big deal out of the study, having dinner beforehand at his favorite Mexican restaurant, and trying to explain the procedure. However, I hadn't understood how strange the experience would be, and he certainly didn't. Technicians hooked up wires to his body, face, and head and connected them to a monitor. I couldn't imagine that he would go through with it—I wasn't sure I could—but he did. I had planned to stay as long as necessary, but after about an hour he said, "Go on home, Mom, I can handle it."

So I did, and received a call early the next morning to come and get him. I don't think I have ever admired his courage more. The diagnosis was sleep apnea, and a nasal mask was prescribed for him. He is motivated to use it because it makes him sleep better and gives him more energy. When it was time for follow-up tests, the doctor suggested repeating the procedure to check on the amount of air pressure needed. We went to the hospital, Billy got all hooked up, and when the procedure began, he said, "I just can't do it." I assured him that it was all right. Billy felt somewhat ashamed at giving up, but I admired his ability to make it through the first test and to wear gear that I would find claustrophobic.

The most persistent, invasive, and frightening physical difficulty has been a strictured esophagus. While Billy had always had difficulty chewing and swallowing his food, a related emergency occurred during his period of supervised living in a cottage connected to a group home. Returning from a night class in Asheville, I entered our house and saw a note from Bill telling me that he was with Billy at a hospital in an adjoining county. I backtracked twenty miles to the hospital to find Billy on a stretcher in the emergency room in a severe panic. He clung to me and cried profusely in fear and desperation. The story of his rescue was such a touching one that I felt it warranted recognition and sent it to a columnist who printed human-interest stories. He told the story well:

> Billy Schulz works at [a regional sheltered workshop] and lives in an apartment under the supervision of the…County Group Home.
>
> One recent evening, Billy had a problem which he has had for years: food became stuck in his esophagus and he began coughing and choking.
>
> While he was trying to bring the food up, his phone rang. E.P. Blevins, Billy's friend, also a member of the apartment cluster, called to talk.
>
> Realizing that Billy was in trouble, E.P. ran the mile from his apartment to Billy's place. When his pounding on the door brought no response, E.P. found Billy at the nearby apartment of Mildred English, who, with her husband Jimmy, is in the Group Home program.
>
> E.P. and Mildred, after working with Billy for a while, realized he needed professional help. They called the emergency squad and got Billy to the hospital, where he received medical care. E.P. also notified Billy's parents in Sylva.
>
> These two young people exhibited courage and judgment attesting to their maturity, sensitivity, and presence of mind. When E.P. was thanked for being such a good friend, he said, "Well, if you can't be a friend, what have you got?"
>
> —Bob Terrell, *The Asheville Citizen*, March 27, 1980

After prolonged medical consultation, we were advised that the esophagus could be stretched, but once begun, the procedure would need to be repeated periodically. We decided to deal with it by avoiding the foods that seemed to cause the problem, mainly stringy meats such as steak and chicken. Sometimes, especially in restaurants, Billy choked on something and went to the restroom to dislodge it, frequently returning to the table with red blotches on his forehead and a pained look on his face. If I saw him in the morning and he had broken capillaries on his forehead, I realized that he had had difficulty during the previous night, and it frightened me as I knew it frightened him. His choking was one of the fears I had in his solitary living, although he had learned for the most part which foods to avoid. This problem plus the sleep apnea made me wonder if he should be living alone.

On one much later occasion, after our move to Tennessee, Billy had an episode so prolonged and with such severe chest pain that I feared he was having a heart attack. I phoned a cardiologist friend, described the symptoms, and was told that it did not sound like a heart problem. It was such a bad experience, however, that we decided to see a gastroenterologist, who recommended dilation of the esophagus. The outpatient procedure was fairly simple in spite of Billy's apprehension. Dr. Fenyves gave Billy before and after pictures and helped him understand the problem and the solution; I was sorry we hadn't done it sooner.

I felt so good about the procedure that I bought steaks for us to enjoy—a big mistake! I looked at Billy's plate, saw the half-eaten piece of meat and his distressed face and knew that all was not well. He had severe pains in his chest and went to lie down. We called Dr. Fenyves, who decided that it was a psychological reaction since the opening was quite large. Billy has adjusted to the idea that he can eat anything, and now chooses to eat what he likes. All of us are able to relax more, especially when dining at a restaurant. Recently we had steak which he ate with gusto, looked up with a smile on his face, and declared, "I love my 'sophagus!"

Billy's diagnosis of diabetes, at age fifty-one, has required some life style adjustments. He manages the disease without medication, noting and beginning to understand nutrition facts, and maintaining his exercise program. Now, after a few months of my checking his blood, he is doing it alone and writing the daily results in a journal. At Thanksgiving, however, he pleaded, "Mom, please don't talk 'bout carbs!"

As I list Billy's physical difficulties, I am surprised at the number of them. However, if I were to enumerate my own operations and illnesses during the past fifty years (and I promise I will not), the list would be much longer. When I think of the possible conditions prevalent in persons with Down syndrome, such as leukemia, epilepsy, Alzheimer's, and heart defects, I am deeply grateful that Billy's health is as good as it is. In spite of my dentist friend's gloomy prediction, I expect Billy to live for a long time.

Billy's appearance does attract attention from strangers, a fact that bothers me far more than it bothers him. Through the years I have adopted many reactions to the stares his physiognomy invites, reactions prompted by my anger at such rudeness. The first, most obvious, and still most effective measure is to return the stares. When Billy was just a little fellow, the children and I were strolling down the beach when a family walking in front of us turned around with one accord and stared blatantly at Billy. It infuriated me, and I grabbed my children's hands, ran in front of the group, turned around, and stared back at them.

This strategy is particularly effective in a doctor's office when we're sitting close to other people and one of them looks pointedly at Billy for a long time. Then I begin looking the same way at them, so that when they turn they see me staring. I know it's silly and childish, but it does work. At one point I approached a person who was staring and said, "You seem interested in my son; would you like to meet him?" Now, that really works!

In more rational moments, I realize that the curiosity comes from others' lack of experience and information, and that other families don't have our background. But I also think the staring is impolite and insensitive. Fortunately, there are many more kind and sensitive people who look at Billy, smile, and say, "Hello!"

There is one reaction in people that has annoyed Billy in recent years. Sometimes people confuse him with others who resemble him, obviously those who have Down syndrome. We attended a wedding recently where a man greeted Billy

with, "Hi, Charlie, I haven't seen you in a long time."

Billy stiffened and said vehemently, "I'm Billy, not Charlie!"

Over the years I have mellowed along with Billy. I have a red-haired friend who told me, "When you have red hair, wherever you are you will be noticed." Realizing that the same thing is true of Billy, I insist that we look our best wherever we go, except—maybe—at the gym.

You're my special mom!

Billy, I'm the only mom you have.

That's what makes you special!

WITH LIMITED RESOURCES and knowledge, I felt that nothing in my life had prepared me to meet the challenges Billy presented to me. Yet, in looking back, I realize that all my life and experiences enabled me to face the difficulties and to embrace the opportunities awaiting us.

As a child, I never felt special. In a family of colorful, strong-willed individuals, I felt pale and uninteresting. Sandwiched between two handsome, intelligent brothers, I knew that my ticket to full acceptance was to be good, to be obedient, to be sweet. That's what Mother expected of me.

Like Billy, I asked, "Was I a pretty baby?"

Mother laughed and responded, "Lord, no, you looked just like a monkey."

In examining family photos, I believed she was right. I had straight black hair, cut in a Dutch-boy style, long skinny legs; and big brown eyes. Compared to John, my older brother, I was homely. When Fred came along, all of us thought he was the cutest child that ever drew breath.

One day when I was in my teens and serving coffee to Mother and her bridge-playing guests, I heard an amazing remark as I left the room. One of the ladies said. "I think it's so nice when the girl is the prettiest one in the family."

Was it possible she was talking about me? Probably not. But, if I couldn't be pretty, I could be nice. I could be smart. And most of all, I could be agreeable. With on-going conflict between my brothers and bitter antagonism between Mother and Daddy, I became the peacemaker, with confrontation my nemesis. Years later, after I had learned to fight my battles, I was thrilled to hear someone refer to me as aggressive.

My mother was the driving force in our family. Bright, ambitious, and hardworking, she expected a great deal from us. She yearned to be aristocratic and one of the things she admired most about Daddy, aside from his good looks, was his family background. He was one of the Virginia Boltons and she wanted to belong to that dynasty. Her solution was to create her own background. Instead of coming from a poor, rural family, with a mother who sewed to support her five daughters, she fantasized that her roots were noble. Instead of being proud of going to a business school (named King's), she told people that she had graduated from Queens, a fine-arts college. She came to believe and to live her fantasy, expecting her children to honor her "background." Many times I heard her say, in criticizing someone's manners, "I wasn't raised that way!"

In living this created life, it was important for all of us to impress other people, always presenting ourselves in positive lights, never breathing a word of our family problems or lack of resources.

In spite of her delusions, Mother was my model of courage and determination, imparting the knowledge that I could do anything I wanted to do. She convinced the three of us that life was a struggle and that the way out was through hard work and reaching for opportunities.

Daddy was handsome, charming, and intelligent. He was born into a prominent family who never wanted for worldly goods and who never "controlled" him. Although he left school after the eighth grade, he was a compulsive reader and, therefore, well educated. From him I inherited a love of humor, and in living with him I acquired the joy of reading, the ability to laugh at myself and life, a fear of alcoholism, and an abhorrence of wasted potential. The good times were wonderful; the bad times were increasingly difficult and frequent as we grew older. His alcoholism led to his downfall and contributed to Mother's bitterness.

A part of Daddy's personality is revealed in his approach to success. One day, after he had returned from a small town, attempting to sell whatever he was peddling at the time, I asked, "Daddy, did you sell anything?"

When he replied that he did not, I said sympathetically, "I'm sorry you had a bad day."

His response was, "Oh, no, I didn't have a bad day; I don't have to go there anymore."

He was probably a sociopath, with no sense of responsibility or awareness of his shortcomings. Mother became the sole support of the family as Daddy continued to drink heavily. He had intervals of disappearing from the family, as in a three-month period that he spent on a boat off the coast of Florida (or so he said). He sent Mother a unique soap-stone carving. I thought it was beautiful but remember Mother's comment: "I'd rather have a roll of toilet paper."

Helping Mother as much as I could and coming to Daddy's rescue when necessary, I tried to make things bearable. However, my parents were so different and at such odds that I always felt pulled between them, loving both but unable to love them together.

My older brother John was my idol. We were close all our lives, and his middle-age death devastated me. Fred, my younger brother, and I were separated by four years and later by geographic distance as he lived in Europe and the northeastern United States. We have grown closer as adults than we were as children. Although I had never heard of the "middle child syndrome" until later in life, I exemplified it, always trying to prove myself and playing the role of the family's peacekeeper.

The place we lived as young children was about half a mile from a wonderful wooded area with deep gullies in it—places designed for fun. We called it "the woods" and all three of us loved to go there. John and his friends made a swimming hole at one gully, where they enjoyed skinny-dipping after school and in the summertime. One day Mother sent me to call John to come home. I crept up close to their constructed pool, watched a while, and then said in a soft voice, "John, Mother wants you to come home." Instantly, a bevy of bare butts dove into the homemade pool.

My favorite activity in the woods was swinging on a gnarled vine from one bank of the gullies to the other. Holding onto the vine, hesitating a moment to garner courage, I would swing free, barely missing the edge of the gully. I also enjoyed picking violets in the spring. Fields of purple, fragrant blossoms begged for the picking. I gathered as many as my skirt could hold, bringing them home like a trophy to my mother, who loved flowers. I also brought home a case of poison ivy, scratching and burning and, even so, looking forward to my next trip to the woods.

Fred, who was much younger than John and me, started sneaking off to the woods almost daily. I don't know if Mother was suddenly aware of the danger, or if she was just more protective of Fred as the baby of the family. Once she discovered his forays, she began spanking him afterward, attempting to teach him to obey her but he persisted in going. Finally, she asked him, "Don't you know I'm going to spank you when you go to the woods?"

He replied, "Yes ma'am, but it's worth it!"

Life in a small southern town was simple. We walked to school, went to church, visited relatives in the summer, and had neighborhood friends. Mother worked at a time when most mothers stayed home, so instead of coming home to cookies and milk, I came home and made cookies. Mother sometimes said that she didn't know where our next meal was coming from, but I don't remember ever being hungry.

We always had a "colored" maid, one who usually became close to the family. It was during this time in my life that I began to see the injustices in our social system. Our maid, Lila, was very important to our family's well-being and we took her for granted as a servant. This doesn't mean that we were unkind to her—we just treated her in a different way. One time when Lila was sick she sent her mother to help the family and since Lila's name was Lila Brown, I called her mother "Mrs. Brown." Mother took me aside and said, "We don't call colored folks 'Mrs.'"

This seemed crazy to me and caused me to pay attention and to become aware of the discrimination we all practiced. Perhaps this was the beginning of my understanding of prejudice.

I loved school. We were never told to do our homework; we just did it. I was something of a loner, although I had one best friend who walked to and from school with me. My family never quite fit socially; we were stuck between lower class (financially) and middle class (culturally).

We lived in the last of a series of rented houses, a pretty white house with a large front porch containing a swing—perfect for courting—and with a pear tree that in the spring became part of the porch. There was a barn in the back yard, left from the days when South Union Street was in the country. We always had a garden, which my dad loved to plant, and I can still taste the sun-ripened tomatoes as I stood in the row and ate from the vine. This semi-rural community was rich with good neighbors, at a time when people sat on the front porch and visited.

Mother liked to tell about the time she went across the street to visit with Mrs. Beaver, the elderly mother of our friend Miss Ella. They sat on the swing, talking as well as possible considering Mrs. Beaver's poor hearing. In making conversation, Mother asked, "Mrs. Beaver, do you smell the honeysuckle?"

The response was, "Yes, honey, I smell your supper. You et onions, didn't you?"

The grandest joy of our childhood was spending the summers at our grandmother's old family home in the mountains of Virginia where, it was said, Robert E. Lee stopped and sat on the porch. It was a magic place, nestled at the foot of the Blue Ridge Mountains, in the Shenandoah Valley. The farm house sat close to the highway, with a lower porch supported by numerous columns and an upper balcony stretching across the front of the house. Watching the cars go by from this porch was an afternoon ritual. My grandmother would ask of my dad, "Who was that going by?"

Never failing with an answer, whether he knew the person or not, he'd reply, "Why, that was Old Man Gugenheimer."

Next door to the house was an old building, formerly a store, where we loved to explore and pretend to be customers in the olden days. On Sundays, we joined the line of people—dressed in hats, newly made dresses, and uncomfortable shoes—in walking down the road to the Baptist Church. The rest of the week we rode horses bareback, swam in the creek, made friends with the hired hands and the local neighbors, went to church socials, and had wonderful, bountiful meals.

As I grew older, I explored the house and yard, and found the ice house within a deep hole at the side of the house. It was delightfully cool there, where they kept vegetables in the summer and preserved them in the winter. My favorite place was the attic, where I discovered real treasures. The ledgers from the old store were fascinating, listing goods—sugar, coffee, nails—transported across the mountains and sold to the local customers. There were other books as well, books to be discovered and devoured in the stillness of the upper floor, books like *Anna Karenina* and *Ben Hur*.

As youngsters, we went to Virginia with Daddy's mother, who loved Virginia with all her heart. When we crossed into Virginia at the state line, she always said, "Don't the air smell sweet!"

She was a dear angel of a woman who enjoyed having us with her. When I was quite young, a summer when it was my turn, Grammie and I went to visit a great-uncle in the little town nearby. He lived in what I thought was a castle: a beautiful white house with steeples, turrets, and porches, set on top of a hill and overlooking the town. I climbed up on the widow's walk, pretending to be the princess who lived there. This uncle and his second wife had six sons and one daughter, a girl with long yellow curls. After so many boys, she was their pride and their delight. One day she and I were cutting out paper dolls and—perhaps in jealousy—I reached up and cut off one of her long curls. I knew immediately that I was in trouble and could be sent home. Grammie took me into the next room. I calculated my possible punishment, and received worse: she put her hands on my shoulders, looked into my eyes, and said softly, "Ain't you 'shamed?"

Oh, how I wanted her to hit me! We did stay for the entire planned visit, and I was on my very best behavior the rest of the time.

Although the Virginia visits delivered cherished memories, there were traumatic occurrences in connection with them, too. When I was nine years old, my family and I drove to Virginia to leave John there for his visit. Returning home to North Carolina we had a terrible accident. Daddy was driving and was unable to avoid a car headed straight at us. Mother was seriously injured, with nerves severed under her right arm as she raised it to protect her eyes. She was unable to do anything for a year, so I learned to take care of her and the household. I bathed her, washed and set her hair, and cooked meals under her direction. During this period I witnessed her remarkable determination. To strengthen her damaged hand, she forced herself to knit and crochet and regained partial use of her right hand.

During the summers in Virginia I had a wonderful, tiny bedroom, upstairs and isolated from the other rooms. In it was a single white iron bed with a table to hold my books, paper, and drawing materials. The window faced a pasture, allowing the freshness of the summer to become part of the room.

When I was about twelve years old, my idyll was interrupted by darkness during weekend visits from a cousin and her husband. Amy's husband began sneaking up to my room and fondling me. The first time he came up I was totally unaware, sitting on the bed reading, when he came up behind me and reached under my blouse for my breasts (about the size of bee stings). I was totally surprised and ashamed, unable to understand why this was happening. I didn't know what to do—he was Amy's husband, so I believed I couldn't tell anyone. One evening as all of us were sitting in the parlor reading, he said, "Come on, Jane. Let's go sit on the porch."

Reluctantly I joined him, not knowing what else to do, and noticing that everyone was looking at us. Now I understood—they knew. I felt totally humiliated, and, because I felt I could not push him away, he forced guilt on me in addition to the shame. I learned to hide on weekends when they came to visit and avoided any contact with either of them. Several years later I discovered, through neighbors' gossip, that he was a known pedophile who had been arrested several times. He stayed out of prison because of the family's influence—the family who protected him rather than me—a prime example of the family shame and pride and of the time in which we were living. It was such a demeaning experience that I totally repressed it.

I recalled the ordeal later, when as a teacher I learned of children who had been abused. The anger and anguish engulfed me in a rush. Decades later, I now remembered what I was wearing that evening on the porch—a red plaid shirtwaist dress that Mother had made for me. My mind's eye photographed the details of the front porch and the swing on which we were sitting. I recounted it to Mother, but she was unperturbed and non-responsive. Had she known? I realized that to her, child abuse, especially sexual abuse, was not a subject open for discussion. I felt the most intense anger toward those who turned away from my distress, and I identified with the children I was learning about.

My visits in Virginia provided my first opportunity to interact with children who had developmental disabilities. Across the road from Uncle Sam's house lived a family whose daughter Frances had what I now know was cerebral palsy, although as children we had no idea what was wrong with her. I don't remember ever discussing it or even wondering about her condition, although she was severely physically and intellectually impaired, with very little understandable speech. My cousins and I sat on the porch of Frances's small, cozy, white house adjacent to her father's garage and service station and played with dolls together, making her laugh. Her family took beautiful care of her and showered her with love. I also met a distant cousin of mine who had Down syndrome. She interfered with adult conversation and annoyed her sisters. She was institutionalized when she was older and I never saw her again.

In looking back at my early experience with persons who had disabilities, I realize that there were notable examples in my own family. Mother had three sisters who were deaf. They visited us from time to time and I was especially fond of Aunt Aggie, who was a beautiful, kind woman. Later my children and I learned some elementary sign language from her and had fun using it; I noticed they were using it to communicate with each other during church instead of listening to the sermon.

I learned a great lesson from Aunt Aggie during one of her visits with us. She and I went to the grocery store, and while we were shopping a man approached me with a card that read, "I'm deaf. Please give me a donation to help feed my family."

As I was reaching into my purse, Aunt Aggie, in her guttural deaf-voice, said, "Don't give to him; he is lazy."

I remembered this as a teacher and a parent, realizing that teaching people to earn their fare is much kinder than giving it to them.

Later I became curious about the etiology of the aunts' hearing impairment, and did considerable research in hearing disorders as a graduate student. I now have developed a tremendous respect for my grandmother, who sent three little girls from one end of the state to the other to a school for the deaf. I can only imagine the anguish and loneliness of that decision in doing what was best for them.

My own high school was particularly exciting as I discovered dramatics, Shakespeare, and art. There were two teachers who had a profound and lasting effect on me. Miss Quinn, my English teacher, required us to learn poetry and to appreciate literature. One day she assigned us the task of learning a poem for the next day. Almost everyone found the shortest poem available, but I learned the entire "Wreck of the Hesperus" and recited all twenty-two quatrains dramatically, striving to impress my teacher and to push myself to the edge of my capabilities.

I have always felt grateful to Miss Quinn for having us memorize poetry, but never so much as in my twenties. Following surgery to correct a detached retina, I was required to hold my head still for three weeks, with bandages covering my eyes.

In this visual void, with little to occupy my time and mind, I recited the poetry I had learned, forming mental pictures that filled the emptiness I was experiencing. Although it seemed impossible to hold my head still for three weeks, I could do it one day at a time. When the surgery failed, I endured another three weeks. During difficult periods in life, I now know I can do anything one day at a time.

Miss Quinn encouraged me to write and applauded my efforts. One day while I was looking out the window, daydreaming, I suddenly began writing. She recognized the creative energy and asked me to read what I had written. This is it, remembered all these years:

> I'd like to take a tree
> And shake its bristles dry.
> To dip it in the sea
> And brush across the sky.

Also the dramatics coach, Miss Quinn urged us to express ourselves in various ways. I participated in many plays, both acting and designing sets. As a result of Miss Quinn's influence and encouragement, I won the school essay medal and membership in the National Thespian Society.

Although I went to school dances, I didn't have a real boyfriend in high school. All I knew about lust and love came from *Jane Eyre* and *Gone With the Wind*, love stories in magazines at the public library, and from my one best friend who did have a boyfriend. Mother had drilled into me the concept of "saving yourself for marriage," and while I wasn't sure why that was so important, it mattered because Mother said it did. Anyway, I hadn't been tempted in that department. Not until Kenneth.

The summer after my junior year in high school I went to the Methodist Youth retreat in Lake Junaluska. A religious assembly community set in the mountains of North Carolina, this place was, and still is, a haven of peace and reverence. We slept in cabins, had workshops during the day, and enjoyed social activities at night. On the last night, during dinner, I was struggling to slice a piece of ham on my plate, oblivious to others around me, when I heard, "Could I cut that for you?"

I looked up with surprise and realized that someone had been watching me, someone who now took my plate, cut my meat into bite sizes, and returned it to me with a smile. We made plans to meet that night at the rock wall. We talked and I found that Kenneth lived in a city not too far from my home, that he was a year older than I, and that he would be entering college in the fall. The next afternoon we again met at the rock wall, sitting in the warm sunshine. He slipped my comb from my purse and began combing my hair, commenting on how silky and lustrous it was. He told me about his college plans and his ambition to write. I was in love.

When Kenneth came to see me on weekends during the following year, I learned about the temptation Mother feared. Being with Kenneth was electric. As my resistance diminished over time, his sense of responsibility increased and I was saved from the proverbial fate worse than death.

During this final school year, I was inspired by another devoted teacher, Miss Cochrane, who saw in me artistic talent and promise as an art teacher like herself. She helped me apply for a loan for college and sent me to her art professor at Woman's College of the University of North Carolina (now The University of North Carolina at Greensboro). The summer after I graduated from high school, I stayed with my Aunt Freda in Washington, D. C., to work and save some money for college.

In looking for a summer job, I saw a solicitation for someone with experience in coloring photographs (this was before color photos were produced) for a portrait studio. Although I had never colored photos, I thought, "How hard could it be?" I applied for the job. Of course they asked me if I had colored photos before and, realizing the job depended on it, fibbed, "Oh yes."

The next question was, "Do you prefer sepia or black and white?"

I had never heard of sepia, so I responded with "black and white," to which the interviewer said, "Great, sepia is much easier."

I was hired. The manager took me to a sleazy building on the outskirts of the city. He showed me to a cubicle containing a stack of photographs, several pots of paint, some brushes, and pieces of cotton. I just sat there for a while, until the girl in the next cubicle commented, "You've never done this before, have you?"

It was time for the truth. She laughed, befriended me and taught me how to do the job. It was a simple—if tedious—process and I became good at it, making a salary of $15 a week.

At the end of the summer, with $60 in my checking account, I went home, made my dresses, gathered my meager belongings, and took the bus to Greensboro. I was completely at home in college, and became president of the freshman class, leader of the dorm, and discovered that boys were attracted to me. As an art major, I was entranced with the techniques I was encouraged to explore: charcoal, watercolor, oil, textile design, and sculpture. I had a part-time job in the art department and spent twenty hours a week lettering slides for the art historian and painting picture frames for the faculty members. Dr. Gregory Ivy, the professor to whom Miss Cochrane had sent me, was extraordinary with water color, and under his tutelage, it became my favorite medium. When we designed textile in repeated motifs, he took me to the department store to purchase the appropriate fabric, knowing I couldn't afford the fabric he would choose. As the recipient of such kindness, I bloomed, and every day was an adventure.

IT WAS SUNDAY AFTERNOON. I sat on the side of the bed in my dorm room, painting my nails with bright red polish, listening to the radio, singing along with Frank Sinatra, "I'll never smile again, until I smile at you." The music stopped and the program was interrupted with the solemn announcement, "The Japanese have bombed Pearl Harbor."

Newscasters announced: "A Sunday morning attack on Pearl Harbor, on the island of Oahu, began The United States' direct part in World War II." Where was Oahu, what was Pearl Harbor? The next morning President Roosevelt declared war on Japan.

Everything changed. We started having dances for soldiers and began to realize that World War II would involve each of us. On a personal basis, I recognized that I didn't have the money to return to college the following year and that it was time to go to work. I rode the bus to Charlotte and took a typing test so I could apply for a job with the FBI in Washington, where my family had recently moved. Daddy had been offered a job in the District of Columbia, so it seemed that he and Mother were attempting to make a new start. Apparently a decision had been made during my year's absence.

When school was out, I reluctantly said goodbye to my dear friends and again got on the bus. By that time I had an appointment to the FBI (I thought that sounded exciting) and set out one day to report for my interview.

This my dad in World War II. An my dad is good lookin. Like me.

I can picture myself: eighteen years old, strolling down Vermont Avenue, dressed in a skirt and blouse with a blue straw hat on the back of my head, pristine white gloves, and wartime nylon stockings drooping on my skinny legs. On the way I passed an imposing, beautiful, black-marble-fronted building on Vermont Avenue just across from Lafayette Park and the White House. I thought, "That would be a nice place to work."

I went in and found that there was an immediate opening for a clerk-typist with Reconstruction Finance Corporation, a federal organization dealing with synthetic and imported rubber. I don't know why my instincts led me there, but it turned out to be a good decision: I was learning to take chances, and this gave me confidence.

Although I had been disappointed that I couldn't return to college, I felt the thrill of a new adventure and quickly embraced the opportunity to live in a beautiful, pulsing city. Washington was a crazy, amazing place to be; there was constant excitement and frenzy in addition to the panic of war. Daddy worked for the District of Columbia government, Mother for a large hospital, and I for the federal government. Fred was still in high school and John, who had married, was in the Army, headed overseas.

Unable to find suitable housing, we all lived in a small, damp basement apartment in the city. We were in such cramped quarters that one night I heard Daddy exclaim, "I'm too young to live like this!" I empathized with his frustration. After I missed a number of my nice high-school graduation gifts, we realized that someone was rifling our apartment during our daily absences. Mother, with her usual ingenuity, made arrangements with an insurance agent who found us a row house in the northeast section of Washington. She turned the place into a lovely home, planting roses in the back yard and tastefully, creatively, constructing rooms of some elegance. I particularly liked my upstairs room, which opened onto a screen porch, also connected to another small bedroom. Fred attended a nearby school. We joined Mt. Vernon Place Methodist Church, a prestigious downtown church, and used the efficient bus system for transportation. It was home.

It was interesting to watch Fred develop from a spoiled brat into a self-assured and determined person. He acquired a taste for classical music and loved to conduct the orchestra as he listened to records, head bobbing and hair flying. He so much wanted to lift the family onto his newly discovered plane. I remember one night when the table had been set for dinner he placed candles in the holders, lit them, and exclaimed, "I'm going to bring culture to this house if I have to ram it down your throats!"

Fred persists in his mission; he is still my mentor on music and art, and accompanies me to museums and the opera whenever I visit Washington.

My brother John was stationed in France at this time, and I truly missed him. We saw his wife frequently and were standing by when his daughter was born; I was delighted that she was named for me. In John's absence, she was taught to kiss his picture each night and bid him good night. When he returned from overseas, she continued to kiss his picture at bedtime.

For the rest of us, life was structured around the awareness of war and the difficulties it imposed on everyone. Most government agencies, including mine, worked six days a week, with Christmas Day the only holiday. At the office I made friends with people who viewed my naiveté with humor and who helped me learn the ropes. Elsie, several years older than I, took me under her wing, covered for me, and became my dear friend for life. I caught on quickly, took a course in shorthand at night, and became secretary to Mr. Hubert, who helped me develop slightly beyond a small town girl.

I still lived at home with my family, for no other arrangement would have been considered acceptable. I had a curfew each night, even though I was working and contributing to the household finances. One night late I forgot my key and crawled in the window. There sat Mother, in the dark, waiting for me. She held a tight rein and it never occurred to me to challenge it.

Washington was full of military men, and I met quite a few of them. Every relationship, however, ended with "going away to war." I learned so much about the real world, and never more than on a train trip to Carolina Beach.

With Mother's permission (which surprised me), I was going to see a young man stationed there, someone I had met at one of the college dances and with whom I had been corresponding. The trip required a long, crowded train ride on an ancient car filled with soldiers and a few civilians. Seated across from me was a young woman who was going to meet her husband. Facing each other, we began to talk; she sang her husband's praises and declared her love for him. Soon we were joined in our double seats by a soldier who was handcuffed to a Military Policeman. The young woman and the prisoner started talking and after a while began making out heavily. I had never seen anything like that taking place in public or private. I tried to avert my eyes, which I am sure were as big as saucers, but couldn't help being aware of the action. As their frenzy mounted, the soldier convinced the M.P. to undo the handcuffs so that he and the woman could retreat to the lavatory. Very soon an alarm sounded; the prisoner had jumped the train.

During this period, our family life was deteriorating due to Daddy's renewed, intensive drinking. Mother was understandably angry, meeting him at the door with, "So you've been drinking again!"

He lost his job and began selling advertising specialties, such as key chains and matchbooks. He was a born salesman and, as Mother had said, "could sell ice to an Eskimo." When he came off a binge, he always craved cookies or cake, and like a good, loving daughter, I cooked for him. He and Fred were in physical and emotional conflict; he and Mother conversed only in anger; but he could always count on me. Instead of condemning him, I enabled him, striving to reestablish peace in the household. However, I no longer felt free to bring people to the house, never knowing what to expect from Daddy's erratic behavior and Mother's certain wrath.

Searching for a safe social outlet, I decided to join the Stage Door Canteen. This venue was carefully monitored to maintain its enviable reputation among a host of organizations set up to entertain servicemen. With a little pull from Mother's hospital board acquaintances, I was accepted into the club as a hostess and found it an extraordinary place. A small stage in the old Belasco Theater accommodated the many famous performers who came to entertain the soldiers, sailors, and marines. One of my favorites was Victor Borge, who had the men and the hostesses roaring with laughter. Little tables scattered around the dance floor were filled with servicemen and hostesses drinking Cokes, smoking cigarettes, and sharing stories of home and family. Music of Benny Goodman, Artie Shaw, Billie Holiday, and Ella Fitzgerald reverberated through the room, with people singing along and dancing to the familiar tunes. I always loved to dance, and when I put on the required red-white-and-blue apron, had more partners than I knew what to do with.

I was dancing with a marine when Bill cut in. He was big and good-looking in his Navy uniform, and outrageously impertinent. His first comment was, "Why don't you comb your hair to the side?"

I retorted, "If you don't like my hair the way it is, dance with someone else."

It turned out that he had been playing a game, asking all the hostesses to change their hair and apparently he liked my response. We kept on dancing, although he was not a good dancer, and soon sat at one of the tables to talk. He said, "Your eyes remind me of my grandmother."

What? Not the kind of thing you want to hear from a handsome man. I'm sure I showed my puzzlement, as he quickly explained that his grandmother was a beautiful woman who had big brown eyes. Oh well, there were all kinds of people at the Stage Door Canteen.

We were not allowed to date the men we met there, a rule designed to combat the idea of a pick-up place for serviceman. As usual I obeyed the rules. Bill met me there each time I was scheduled to be a hostess, and we talked a great deal about our families and our postwar dreams. The thing that impressed me most about him was his devotion to his family; it seemed to be the kind of family I had always wanted. I was beginning to like him and to look forward to our visits.

I was caught off guard when Bill called me at the office to inform me that he was being reassigned to duty in Norfolk, Virginia. He suggested that since he would no longer be going to the Stage Door Canteen, it would be "legal" for us to go out together. That seemed reasonable, and he proposed that we have dinner together that very night. Going out to dinner always called for gloves and a hat, which I hadn't worn that day. I responded that I didn't have a hat to wear. "Don't worry, I'll bring you one."

As I went to the lobby to meet Bill for our first real date, he presented me with a fresh gardenia to wear in my hair. What could be more romantic? I melted, pinned the flower in my hair, and joyously joined him for dinner. After dinner we went to meet some friends of his, one of whom confided in me, "Bill says you're the girl he's going to marry."

His presumption really angered me, and I assured the friend that we had no intention to marry. However, I must admit that I was flattered that he was so deeply smitten.

We spent a whirlwind week, going from one impressive club or restaurant to the other. I thought he must be wealthy but learned later that he had played poker all week to afford our dates. At the end of the week he left for Norfolk, expecting to be sent overseas. Both of us realized that we were in love and that we wouldn't have much time together.

CHAPTER 8

The Knot

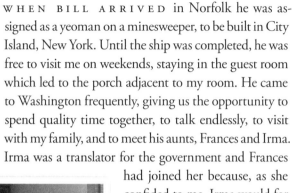

My mom and my dad got married. In 1944. In Washington. An I not there.

WHEN BILL ARRIVED in Norfolk he was assigned as a yeoman on a minesweeper, to be built in City Island, New York. Until the ship was completed, he was free to visit me on weekends, staying in the guest room which led to the porch adjacent to my room. He came to Washington frequently, giving us the opportunity to spend quality time together, to talk endlessly, to visit with my family, and to meet his aunts, Frances and Irma. Irma was a translator for the government and Frances had joined her because, as she confided to me, Irma would forget to wash her underwear. They were fascinating women who became good friends and gave me an indication of the kind of family Bill came from. In between visits our courtship continued by mail—letters each day written in creative format and extravagant language.

Bill proposed to me three months after we had met. He gave me an engagement ring created with a diamond from his father and a simple design of Bill's choice. Mother took Bill aside to talk to him about how he would be expected to treat her darling daughter; Daddy welcomed him by showing him where he kept his liquor.

When Bill got a leave, we took a trip to Milwaukee for me to meet his family. His parents, one of his brothers, and a sister lived in the home, a large house in an old established neighborhood. Two other brothers came from out of town to look me over, and we visited a number of Bill's relatives for the same purpose. They were cultured people of strong German backgrounds; they welcomed me graciously. I was overwhelmed by the attention and astonished by the abundance and magnificence of the meals—these people were dedicated to good eating! Bill's father, a robust, imposing man, urged me to eat, so I resorted to hiding part of my food under baked potato skins when possible. I loved his parents and was eager to be part of this endearing family.

Mother and I began making plans for the wedding, to take place at Mount Vernon Place Methodist Church, with Dr. John Rustin officiating. My brother's wife, Peg, would be matron of honor and my friend, Elsie, a bridesmaid. Bill's shipmate would be best man and my brother Fred, usher. We bought my dress, ordered bridesmaid dresses, engaged a photographer and planned for a reception at our home. With Bill in his Navy uniform, everything would be in white, a distinct departure from the varied pastel dresses currently in vogue. It would be a Cinderella dream come true. Fortunately we had decided to send announcements rather than invitations. We scheduled our wedding for May 26. On May 20 Bill called me at the office, saying, "I'm being transferred to a ship on the 26th, we'll have to get married tomorrow."

Without questioning his decision, I went into Mr. Hubert's office and, like a child, announced that the tea he and his wife were having the next day would have to be canceled. In his administrative manner he responded, "We'll just turn it into the wedding reception."

That evening was busy in our household. Bill's family had to be notified to cancel their trip, Peg was up late hemming her dress, and the bridesmaids' head-pieces hadn't arrived so Mother fashioned beautiful coronets from roses in her garden. Friends were notified by phone of the change in plans. As we neglected to call the photographer, Frances and Irma took the only photographs we have and represented Bill's family well.

Although hurry-up weddings were not unusual in 1944, the newspaper feature writer was intrigued with our story and recorded it well:

> Due to the unexpected change of orders of William H. Schulz, petty officer, second class, U.S.N.R., arrangements for his wedding to Miss Jane Eloise Bolton were hurriedly made and the ceremony took place Sunday, May 21, instead of the later date originally selected. Receiving word only a day before the wedding of the new orders of her fiancé, Miss Bolton completed her plans and the wedding was one of the prettiest of the season.

Following an accurate description of the ceremony and reception, the reporter closed this way:

> After the reception the young couple left for a short wedding trip and the bride now is with her parents until her husband receives his new assignment.

We had only a one-night honeymoon. Bill went back to Norfolk early the next day, leaving me a huge bouquet of Talisman roses.

Bill came to Washington for visits until he was assigned to City Island, New York, where they would build his ship. I joined him there for a week, staying in an upstairs apartment in a local resident's home. After Washington's frenzy, it was a rest for me. I compiled our photographs and clippings into a scrapbook, slept late, lounged on the beach, and met him for lunch in the cozy village. He proudly introduced me to his friends, called me "Schatzie" (German for little treasure), and treated me like a princess. I felt beautiful and adored. I knew that I would be with him forever.

When the minesweeper was commissioned, Bill was assigned to Staten Island where they were to remain until further orders. I joined him in New York City for several weekends filled with interesting experiences. The hotels must have been guarding against prostitutes, because I was certainly treated in an unusual manner. On my first visit I arrived at the designated hotel, clad in my best suit, perky hat, and Mother's fur piece, prepared to be treated like a lady. The man at the desk refused to let me go to the room Bill had reserved because I didn't have a copy of our marriage license. I was humiliated and had to sit on a bench in the entrance until Bill arrived.

Sometimes Bill couldn't join me until the day after I arrived, so I was left to amuse myself. One evening I went down to the hotel dining room to have a quiet dinner and was seated next to a young businessman, who initiated a friendly conversation. As the music started he asked me to dance; I agreed. As soon as we got on the dance floor a hotel employee tapped my partner: "We don't allow that here." Humiliated again, I went to my room in tears.

One afternoon, attempting to pass the time until Bill's arrival, I went to a movie in the afternoon. I had just begun to watch the feature when a man sat next to me and put his hand on my knee. I fled to my hotel room, grabbed my book and waited for Bill. Obviously I was not prepared for wartime in the city.

Eventually I left my job and joined Bill on Staten Island, where we had an upstairs apartment with use of the kitchen and a shared bathroom. I had not cooked much beyond cakes and salads without direction, so we had some interesting meals. Our divergent backgrounds became clear: I had never tasted lamb, and he had never eaten turnip greens. One night I made an apple pie and he woke me up in the middle of the night to tell me how good it was. He was always appreciative of my efforts and ate anything I put before him. It was a good place to begin a marriage.

Frequently we took the ferry to New York to go to plays (servicemen were admitted free of charge) and to have dinner. Coming back on the ferry late at night, we would huddle together on a bench and never feel the cold. We were on Staten Island for a month, a priceless month that was a magical experience for both of us and for our marriage. At the end of the month, Bill had to live on the ship. We assumed he would be going overseas, probably to Japan, and he wanted me to be in Milwaukee with his family.

I arrived in Milwaukee on New Year's Eve, and when I smelled the family's traditional pickled herring, my reaction made me think that I might be pregnant. I got a receptionist job with Bill's Uncle Irv, a surgeon, who later confirmed my suspicion of the pregnancy. Irv's wife helped me figure out what they then called the ETC (expected time of confinement).

Things were so different then: we didn't disclose our "condition" or wear maternity clothes until late in the pregnancy. I began taking a jar to my bedroom at night so Bill's parents wouldn't hear me using the bathroom. I continued to work, but when my dresses became tight I went to Washington for a visit with Mother and Daddy and bought some maternity clothes. The dresses were ugly, and the wartime shortage of rubber meant there was no elastic. I wore a strange over-the-shoulder contraption to hold my stockings up.

Although Bill served on a minesweeper in New York Harbor, he never went overseas and was transferred to a base in Illinois, where we again found an upstairs apartment and waited for our baby.

We were completely naïve and unprepared for parenthood. I spent ten days in the hospital, in a seven-bed ward, coming home to no washing machine and a baby who had diarrhea. Bill and I learned together, sharing feedings, washing diapers, and playing with our beautiful baby.

With the war's end, we moved to Milwaukee and into the family home. Bill's dear mother had died, without seeing her grandchild, and we spent what seemed like eons with his loving father and his contentious sister. Housing was scarce; we searched the ads and visited a number of the places listed. Several were willing to rent to us if we would pay for them to add on to their house, or finance any number of projects. We placed our own ads, attempting to be creative enough to entice people to rent to us.

We finally found a duplex for sale and talked with friends who were in our same situation. We bought the house jointly with $100 down, were unable to evict the people in the upstairs unit, and spent a year in a two-bedroom, one-bathroom house with another couple and their two children. Jean and Otto had bought a piano, an albatross in such close quarters, for $10. We moved it from room to room; it ended up in the kitchen, where we used it for a buffet table. Since they couldn't get it upstairs when their apartment became available, they had to pay someone $15 to haul it away. It's a tribute to our humor and acceptance that we remained close friends.

Once we were able to occupy our own part of the house fully, we were blissfully happy, painting and decorating our home together. Bill was working at a bank during the day and going to business school at night while John and I were reading stories and venturing into the snow. Bill's dad was a frequent visitor, bringing us goodies from the bakery and playing with his grandson.

About once a year John and I would fly to Washington, taking a midnight plane to save money. Mother and Daddy had divorced while I was away, and although I knew it was inevitable, it made me sad. Like most children whose parents divorce, I felt I could have done something had I been there. Daddy moved into a shabby apartment and began selling advertising specialties only as the need arose. John and I always visited with him, listening to his stories, laughing at his jokes, and sharing meals.

The phrase "miscellaneous items" would have little meaning to most people. To me it evokes a picture I will never forget. Daddy put a number of the products he was selling—matchbook covers, key chains, and the like—into a box, presenting them to John as "miscellaneous items." He and John sat on the floor examining them and reading their messages. For years this was John's favorite possession, reminding him of his close relationship with his granddaddy. However, when he asked if he could spend the night alone with Daddy I also saw painfully the disappointment in his eyes and the hurt in Daddy's when I said, "no."

We had good friends in Milwaukee, but the winters were hard on me, and Bill didn't like his job at the bank. Friends of mine from North Carolina offered Bill a job and I was hopeful that it would work out. Bill went south to interview and returned, bringing me a magnolia blossom, to announce that he had accepted the job as salesman for a brick-manufacturing plant.

It was a welcome move except that we had to leave Bill's

dad, who was so close to us and especially to John. He died soon after we left Milwaukee, and I truly believe it was from loneliness.

Sanford was a lovely town. Bill adapted well to the South and we made many friends through our church and his membership in the Junior Chamber of Commerce. Somehow, his job didn't work out well. He said one of the men "had it in for him," so he decided that we should return to Washington for him to go to school. We stayed with Mother for a year while Bill went to school, but we missed our friends and lifestyle in Sanford, and returned there to live.

We remained in Sanford until I was pregnant with Billy. John was doing well in school; Tom, our second boy, was a great joy; Bill and I were happily married. Our only troubles seemed to be financial. For one reason or another, Bill seemed unable to hold a job. I worked as a secretary before Tom was born and again when he was old enough to stay with a neighbor. Bill had been selling insurance and doing well but always wanted to "make it big." Thinking it would be a lucrative business, he opened a hamburger place near the swimming pool. Supposedly supervised by him, the business was operated by young people who cheated him. His insurance business suffered from this distraction and we sank head over heels in debt. The restaurant was a disastrous venture that ended in bankruptcy. At the end we were eating the remaining purchased shrimp which we estimated cost us three dollars each.

My brother John offered Bill a position with his insurance agency and transferred him to Jacksonville, North Carolina, to sell insurance to the marines. We made a hasty retreat, deep in debt, to try another job, another town, and to wait for another baby.

CHAPTER 9

The Awakening

I not talking bout names. I talking bout Santa Claus!

IN THE SAME WAY THAT WE HAD MOVED to Jacksonville for new work and a new baby, two years later we had moved to Columbus, expecting Mary's arrival. But this time, our future looked bright; we were finally able to own a home, we made friends, we put down roots, we had a degree of permanence: Columbus was home.

Even with the extra challenge of boosting Billy's development, our family members began to thrive. John was

in school; Tom, Billy, and Mary were at home with me. Bill and I were involved in John's activities and in touch with his teachers. At home, Tom, Billy, Mary, and I maintained our daily routines of playing, reading, keeping house, and taking walks about the neighborhood.

I was doing exactly what I felt I was destined to do—raising a family. Although I had worked in the past, I had no desire to leave my children and couldn't imagine a more pleasant life. We had fun together of our own making. One hot Georgia day we decided to make a swimming pool. There was a large drainage ditch between our yard and the street. The children and I took our massive army camping tarp, fitted it into the ditch, and boarded off the ends. The hose reached from the outside faucet and we filled the ditch until we had our own swimming pool. This provided a couple of days of great entertainment for us, and for our neighbors.

Christmas was the greatest event of all. Bill especially enjoyed decorating and planning surprises for the children and for me. Long before theme decorations were in vogue, he envisioned one year to have a gold tree and corresponding decorations. The whole family made loops from gold wrapping paper and tape to form chains for the tree; we spray-painted pine cones to drape from a garland on the wall, and purchased gold balls in graduated sizes, which Bill meticulously spaced on the tree.

Billy got into the Christmas spirit with the rest of us. A firm believer in Santa Claus, he became concerned when he realized we didn't have a fireplace for Santa to enter. Bill constructed a cardboard chimney and put it on the roof—Billy was not convinced. Finally we told him we would leave the front door open on Christmas Eve. (In later years, when our children matured and our group grew larger with extended family, we decided to draw names for giving presents.

Still Billy talked about what Santa would bring. I explained, "Billy, we drew names, remember? Those will be our gifts." In a huff, he declared, "I not talking 'bout names; I talking 'bout Santa Claus!")

Bill was working day and night and apparently doing well selling insurance to military personnel. It was a shock to me when I found we were in debt again. I didn't understand how that happened, as Bill had been managing our finances. One day he announced: "You will have to go to work for a short while until we can get caught up."

I was devastated at the thought of leaving my little girl and sweet boys, especially Billy, who needed me so much. However, there seemed to be no other solution. Could I resist and let the debts soar as they had in the past? I believed it was a temporary plan, and knew that I had no choice.

It is difficult to acknowledge the degree to which Bill's wishes were law. I later talked with a psychologist who related that it's not unusual for women to be in control in the workplace and completely dominated in the home. Bill was a good man, devoted to me and his children, but he was also the product of a German family in which the father ruled. I had been an obedient, submissive child who never questioned her mother's authority; in many ways, marriage simply redirected my management. I now find it difficult to believe that I was completely nonresistant to Bill's judgment and wishes.

Writing about our lives has revealed to me one of my major character flaws: my reluctance to stand my own ground. My efforts to avoid confrontation made me almost subservient to my husband and to my mother. Now I understand my docility was related to my earlier family role, combined with the experience that it was the easier route.

My dependence on Bill was exemplified by established practices. We had one car, which he always drove wherever we went. He either took me grocery shopping or did it himself. He bought furniture without consulting me; I still have pieces that I would not have chosen. One example of his dominance still amuses the children and me, as it completely describes his method of operation. He went to buy a new car and phoned to ask whether I would like brown or green. I responded that I would prefer green, having never liked the color brown. When he arrived in a brown car, I told him, "I really don't care what color car you got. I just wonder why you asked me."

He answered, "I thought you would say brown."

The frequency with which Bill traded cars bothered me. Once I sarcastically remarked, "You trade cars when the ashtray is full." He explained in great detail the rationale for never totally owning a car: it made more sense to keep a new one, one that didn't lose its trade-in value. I bought his explanation, as I always did. I finally discovered that this was another of his elaborate financial maneuvers: when you trade cars, you skip one month's payment.

Bill's lack of judgment in handling money continued to be a source of contention between us and despair for me. Rather than taking control of our finances, I accepted his authority. There were many instances of overspending, always indicating his wish to be magnanimous, to afford the best for his family.

He delighted in buying gifts for me, particularly clothes. He had excellent taste and spared no expense. Bill knew how much I enjoyed my bath. With the children in bed, the chores done and the house quiet, I took a nice warm, leisurely bath each night. On my birthday, Bill gave me soft and pretty, luxurious bath towels. That evening, with the cares of the day behind me, I slipped into the bathroom and turned on the faucets for my bath: nothing came out. Bill hadn't paid the water bill.

I had been looking for a second-hand piano so Mary could learn to play as I had always longed to do. For an anniversary gift, Bill had a brand new piano delivered to our home. I should have sent it back; instead, I thanked him and arranged for piano lessons for Mary. In several days I received a book of coupons in the mail from the piano vendor.

Later, when Bill bought a boat, someone asked me, "How long is the boat?" Beginning to get the picture, I answered, "Twenty-four months."

It has taken me forever to figure out how I could possibly have maintained such a flawed relationship. I desired to establish and maintain the kind of family that Bill had come from, a stable home in which the father, the breadwinner, was in charge; a home in which the mother created a haven, a pleasant and safe place for children to grow up and for the husband to delight in at the end of a weary but profitable day. This dream always eluded me. I later learned I did not have a true picture of Bill's family, but I foolishly and hopelessly pursued my illusions.

Given our history, it was natural for me to accept Bill's decision that I would look for a job; it seemed the only way out of our financial dilemma. We had a friend who worked for the superintendent of Ft. Benning schools at the post where Bill was selling insurance. When she found I was looking for work, she mentioned that there was a vacancy in her office. I applied for and got the job as secretary to the director of instruction, later becoming secretary to the superintendent. It was an interesting job, one in which I learned a great deal about school administration and administrators, school finances, curriculum, and teachers. Little did I realize that I would return there as a teacher myself.

My return to the work force brought about many changes in the family routine. At that time there were no daycare accommodations for children whose mothers worked outside the home. Those who did work hired maids to stay with their children and do the housework. It was difficult to find people who were dependable, and I was never sure from day to day that someone would show up. We did have several maids who became dear to the children and were deeply appreciated by me.

One memorable young woman, Equila, stayed with us for several years. I learned from her, and from others, how hard life could be for disenfranchised people. Equila's living conditions must have been extremely poor, as I realized one cold, dreary morning. When I commented on the weather, Equila responded, "Yes ma'am, when I went in to change my baby's diaper, it was froze on him." Such experiences added to my growing concern for others and my constant awareness of many discriminatory situations.

I tried to use my working, and having a maid, as a vehicle to give me quality time with the children. Sometimes this idea worked; at other times I was too tired to play. I hoped they would be in a better environment when they were in school. At this time, Tom was attending a school within walking distance of home, and Mary would soon be entering kindergarten there.

It was time to investigate a situation for Billy, so I went to see the director of special education to determine what classes would be available for him. It was the accepted and standard practice at that time for all children with special needs to attend separate schools; I thought registering him would be routine. The director was a pleasant person, as well as the mother of a child with developmental disabilities, who told me matter-of-factly, "He won't be eligible to attend school until he's eight years old."

This made no sense to me. Mary, who was very bright, was ready to enter kindergarten at age five. Why was Billy, who certainly needed more help, not eligible for school attendance at the age of six?

Instead of finding answers, I was confronted with additional questions: why did tax dollars not extend education to all children when they reached school age? How could I explain to Billy that his brothers and sister went to school and he could not? What could we do as a family to remedy the situation? It was clear to me that I would need to be at home with Billy and to resume my job as fulltime mother and homemaker.

The next morning at breakfast I said to Bill, "I need to quit working and stay at home with the children." Without hesitation he replied, "No, you'll have to work for a little while longer."

It was at this moment, on this morning, that the path of my life changed. I went to work, sat at my typewriter, and looked into space. Then, what I can only interpret as a visitation, or God speaking to me, came as the strongest force I have ever felt. I actually heard a voice say, "You are going to be working for the rest of your life."

I felt calm, resolute, and in control. As I sat with my hands on the keyboard, I said out loud, "Then it will not be behind this typewriter."

"BUT MOM, I thought you were *twenty*-seven!"

Mary's high-pitched voice permeated the registration hall of Columbus College as I solemnly continued to fill out the appropriate forms. She had wanted to accompany me on this significant occasion, and I welcomed her presence to lend a trace of normalcy to the event.

There were several professors who appeared to be much older, but all of the students were as young as my John. I was somewhat intimidated, registering as a sophomore, when I had been out of college for twenty years. I felt much more acceptable when my advisor, Dr. Mahan, kindly said to me, "I really like having mature students in my classes."

I immediately registered for her psychology course as well as the sociology class she recommended. It was a momentous event, requiring all the courage I could muster. And yet, in spite of the strangeness, I felt exhilarated.

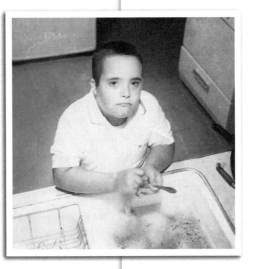

The newly formed Columbus Junior College was housed in an abandoned hosiery mill, awaiting completion of the permanent building. I found it ironic, as I had grown up in a mill town. One night when my brother John was visiting, he and Bill picked me up after class and he remarked teasingly, "Gee, Sis, I knew things were rough, but I didn't realize you were working the night shift!"

I converted my table-top sewing machine into a desk in our bedroom, found a reading lamp, and was ready to delve into general psychology, which had always interested me. The first night after class I put the children to bed, settled my books at my desk, and began to read

Billy Schulz do the dishes, mommy.

the textbook. The language was difficult, the ideas strange, and I began to cry. Then I raised my head and declared, "What the hell, I can do this!"

I continued to work as secretary to the superintendent of Ft. Benning Children's Schools, attending college at night. My co-workers were surprised at my ambitions, and the administrators somewhat skeptical of my ability. One director, with a brand new doctorate, saw a book on my desk that I was reading for my sociology course, and exclaimed "*You're* reading *that?*"

Such remarks made me more determined to pursue my course.

It was during this second quarter of my renewed education that I discovered that Billy was not eligible for special education, so I began to search for a plan that would serve both of us. This was the beginning of my advocacy role and my career direction—the beginning of my alliance with Billy.

It is providential how events came together. I had always wanted to be a teacher, but due to my financial inability to continue college and my early marriage, it had seemed impossible. Now, given my frustration about Billy's lack of education, I considered my options and discovered a solution to both situations.

At that time, the 1960s, the state of Georgia did not require teacher certification or a college degree for kindergarten teachers. My teaching experience was limited to Sunday School and raising four children, but I felt sure that I could teach kindergarten. In my excitement at the idea, I also fed into the formula the following facts: Mary would be entering kindergarten, John would be in college, Tom in school, I would take Billy with me, and thus there would be no need for child care. Although my salary would be diminished, I would save money and also be at home when the children were there. Bill shared my enthusiasm, and only one challenge remained: finding a teaching position. Never doubting that one would be available, I wrote the following letter to the director of personnel at the county school office:

> I am enclosing an application for a position with the Muscogee County schools as a kindergarten teacher for the school year 1962-63. I would like to supplement the application with some additional information about my background.
>
> I attended Woman's College of the University of North Carolina for one year, where I majored in art, with the intention of teaching. I was financially unable to return to college and obtained a secretarial position in Washington, D. C., where I attended a business college at night. Since that time I have intermittently held several secretarial positions. I am presently employed as Mrs. Hazel Scudder's secretary in the Fort Benning Children's Schools. Since I still have the desire to teach, last fall I enrolled in night classes at Columbus College. I have completed twenty quarter hours and plan to complete ten hours in the spring quarter. Upon fulfillment of my contract with the Fort Benning Schools in June, I will enroll as a full-

time student in the summer quarter at Columbus College to complete my second year of college work. I wish to continue working toward my degree in elementary education by attending night classes at the University of Georgia extension for the third year and Auburn University for the fourth year.

Since I am eager to begin my teaching career, I hope you will give my application every consideration possible. I would like to request an interview with you on any Saturday that would be convenient for you.

It never occurred to me that I would not be hired, and during the summer I received a letter appointing me as a kindergarten teacher and enclosing a contract with an annual salary of $2,300. The additional stroke of good fortune was my assignment to Benning Hills School, which was not far from our home. Full of confidence, I went to meet my principal and obtained his permission to bring Billy to school with me.

There was a final hurdle—a huge one—that remained. It is hard to realize or understand that I almost never drove a car; it was clear that I would need to drive to work. During the time most young people learned to drive I was away at school, then living with my family in Washington where we relied on public transportation during the war. After my marriage, we couldn't afford a car for years, and when we did get one Bill always drove. In my job at Ft. Benning I rode to work with Mother, who also worked on the post; Bill picked me up after work and frequently for lunch. I didn't even have a Georgia driver's license! When I received my appointment as a teacher, Bill bought a second car from a soldier who was being transferred: a green 1952 Plymouth that cost $35. For me it was the key to independence.

We have many stories about that Plymouth. Once John drove it on a fishing trip, mistakenly leaving his catch in the trunk; I discovered it when I was overwhelmed by the stench. Another time, the brakes gave way as I was coming from Benning Hills School down a steep incline into a major intersection, pulling on the emergency brake with all my might. But it was my first car, and it served the purpose: getting Billy and me to school.

Billy loved going to school. Although his classroom was adjacent to mine, I rarely saw him during the school day—both of us were busy. His teacher accepted him wholeheartedly and also helped me a great deal in my new role as teacher. Billy's excellent social skills made him a successful student and a friend to the other children. He learned to take his turn, to behave in the lunchroom, stand in line, and to go to the bathroom on schedule. It was one of his best school years. We became pioneers in the mainstreaming process, a concept that was to become my mission.

On the first day of school our house was frenzied with excitement: all of us were going to school! Bill had taken John to Charleston for his Citadel experience; Tom looked forward to another successful year; Mary entered kindergarten at a school within walking distance, with a teacher we knew to be one of the best. And, magically, Billy and I were riding to school together in our very own car, dressed in new outfits and carrying brand-new lunch boxes. He went to his classroom, took his place, and was ready to learn. And so was I.

As I stood before 43 kindergartners, their faces lifted to me in expectation, I felt at home and received the revelation, "This is what I am meant to do."

I had no idea what to teach, but I knew who could help me. Each day Mary came home with her contagious enthusiasm and remarkable memory, declaring, "We had a wonderful day!"

She detailed everything her class had done as I took notes, and that's what my class did the next day. That continued until I caught on and developed my own strategies. She and I went to the classroom every Sunday afternoon to fix bulletin boards and arrange materials. Mary was my education teacher.

I found the children in my kindergarten class enchanting. They were as excited about starting school as I was, and we fed on each other's exuberance. With so many children there was a need for established discipline and I had picked up a few tips from talking with other teachers on the staff. The technique that served me best was useful when the noise and activity levels became too high for me to be heard. I made a rule that if I turned off the lights, the children were to put their heads on the desk in front of them. It worked like magic, and I can still see those little heads flopping down in a flash when I gave the signal.

I brought records from home and we sang "America the Beautiful" (they called it "purple mountains"), the songs from *Sound of Music*, and all of the Burl Ives songs. We had a story rug and read incessantly. There were, of course, prereading and writing exercises required, but we did them so we could have a story. I found myself reading to Steve, whose big brown eyes never left mine. The children thought I was beautiful, frequently calling me "Mom," and also thought I could sing. It was so much fun that I often wonder why I left it.

The group picture of my first class stimulates my recollection of special events and children: Dennis, who threw up at will; Chuckie, who ran to see the spill, fell in it and cut his head open on a desk; Fritz, who wanted me to go camping with him and his dad; Kelly, a beautiful little girl who swore like a sailor. Naturally problems arose from time to time, but we respected each other enough to work them out amicably. I envy today's teachers who have smaller classes and teaching assistants, as I remember thinking that if only there were a measles epidemic I would have a manageable number of students. One great benefit of the work was that kindergarten lasted only for the morning, so that I could take Billy home, be there for Mary, have lunch, and collapse. I think of my kindergarten years as one of the happiest periods in my life.

In June of 1963, after Billy's first year, we received a letter from the guidance center of the school system stating, "This office can plan a place for Billy in the Special Training Class at Edwina Wood School in September. Billy will be assigned to the younger group. We hope Billy will profit from this class." Although his kindergarten experience had been totally positive, we thought, "Now he will really learn."

All of us looked forward to Billy's first day at his new school. As the time drew near, however, I realized that it would also be my first day of the school year, a day I could not miss. To complicate matters, Bill was out of town. I called on our friend Mary Ann McDonald, who readily agreed to transport Billy. Early that morning, I drove Mary Ann to the post where she could pick up her husband's car and then deliver Billy to his school. I can still picture her: a baby in her arm and two little ones at her side, gently holding Billy by the hand. After the first day, a taxi picked Billy up every morning, took him to school, and brought him home.

Although I missed Billy's company to and from kindergarten, Mary drove to my school with me because I had discovered a marvelous first-grade teacher, Mrs. Blake, and knew Mary would be at home there. We had a glorious time riding in the old Plymouth, singing with the radio, and "fixing up" my room. Perhaps I was a little selfish in wanting her with me, but it worked out beautifully for both of us and I was confident that Billy was in the appropriate learning environment.

The first day I visited Billy's special class I was taken aback by a group of "different-looking" children. While I had had no difficulty in accepting Billy and his differences, this was the first time I had seen or even imagined him as part of a special needs group. I wanted to run! I felt ashamed of my reaction, but later found that it helped me to understand the reactions of others. I also found that as I learned the children's names, they became Sonny, Mary Jane, and Iris instead of different-looking kids. I became involved with the class and their activities and grew fond of the children. Somewhere along the way I had begun to change.

Soon after Billy was born, when I was seeking information and understanding, I had encountered an article written by a parent named Dan Boyd.[1] It was a sensitive and moving piece in which he discussed his growth as the parent of a child with mental retardation. He enumerated three stages of growth: the first

---

1   Boyd, Dan (1951). "The Three Stages in the Growth of a Parent of a Mentally Retarded Child." *American Journal of Mental Deficiency*, pp. 127-129.

stage where he was concerned almost wholly with himself and the effect on him of having a child with a disability; the second stage, when he began to think less of himself and more of his child; and the third stage, when he began to think of what he could do for others and the realization of how much parents could accomplish when acting together. This article and its philosophy had never left me and was becoming part of me.

Added to this awareness was an incident occurring at registration in the beginning of my second year as a kindergarten teacher. A parent approached me and said, "I understand you have a handicapped child, and since my daughter has problems, I want her to be in your class."

Sandy had severe emotional problems and presented me with a great teaching challenge and learning opportunity. I discovered when she was agitated and disoriented, that if I kept her by my side whenever possible and touched her frequently, she became calm. I also learned that I enjoyed working with her and heralding her small successes. I began to see the power of my experiences with Billy as potential strength in teaching.

Unfortunately, the quality of instruction in Billy's classes at the special school was not at all what I had expected, and there were no other choices. If a child was mentally retarded, physically impaired, or disabled in any way, the special school was the only placement available, and many parents were grateful for it. I heard one parent say, "My child is in special education and I want all my children to have it." My experience was quite different.

Billy's teacher was a gentle woman, kind to her students and fond of each of them. However, her only expectation was for them to behave and play well together. Frequently when I visited, she was at her desk and the children were playing with blocks on the floor. It seemed a step down from Billy's kindergarten experience.

There were some social opportunities for the class that Billy thoroughly enjoyed. One particularly important event was participation in the local TV program *The Children's Hour*, hosted by the beloved Miss Patsy. Frequently the special education classes at the school were invited to appear on the program, to enjoy music, and to play games. One time Miss Patsy took Billy's class to Callaway Gardens, about forty miles from Columbus. I heard that—on return to the city—it was discovered that one child was left behind. The student showed amazing ingenuity and independence by hitchhiking safely home. However, after learning about that event, I always volunteered to drive children on such outings and to help supervise, especially where a potential danger, such as playing in water, was present.

Billy was also becoming independent, in getting ready for school and in activities at home. Bill wrote to his aunts:

Billy is growing fast (mostly around the waist). His speech is improving all the time, and it amazes us to hear complete sentences and even two sentences come out now. He is a little clown and going through a cute stage. The other night we had a "Fashion Show" and Billy and Mary put on a show. Billy is making our life a joyful one with his antics and love. He has been learning to help around the house, and here is a snapshot as proof that he does help once in a while. Just a short time ago, he got up from the table and said "Billy Schulz do the dishes Mommy." And the dishes were clean!

We supplemented Billy's instruction at home, reading to him, stimulating his speech with pictures and records, and including him in family cultural and church activities. Tom and Mary were his models; he adored both of them. Billy and Mary played music on their little portable record player, learned the words, and created their own dance routines. Their favorite songs included: "What Locks

the Door?", "Who Will Answer?" and "One Little Dress at a Time." I loved going into their bedroom for their shows and rewarding their creativity by clapping enthusiastically.

As our other children engaged in extracurricular activities, we realized that there were no organized events such as scouting, music, art, and theater for children with special needs. In keeping with my newfound philosophy, I started a Cub Scout program for exceptional children. We were able to use a small outbuilding at our church and soon had about six members. With help from other parents and my own children, we enjoyed the prestige and benefits of a real scout program. Billy can still recite the Cub Scout pledge, ending with "an to obey de law of de pack." Our group joined other packs in outdoor activities and programs, adding new flavor to the regular events.

I continued my evening classes at Columbus Junior College (now out of the hosiery mill and into a brand-new building and campus), completing my sophomore year. In an effort to earn my degree sooner, I also took some early afternoon classes, following kindergarten. I took one class in English literature, a favorite of mine, as soon as my own students left. My professor read to us in a soft, monotone voice, and after a riotous morning with more than 40 five-year-olds, I could hardly stay awake. During one such reading, someone came to the door to announce that President Kennedy had been shot and killed. The professor did not miss a monosyllabic beat.

By the end of this term, my career began to focus in a logical, inevitable direction: I would be a special education teacher. This desire evolved from my dissatisfaction with some of the special classes I had seen and the insight I had gained from working with Billy and other children who had special needs. As I later learned, this decision proved to be a wise and timely one.

IN THE EARLY 1960S, during the Kennedy administration, there was a climate of concern for people who had been disenfranchised, first of all through racial discrimination, and later for people with disabilities. This trend was sparked by the presence of a child in the Kennedy family with mental retardation and led to concerted efforts and funds to train teachers in this field. Therefore I was able to obtain student loans and grants for most of my college education.

After my sophomore year at Columbus College, with Bill's help, I made a huge decision: I would go to college on a full-time basis and become a special education teacher. The nearest university was about fifty miles from where we lived, in Auburn, Alabama. Although I loved kindergarten and knew I would miss the children, I felt another calling. I resigned from my kindergarten position and applied for admission to Auburn University; I was accepted as a junior. That meant, among other things, that I would have a parking space.

The driving issue again! There was no way that the old Plymouth would make a trip of over a hundred miles a day, so we found a neighbor who wanted to sell his 1955 Chevy, which looked pretty good to me (my son John tells me it is a classic now). The Chevy had one interesting characteristic: since the windshield wipers were operated by a vacuum system, they would cease to operate if I pushed the accelerator while going up a hill. So, if it rained, I tried to avoid hills, no small feat on the old Auburn road.

Hi, Mom!

A new challenge addressed the unbelievable fact that although I had become familiar with city driving, I had never driven out of town. I was so frightened on the day of registration: driving a new-to-me car on a country road I had never encountered before, going to a large campus I had never seen, registering for classes among thousands of students—most of them younger than my oldest son. I was so nervous and lost that I doubted the wisdom of my decision. I felt very much alone and wondered, Can I really do this? After driving to Auburn that day and going through registration, I felt I could do anything.

In rearranging my life to accommodate a daily two-hour commute, I developed strategies that would serve me for the rest of my life. The most useful technique is one my family and I refer to as the "Alabama Bridge." In going from Georgia to Alabama, I crossed a bridge which, for me, meant leaving one life behind and assuming another. In Georgia, I was wife and mother; when I crossed the bridge I was a student. As I practiced this technique, I could feel a change that was almost physical as I drove over the bridge. On the return trip I could visualize my children at this point. The Alabama Bridge strategy has enabled me to focus on any task at hand and to submerge other concerns for the time being. It transfers into every task I encounter.

In going into Alabama there was a change from Eastern time to Central time, which meant I could leave home at 8:00 for an 8:00 class. This helped with getting the children ready for school, but meant allowing two hours to return home. I struggled with converting one time to another, finally keeping an extra watch in the car set on Central time, and automatically reaching for it as I approached Auburn.

There was an old story about a man who asked what time the bus left from Columbus to get to Dothan, Alabama. He was told, "Eight o'clock."

"And what time does it get there?" he asked.

The answer again: "Eight o'clock."

"Do you want to buy a ticket?"

"No ma'am, but I shore want to be here to see that bus take off!"

I had decided to begin my college work during the summer rather than the fall, following my last kindergarten year. It was a good time to make the transition, since there were a number of teachers returning for certification in the summer, people actually my age and older. For my first summer session I was also awarded a scholarship by the Georgia Association for Retarded Children in the amount of $150, an award that was most welcome. This was one of twenty grants the state gave to encourage teachers to enter the field of special education.

I soon found that there was a car pool from Columbus for commuting students. I signed up for it and discovered the drive was pleasant in the company of young people dedicated to getting an education as well as to finding a date for Saturday night.

In my first special education class, the instructor told us that there would be a summer demonstration class, providing college students the opportunity to work with children who had disabilities. They actually needed children for the program, so I decided to bring Billy with me each day. It was a wonderful situation for both of us: company for me and a learning situation for him. There were even young college students to care for him when I was in class and he was not. One day as I was going from one class to another, I heard "Hi, Mom!" and looked up to see him waving from the front seat of a baby-blue convertible, sitting close to a beautiful red-headed young woman, both of them laughing heartily. Billy was a big hit on campus.

During that first summer, my class visited various facilities supposedly designed to educate children with mental retardation. A major event was the trip to Partlow, a residential institution operated by the state of Alabama. This visit affected me more strongly than any experience I had ever had. As a group, we walked into one expansive barn-like room, furnished with two long benches facing each other, no other furniture in the room, no curtains on the cloudy windows, and absolutely no stimulation of any kind. I stopped in the doorway, mesmerized by the dreariness of the place. As I began to focus, I saw that on the benches sat little boys appearing to be around the age of ten or twelve, hands by their sides, staring blankly about them. This image was my nightmare for months to come, an image still present in my mind. I was so struck with the horror of "nothing to do" that I swore to myself, "That will never happen to my little boy."

Yes, the demonstration class was a good thing, and I knew I would continue to involve Billy in any activity I had a part in. Thus began our summer treks to Auburn. After several years, I became the teacher of the demonstration class, bringing Billy and other children with me from Georgia. The college students, most of whom were teachers seeking certification in mental retardation, observed the class and kept notes, which I later read and commented on. One student wrote:

"The teacher has a good rapport with the children; one student even calls her 'Mom.'" Billy had also learned the Alabama Bridge concept; he became my student when necessary and my loving child at other times.

During that first summer we met Steve Hinton, who was also in the demonstration class. Steve, who has Down syndrome, was a warm, sensitive, loving child who became Billy's best friend and my ardent admirer. His parents, Margie and Bodie, were professors at Auburn who, like me, were devoted to finding the best education possible for their son. Steve had skills beyond most of the children in the class, reading at about the second-grade level and writing legible and interesting letters. One teacher who observed the class said that he had never seen a more beautiful friendship than the one between Billy and Steve.

It was such fun to be teaching again. We had freedom to build our curriculum around the students' interests and to take field trips to introduce them to new experiences. One of the favorite field trips was to the School of Veterinary Medicine, especially to the large animal clinic, where the children watched with amazement as a horse was strapped to a huge door-like stretcher and tilted up for treatment. My own favorite field trip was to Calvin's home. Calvin was a tall, string-bean boy of about twelve who spoke in a high pitched voice with minimal facial expression. He proudly showed us his grandmother's garden and identified the insects we could see. This led to a study of insects, their body parts and names.

When I think of Calvin I remember one day when I wore my new chartreuse shoes, perfectly matched to my bag. As we sat in a circle, Calvin noted, "Ms. Schulz got some new shoes." I responded, "Yes, Calvin, do you like them?" "No ma'am, they too green."

The summer had been a phenomenal success. I completed my first courses in special education, Billy had experienced broader educational opportunities, and both of us had new friends. He was ready to return to his regular school, and I could hardly wait for the fall quarter when I would indeed be a full-time student.

Billy returned to the same teacher, and most of the same classmates, in his special school. There was little difference in the curriculum and in learning activities for this new school year. The comments on his report card reflect the level of achievement expected and attained: "Most of the time Billy is so gentlemanly. Billy is helping teach good manners to the others. Billy is quite cooperative." He received all Ss (satisfactory) on his report card and was assigned to the same class for the next year.

I continued commuting to Auburn, following a standard course of study. My fellow students were generally much younger than those I had been in class with during the summer. I continued to use the car pool, which meant I didn't have to travel alone. Sometimes this was good and sometimes inconvenient, but I learned a great deal from the young students. After their initial reluctance, they became at ease with me and confided all sorts of things in me, sometimes to my consternation. The same thing was true on campus. I sometimes felt that I learned more in the Student Union than I did in the formal classes.

As I continued to pursue my education, I found that I had learned a great deal from Billy that served me well in my college classes. I also learned that I knew more about mental retardation than some of my professors. For example, in a speech class, the professor declared, "There are no girls with Down syndrome."

I had just dropped Billy off at his school where I saw Iris, Mary Jane, and Cindy, all of whom had Down syndrome. I didn't yet have the courage to disagree, but began to feel more confident in my own practical knowledge. One day I was outraged in class to hear a professor declare, "A Mongolian idiot would know that!"

In a special education class the teacher, who had worked for a number of years with special needs students, stated that mentally retarded children have no creativity. I came home that day to find that Billy had turned a chair over, placed a blanket over the ladder back, and was riding his homemade horse. No creativity? As I became more secure I was able to contribute my practical knowledge in class, being careful to protect Billy's dignity.

Sometimes I felt that I was neglecting my family, but I realize now that it was also a learning time for them. We had study time every night; all of us were doing well. Mary and Tom were learning what was called the "new math." Ironically, so was I; guess who was having trouble with the new concepts? Both of them had excellent teachers. Mary's teacher left an amazing impression on me when, during her last year before retirement, she attended summer school in preparation for teaching the new math. Tom's teacher, "Tiger" Williams, demanded and got wonderful results from her students. I, on the other hand, had a teacher who declared, "I don't care whether you get this or not." My children, sharing their new knowledge, saved me from total math failure in school.

My family made my education possible. Bill was wholly supportive and willing to assume the responsibility of transporting the children, shopping for groceries, and being there when I was not. When someone asked Mary when she learned to be such a good cook, she replied, "When Mom was in college."

We had complicated arrangements for sitters and for extracurricular activities. Bill was always there to help—a big task since by then John was away at college. By the end of each week, commuting for five days and coming home to study, prepare meals, and take care of the children, I was exhausted. It was an unspoken rule that I could sleep Saturday morning, and I frequently woke up to Bill's fresh coffee and the children gathered atop my bed—a glorious awakening.

I was not the only family member who was busy. Bill was having an amazingly productive year. He was doing well in his insurance business, but wanted to do better and conceived the idea of a "Million Dollar Month." He believed he could sell one million dollars worth of life insurance during the month of March and designed a campaign with that goal in mind. We made a scroll, which he put in a tube and carried with him every day, listing each person who bought a policy and who wanted his name inscribed on the scroll. Even his supervisors declared it was a corny idea but saw it working! Bill also promised each purchaser an invitation to his Million-Dollar Month dinner, a significant event shared by the family as well as dignitaries (including my brother John) from the home office of the insurance company. The realization of this project brought Bill the success and honor he had longed for and promised great financial rewards, which we needed.

Each year Bill and I attended insurance conferences at such places as The Greenbrier, Lake Placid, and the Fontainebleau in Miami. We usually added a few days to the trip to give ourselves a real vacation. It was great fun to wear cocktail dresses with matching shoes, to go horseback riding, to attend banquets and dances, and especially to be with my brother John and his wife.

Being away from the children from time to time brought renewed vigor to our marriage, although I was always glad to get back to my family. Mother usually stayed with the children at night, supervising their activities. Both she and the children were relieved when we returned.

Bill became a celebrity in his insurance company. He earned the much-coveted distinction of Agent of the Year and was presented with a number of awards at the August conference at The Greenbriar Convention Center. As his wife, I even received a special gift (an Auburn sweater) for encouraging Bill in his terrific achievements during the past year. Both of us were elated with his success and, needless to say, had a marvelous time at the conference. The August bulletin was filled with his achievements and we, the family, were justifiably proud of him. Bill was finally winning.

Unfortunately, in the November bulletin, the following notice was printed:

GET WELL SOON, BILL!

We are very happy to report that William H. Schulz—Big Bill to his many, many friends—is recovering nicely from a recent serious illness. Bill, as you know, is FBL's Salesman of the Year and Million Dollar Month star agent with Armed Forces Insurance Service. We understand that he will be hospitalized for several more weeks, and we know he would appreciate hearing from you. The wishes of the entire Company are with you, Bill, for a speedy recovery!

Prior to the Million Dollar Month endeavor, Bill had determined that he would lose weight and had a prescription from his physician which not only curbed his appetite, but gave him tremendous energy. He was getting up each morning at about 4:00 and working until late in the evening. I realized too late that he was on "speed" and that the side effects were devastating.

One night, as Bill and I were hanging new wallpaper in the breakfast room, he experienced severe chest pain. I took him to the emergency room. He had suffered a myocardial infarction and was seriously ill, remaining in the hospital for several weeks. While he was there and I was only allowed to visit him for brief times, I went by the hospital on my way to Auburn and again on my return, knowing that it would alarm him if I were to drop out of my classes.

At the same time, Tom limped into the kitchen one Sunday afternoon with a huge gash in his leg from an accident on his bike, stating calmly, "Look, Mom, I think I hurt my leg." Although his accidents were legion, this particular trip to the ER included hospitalization, where he underwent a skin graft. During the treatment he acquired a staph infection and remained there for several weeks, overlapping the period his dad was there.

I somehow managed to finish the quarter at Auburn and to help Bill recover at home. Although he made a great deal of progress, his former energy never returned. His business suffered during his illness, with a number of the policies acquired during the Million Dollar Month cancelled. He was crushed physically and psychologically. During the following quarter I was student-teaching in Columbus and did not have to commute to Auburn each day, fortunately giving me time to help Bill in his recovery.

My student teaching was one of the most enjoyable periods of my school career. My supervising teacher, Mrs. Coulter, was an exemplary teacher, and I learned a great deal from her about understanding and teaching children. Her class was housed in an old school building in downtown Columbus. It had an old-fashioned cloak room, oiled floors, and plenty of space. She was a creative and sensitive teacher, using every opportunity to help her special students acquire the skills they needed. For example, over the summer Mrs. Coulter had collected broom handles. In the makeshift shop in her classroom, she had a vise and a saw, which she taught the children to use in making "counting circles." As they made circles out of the broom handles, sanding away the edges, they learned the concepts of round, smooth, and rough, and in using the circles as math counters, learned that they could use the things they made. I loved her and the children and knew I had found my place.

At the end of my second year at Auburn, I graduated with honors, cheered on by my family in the stadium. During my senior year, with a cherished senior parking sticker, I had taken several graduate classes and realized that my education was incomplete. I applied for and received a grant which would pay my tuition for a master's degree.

My graduate work excited me. I continued to teach the demonstration class in the summer and to take Billy with me. My master's degree was to be in psychology, with major focus areas in intelligence testing and behavior modification, both of which served me well. This focus also enabled Billy and my other children to have a new experience: being tested by a number of my peers.

In learning to administer intelligence tests, we were required to give a number of practice tests, and our children proved to be good subjects. Billy was tested so frequently that he soon learned to say, with authority, "Peat the question please." It also afforded me some valuable experience and later became a source of income.

I had learned to use every opportunity to further Billy's education. Somewhere along the way I had met Dr. Douglas, headmaster at a private school in Columbus. He asked me to be a teacher in his summer school and I accepted, with the agreement that Billy could attend the school tuition-free. It was a unique program, with one hour devoted to activities in the gymnasium to improve general physical development, plus activities in the visual-training room where various instruments and exercises were employed to strengthen visual skills. The other hour was spent in the classroom in a program of reading readiness, writing, and the development of number concepts: my domain.

With Dr. Douglas's permission and help, I used the situation to develop my master's thesis, "An Analysis of the Achievement of Two Mentally Retarded Children in a Perceptual-Motor Development Program." A delightful girl named Margaret joined Billy as the subjects of my study. During the gym activities I became aware for the first time of Billy's fear of heights, a problem that Margaret shared. They were forced to hang by their knees from a bar and to climb a knotted rope, activities that terrified both of them.

In the visual-training program, Dr. Douglas, in encouraging rapid eye movement, employed an exercise using two thin rods, one tipped with gold, the other with silver. The child was to look from one to the other at his command. "Gold, silver" became household words as Billy complained about the activity. We laughingly remarked that Billy had been taught to look cross-eyed.

Billy and Margaret seemed more comfortable with their academic activities and made considerable progress, learning to write numerals, some words, and their names. In teaching them, I remember wishing that Margaret had been named something short, like Sue.

After receiving the master's degree, I returned to Ft. Benning, where I had been a secretary, to teach. The first year I was a coordinator of special education, working with the special education teachers, administering intelligence tests, and counseling with parents when necessary. During this time, one experience totally changed my way of thinking about parent-professional conferences. As part of an army post, we were privileged to have a psychiatrist working with us and invited him to join us for a conference to discuss a problem with a student. In charge of the details of the meeting, I had also invited the child's mother (the father was overseas), the special education teacher, and the principal. Our task was to discuss the extreme behavior problems exhibited by the student, Mike—behaviors that interfered tremendously with his and others' learning. I was confident I had arranged the meeting thoroughly and was taken aback when the psychiatrist asked, "Where is Mike?"

I responded in surprise, "Why, he is outside with Henry." Henry was our custodian who had such a good influence on our kids.

The psychiatrist looked me in the eye and asked, "Well, if we were talking about you, would you want to be here or outside?"

After that experience, I always included the child when possible. I found that the student usually could contribute some insight and that the atmosphere was more professional.

Parent conferences often provided me with opportunities for insight. As I was talking with the mother of a child who was mentally retarded, she exclaimed "You just don't know what it's like!" Since most of my prior experience had been as a mother, I wondered how many times I had shared that feeling. Now, as a teacher, I resented her outburst, for I cared deeply about her child and had spent a great deal of time in trying to meet his needs. I *did* know what it was like, and told her so. As we exchanged points of view, I understood the value of honest communication between parents and teachers.

Another part of my job was evaluating children and making recommendations for their placement. This was some time before the passage of the Law for the Education of Handicapped Children, and decisions were made by administrators, sometimes without regard for parents' feelings or agreement. One day I met with the principal of a school at Ft. Benning and made my recommendation for special education placement for a particular student. Without hesitation, the principal phoned the child's mother and said, "Your son is retarded. Take him to the special class in the morning." I often think of that conversation when I hear people complaining about the rules and regulations in place now. The rules may seem cumbersome and inefficient, but they are in place to ensure we handle decisions professionally and with humanity.

In a contrasting situation, I evaluated one child who was in a special class and found that he was functioning within the normal range of intelligence and should have been in a regular class. Because he had some behavior problems that were disturbing to the fourth grade teacher, the principal refused to move him. Strongly believing in the rights of the child, I pursued the issue with the superintendent, whose secretary I had been in years past. She agreed with the principal, a friend of hers, and determined that the child in question should remain in special education. After several disturbing experiences of this sort I, possibly identified as a trouble maker, was moved to another school and out of the evaluation business.

My second year at Ft. Benning was as a teacher at the junior high level. All of my previous experience had been with younger children, and although I resisted the change, I realized with surprise that I loved it! It was an amazing year with some of the most engaging children I have ever known.

The class was designed to serve children who were mentally retarded, but actually included children with various diagnoses. An example of a child with a different disability was David, who entered the classroom with a bang. We had a metal thermometer on the wall, untouched until his first day. David walked by the thermometer, which fell and cut a gash in his leg. For a basket-weaving activity, I put the reed-soaking bucket of water under a table to forestall any accidents. While we were working I heard David say, "Mrs. Schulz, you won't believe what I did." By that time I was accustomed to his incidents and knew that he had stepped into the bucket. Like David, his desk was a total disaster and one of our Friday chores was for some of the students to help him clean out his desk. I knew that David was not mentally retarded but that he had some slightly different disorder. When the physician put him on medication, his behavior changed noticeably, and some mornings afterward the other children would note, "David forgot to take his medicine." Later, when the condition of learning disabilities was identified, I knew where David had belonged.

Tyrone was an unforgettable character as well. He sat in his chair and read *TIME* magazine whenever he could get away with it. Trying to get him outside and involved in playing dodgeball, I said, "Tell you what, Tyrone, I'll play if you will."

His instant response was, "Tell you what, Mrs. Schulz, I won't if you won't."

Edwin was a student who asked me, "Could you teach me about fractions? My other teachers wouldn't let me do fractions." Hearing his challenge, I discovered some strategies that worked for the entire class. Remembering my own earlier problems with math, I was motivated to develop hands-on techniques and materials that worked in teaching abstract concepts.

Sometimes the students' understanding of themselves broke my heart. Bill and I had been to see the movie *Charly* based on the book by Daniel Keyes, *Flowers for*

Algernon. The film touched me so deeply that I sat in the car and cried on the way home. Specifically, when Charly threw his jacket over his shoulder, he looked just like Tony, in my class. The next morning I was so full of the film that I told the students about it, describing the premise that it was science fiction, in which someone was made extremely intelligent in a scientific experiment. Alicia exclaimed, "Oh Mrs.Schulz, wouldn't that be wonderful if it could happen to us!"

I grew so close to these students and we talked openly about their learning problems. One day, one of my students came in crying, "That girl called me retarded!" First I had to respond to my student when she asked if it were true. In a moment of inspiration I suggested that we look up "retarded" in the dictionary. It said "slow," so we dealt with that as a class, agreeing that they were indeed slower than others in learning; that was the reason they were in a special class.

My second step was to find the girl who made fun of my student and say to her, "My students know they're retarded, but they don't want to hear it. Understand?"

My third step was to ask for a spot at the next teachers' meeting to discuss the necessity for some instruction in sensitivity for students and faculty. This was the beginning of my career in teacher training.

I was attempting to integrate my special needs students into regular classrooms where possible, and I managed to enroll them in classes in home economics, shop, and physical education. There were some disappointments, such as finding Paula, a girl who desperately needed physical activity, sitting on a bench watching other children shoot baskets under the direction of the physical education teacher. On the other hand, one of my most thrilling moments as a teacher came when the home economics teacher requested, via the intercom, "Would Alicia please come to the home ec room to demonstrate how to put in a zipper?"

My supreme reward with the junior high class was at the end of the year. They had discovered that my birthday was in May and planned a surprise birthday party for me. Totally on their own initiative, they had arranged for the principal to call me to the office and magically produced flowers, a cake, and a cardboard crown for me. Never have I been so touched, not just by their thoughtfulness and devotion, but by their ability to plan and execute a complicated event.

While I was involved in such a satisfying teaching experience, I was becoming more and more dissatisfied with Billy's situation. He had been promoted from one level to a higher level, again receiving all S's and the following remarks: "Satisfactory work this six weeks... Billy continues his satisfactory work... Billy has continued his fine work throughout the year." Although his marks were good, there was no indication of *what* he was learning. His teacher at the primary level, Miss Rainey, worked diligently to provide a stimulating environment and activities for her students. I could see progress in his prereading and writing performance and hoped that it would continue.

Billy received a certificate for good citizenship and another certificate for satisfactory completion of the primary Trainable Mentally Retarded class in May of 1968. He was twelve years old and eligible for the intermediate class.

While in graduate school, I had substituted for the intermediate class in the teacher's absence; on other occasions I had observed the teacher, and knew that there was very little instruction going on in that particular classroom. There was one addition: this class had a television set, which was on all day. The teacher sat and watched her programs most of the time while the students did as they pleased. I knew that we couldn't afford a year of non-teaching and non-stimulation. We had to do something. Little did I know that our decision would place us in the middle of a social revolution.

IN 1963, the first year I taught kindergarten, Martin Luther King, Jr. led a march on Washington to protest racial discrimination and to demonstrate support for major civil rights legislation that was pending in Congress. The civil rights movement had major implications for special education as the precedent to extend the concept of "separate is not equal" to children with disabilities. My family and I were also deeply affected by this movement.

This my science project.

The horrendous events taking place were more than newspaper stories to us; we were living in the midst of them. Since childhood I had been aware of the injustice in our discriminatory practices and abhorred the separate facilities and schools common in the South and in other places.

Following President Johnson's election and dedication to the civil rights movement, the desegregation of public schools proceeded steadily, although the proliferation of private schools often made integration an elusive goal. As a family we became involved in the legal and moral changes that were finally occurring.

The pattern began with some black students and teachers being merged into white schools. In fact, the year I taught kindergarten, taking classes at night, the first black student was integrated into Columbus College. I remember discussing this move with our janitor, a black man, who asked me honestly, "Who's he going to laugh and joke with?"

That was the first time I realized how difficult the process was for everyone, blacks and whites, to understand.

Billy was the first integration pioneer in our family.

My dissatisfaction with Billy's school situation led me to see the director of special education about options for his next step. By this time we were on a first-name basis. I said, "Ann, I have visited the intermediate class several times and saw nothing educational going on there. What other class is available for Billy?"

"Well, Jane, you could send him to Talbotton Junior High." She chuckled, because Talbotton was an all-black school, and all integration efforts thus far had consisted of black children attending formerly all white schools.

I asked, "Well, could I visit?"

I met with Mr. Washington, the principal of Talbotton Junior High School, and was warmly received. With his permission I visited Mrs. Sanders, the special education teacher, and observed her class. It was a total learning environment with busy, interested students doing actual schoolwork—something I had not seen in other special classes. In discussing the possibility of Billy's entering her class, Mrs. Sanders asked, "Would you give me permission to spank Billy if he needs it?"

I felt this was a test of my faith in her, and responded, "Yes, if he needs it."

With the teacher's permission, I brought Billy to visit. We went to an assembly program where we were the only white people in the auditorium. It was my first experience as a minority member, and the welcome we received was heart warming. Comparing the events to other integration settings caused me embarrassment for my race. Billy, apparently, didn't notice anything different, and felt quite at home in the school. Bill and I became members of the National Congress of Colored Parents and Teachers.

Mrs. Sanders frequently picked Billy up and took him to ball games; it was obvious that she was pleased to have him in the class. She involved her students in a number of competitions; in an art contest, Billy won an award. His picture, with several of his classmates, was featured in the local newspaper.

I took the picture to show to my students at Ft. Benning and told them it was a picture of my son. One student looked at the picture and asked, "Mrs. Schulz, which one is your boy?"

Billy attended Talbotton Junior High for a year until we moved to Alabama, certainly one of his best school years—and was involved in many activities, such as the county-wide science fair. Bill and I stood on the balcony of the municipal auditorium, where the fair was housed and observed our three children demonstrating their projects. Tom had built a wooden maze to show that earthworms could be trained; Mary illustrated the nesting patterns of hamsters (in spite of the trauma of a deceased hamster discovered during breakfast time that morning);

and Billy was explaining to passers-by his posters about poisonous plants, "Poison ivry, poison oak, and poison sumac."

In addition to Billy's experience in Mrs. Sanders's class, as a family we participated in several aspects of the racial integration movement of the 1960s. Living in Georgia and later in Alabama, we were in the heat of the battle. Each of us had a unique part in that history, a painful time in the South.

Tom related a troubling experience when he was traveling from Atlanta to Columbus after participating in a track meet. When the group entered a restaurant for hamburgers, the owner, who by then was required by law to serve all customers, sprinkled the food served to the black students with so much pepper the hamburgers were inedible. The coach was infuriated, sent the team outside, and dealt with the situation in a manner never revealed to the students. Tom was surprised and outraged at this blatant act of discrimination.

In an effort to integrate schools throughout segregated neighborhoods, one of the Supreme Court decisions upheld busing children from one school district to another as a legitimate means for achieving racial balance in schools. In accordance with this ruling, Mary, as a third grader, was bused across the city of Columbus. She attended class in an ancient, rundown school with pigeon droppings covering the front doors. Although she had a good teacher, the point of the long trip was lost to us, since we lived within walking distance of the school she had attended in second grade, and since she doesn't recall whether there were black students in the school.

At the same time, John—who had graduated from college with a degree in English—was one of a small group of white teachers in an all-black high school. He writes of his experience, which is also a picture of the times:

> I remember that all of the black kids were freaking out over the Jackson 5 and their lead singer, little Michael.
>
> I had taught in the white schools for two or three years when I volunteered to be transferred to Carver High School as part of a "pre-integration program." This program sent a few white teachers to each of the black schools and a few black teachers to a few of the white schools.
>
> I ran into some animosity, but not much. Mostly, I was looked at with a mild curiosity. I was readily accepted by most of the black teachers and a lot of the students. The kids? Hell, they were just like any other kids. Apart from cultural differences, they were similar to the white students. They had identity problems, love problems, family problems, and other concerns that were identical to those that I had observed with white seventh and eighth graders.
>
> The part of moving to the all-black school that I found to be completely different was the way the black teachers were treated by the administration. The black teachers seemed to be very concerned with keeping their jobs. This was understand-

able due to the lack of professional opportunities for college-trained black people at the time. The administration was oppressive. I got the impression that prior to the coming of the whites, the teachers had been used to paying a "kickback" every month to the principal. I was never able to confirm this suspicion, but the evidence was pretty strong. The principal was not merely respected as in the white schools; he was feared. I have two illustrations:

At the white schools, we were used to having our paychecks placed in an envelope and brought around by someone who was called a teacher's aide. When the first payday at Carver rolled around, I had not received my check by the end of the day and went to find out where it was. There was a line of teachers (60 of them) formed at the door to the principal's office. I stood in line with Betty, another white teacher, and waited. The line moved slowly through the dimly lit hall. When I got as far as the door, I was able to see that the principal was sitting behind his desk holding a stack of checks. He would look up at the next person in the line, shuffle through the checks, pull one out, examine it, and grudgingly hand it over. I certainly didn't feel that I was being treated like a professional, and having been in similar lines at the public-works camp, I resented it.

I turned to Betty and said loudly: "Kind of reminds you of field hands after a day of picking cotton, doesn't it?"

Betty laughed. Everybody else in line got mad. I was asked to explain how they did it in the white schools. Suddenly, the teachers were no longer angry with me, but with the principal. They could feel that, as Bob Dylan kept telling us, "The times they are a-changin'."

The following month, right after lunch, a young teacher's aide brought me my check in an envelope. After this incident, I felt a bit of closeness with many of the teachers, but the principal decided to make life hard for me. One day, soon after the payroll incident, I came to school wearing a tailored black suit and a white turtleneck. I was sent home to put on a tie. My pay was docked.

One short incident will show that kids are kids. It was Martin Luther King Day. The students had decided to demonstrate and were totally unmanageable. They dressed in black, which gave them an intimidating look, and they marched around the parking lot. The police had been called, and all whites had been warned to stay in the building. A riot was in the making. I was in my mid twenties and totally invincible, so I walked out with my camera to take pictures of the demonstration. All of a sudden, the ferocious kids started waving their arms, jumping up and down, and yelling: "Take my picture, Mr. Schulz! Mr. Schulz, take my picture!"

Several years later, while I was in graduate school, I taught a summer course at Tuskegee Institute (now Tuskegee University) in Alabama, a college established by Booker T. Washington to offer black students opportunities for advanced education. I found it to be the most beautiful campus I had ever seen, with huge trees meeting across walkways leading to distinctive buildings. I loved to walk under those trees, but here I was not greeted with enthusiasm or even courtesy. Again I was in the minority, but at a place and time where white people were not expected to be. Although my class members were accepting of me, the students I passed on campus were not; they simply stared at me and turned away.

My task was to teach a group of teachers who were seeking certification in the area of mental retardation. They were excellent, highly motivated students except when they were required to write; I discovered I had to have them respond orally to avoid failing them. I had known that the black schools and colleges were lacking in buildings, professors, and resources, but hadn't realized the academic poverty now revealed in the teachers' underdeveloped writing skills. In this time of student integration, I believed the playing field for students should have begun with the teachers.

Even after the Supreme Court's ruling that separate was not equal, I saw special education classes being used to segregate students. In fulfilling another part-time job during my graduate work, I served as a psychometrist and recommended special education placement of several white children in one school. The administrator of the school refused to put white students in a class with a black teacher and black students. In some school systems this practice was actually used as a means of racial segregation, contributing to the minority imbalance evident in a number of special classes.

Racial desegregation contributed to focusing attention on special classes predominately composed of students from minority backgrounds. In carrying out the decision of the Supreme Court in *Brown v. Board of Education*, the Office of Civil Rights required some school systems to eliminate special classes that were interpreted to be vehicles for segregation.

Another issue that related to special education was unfairness in evaluating the intelligence of children, the procedure used to determine whether or not special education might be indicated. Further experience in psychological assessment made the inequality of some of our techniques apparent to me. Employed on a part-time basis by the state of Alabama, I visited a number of schools, giving intelligence tests required by state law. In registering for graduate courses, I tried to leave one day a week free to visit the schools, mostly rural, for the purpose of testing children who were not doing well in school.

One school I particularly remember was in a community known as Smith Station. I loved going there, driving into the Alabama countryside and meeting dedicated teachers and administrators who wanted to meet the educational needs of their students. Unfortunately, there were no suitable spaces for testing. In my university courses I had learned that the ideal environment for establishing rapport and deriving the clearest answers on a test was a quiet, uncluttered room, with no interruptions. In contrast, I frequently had to administer tests in a storage room, sometimes full of audiovisual equipment, with noisy traffic and frequent interruptions. I did my best but felt that the children, easily distractible even under good conditions, were limited in their ability to perform.

I also learned, as many researchers were pointing out, that the intelligence tests we were using were inherently culturally unfair. For example, one of the words presented for definition was "spade." For a rural, farm-bred youngster, it might mean "what you do to keep your dog from having pups." This was, of course, an incorrect response according to testing standards, and, with similar misinterpretations, could contribute to a lower score—perhaps leading to indication for special class placement.

These issues, coupled with parental concerns and advocacy, led to the passage, in 1975, of Public Law 94-142, The Education for All Handicapped Children Act. The main thrust of this law is directly related to the tenets of *Brown v. the Board of Education* in requiring equal educational rights for all children, regardless of race or disability.

In looking at the impact of *Brown v. the Board of Education* 50 years after its ruling, Ellis Cose, in *Newsweek* (May 17, 2004) pointed out that the real issue may have little to do with desegregation as such. It may, in fact, be about decently educating those who begin with the least and letting us see children of color, disability, and ethnic diversity in a wholly new and beautiful light.

OCCASIONALLY Billy will forget something he was supposed to do, answer a question incorrectly, or misunderstand a direction. He will say, "I'm so dumb!"

This bothers me, and I say, "No, Billy, you are smart!"

"Are you sure?"

He can charm people, have fun at a party or family gathering, discuss television shows and movies, do a slide presentation, and hold down a job. Are these accomplishments signs of intelligence? If so, how smart, or how intelligent, is he?

For centuries people have tried to define intelligence. Current concepts range from a multifaceted approach used to identify children who are gifted and talented to the generally accepted standard for identifying those who have mental retardation. Most assessments, however, begin with the concept of the intelligence quotient, or IQ. Using the standard of 100 as the average IQ, a statistical measure enables psychologists to determine the degree to which a person scores above or below what is considered average.

The Association on Mental Retardation, an organization comprised of professionals from medical, psychological, and educational backgrounds, added to the definition of mental retardation the concepts of adaptive behavior and developmental period (occurring during the time from birth to the eighteenth birthday). Other disabilities have additional or different criteria for identification, but most begin with measured intelligence.

Peat the question please

While the IQ is evaluated by psychologists, adaptive behavior is based on observations by professionals or parents. We all know people who are considered brilliant but who exhibit little common sense. On the other hand, there are people whose measured intelligence is below normal but who are able to function reasonably well in day-to-day situations.

Billy's IQ reports have been fairly constant throughout his life, indicating that he functions in the moderate range of retardation, as distinguished from mild and severe. His past experience in test-taking, as the subject of my peers in college courses, has made him comfortable in testing situations. His most recent evaluation, required by vocational rehabilitation for job placement, contained the following comments:

> William was friendly and interacted easily with this examiner. Motivation was good and he maintained good interest and effort. His activity level was normal and appropriate persistence was observed. Attention and concentration were good throughout the evaluation.
>
> Examination of Billy's scores on verbal and performance tasks indicates that he performed equally well on both, with a slightly higher rank on performance items. The overall conclusion was that "William can be expected to perform at a level which is significantly lower than same-aged peers."

An added remark shows sensitivity on the part of the psychologist:

> He has good social skills and should make a good employee at his level of functioning. All results must be interpreted along with other relevant information from those individuals who know him well including his mother.
>
> Billy's strengths lie in his adaptive behavior and social skills. He compensates for his inadequate academic abilities in many ways.

One of the benefits to living in a university town is the availability of tutors, many of them, in our case, from the reading clinic. Students always enjoyed working with Billy, commenting on his motivation and interest in learning to read. The most successful measures in teaching him to read were words related to his surroundings. One clinician commented, "Since Billy found it very difficult to remember and master phonetic sounds much of his word study was of the visual type." We have collections of workbooks from tutors and from his school days containing pictures of objects familiar to him with the labels beneath the pictures. He recognizes these worksheets but without the picture often does not recognize the words.

In our teaching at home we have emphasized recognition of essential words such as "Danger," "Exit," "Men," "Women," and "Stop." He recognizes the names of families and friends but needs help in writing them. He scores at about grade one or two on a standardized reading test. I think he realizes that reading is a sign of normalcy and correlates with "being smart," so he avoids attempting to read aloud in front of people.

And yet...Billy identifies the names of every store we pass. He follows *TV Guide* religiously and can tell me the time and channel of any program I want to watch. In church he picks up on the last syllable of the word in hymns and follows one beat behind, but he does follow. He is so clever at this technique that people assume he is reading. Nancy Tate, a staff member at our church and one of Billy's favorite friends, called at Christmas time to ask if he would read a story at one of the services. She was surprised to learn that he would not be able to read even a paragraph. He can microwave a product for the appropriate time and setting as stated on the directions. His latest accomplishment is

reading the daily weather report in the newspaper, and he loves to share this skill when his brothers visit. But the most amazing ability he has is his ability to function without reading. My favorite example occurred a number of years ago when he, his father, and I were dining at a new restaurant. He excused himself to go to the restroom and when he returned I went, myself. Instantly I saw the labels on the restroom doors: Pointers and Setters. I was concerned that he could  have entered the wrong room and, on returning to the table asked, "Billy, how did you know which restroom to use?"

He calmly replied, "I watched to see who came out."

Some of the same measures are used to help Billy in his writing. When he needs to compose a thank-you note, we have a choice of procedures. He dictates what he wants to say and I type it on the computer or write it on paper, then he copies it in his precise and beautiful printing. It's an arduous task for him, one that we break into segments of about two notes at a sitting. He always acknowledges Christmas and birthday gifts, although sometimes it takes weeks to complete.

Billy cannot manage to compose a letter, but he does write notes to me, especially when we need something at the grocery store. I have a collection of these notes and find his spelling and structure fascinating. The point is: the notes do

> Dear mrs schulz
> How are you getting along.
> How are Things with you.
> iT MUST been preTTy i
> when you goT up Thismorn-
> ing.
> Tell mary and Tommy and
> Billy I said mind you.
> Tell Billy I said To Do
> his best in school and
> To work hard.
> I am noT going off To schoo
> l I might go To school
> in Montgomery.
> write me real very soon
> if you wanT To.
> I am going To give you 14 days
> To write.
> I am going To make a song.
>
>
> love STeven

communicate. On occasions when Billy has written letters to me, I know he had help. I also know that they express his language.

Billy's friend Steve, from Auburn, wrote wonderful letters which he composed and sent. Examples on these two pages reveal his ability to express himself. The best of friends, Steve and Billy were quite different in the range and type of their abilities. Where Steve excelled in one area, Billy excelled in another. Individuals with Down syndrome are as different within their classification as are others in

> Thank you for letting
> Billy go to camp with me.
> what is your plans after
> Billy and I come back
> from Blue lake.
> let me know when you write
> me back about the plans.
> hope to see you real soon.
> Tell Billy I will write him as soon
> as I can.
> Tell Billy I said to please
> write me soon.
> is Billy getting along all right
> with his new friends.
> Tell mary and Tommy and
> Billy I said to mind you.
> How much has Billy learned
> in school.
> summer school is real fun.
> There is a girl in class
> They think she is going
> deaf.

the general population.

When Billy received checks as gifts and later when he had a checking account, he learned to sign his name in cursive writing. I wrote my version of his name, and Billy practiced tracing it until he developed his own signature. I am fascinated by the fact that Billy, now in middle age, is still learning to read and to write.

Billy's math skills are notably undeveloped. In his early childhood, we counted everything: setting the table, counting people, placing the corresponding number of chairs at the table. But even today, if you ask him to put plates on the table, he names the people expected on his fingers to determine the plates required, then counts the plates. Daniel, Billy's nephew, attempted to work with Billy on math skills and was amazed to find the gaps in his understanding.

Perhaps Billy's most difficult area is in dealing with money. When he was young, I attempted to show him how to spend and expect change for a purchase. One day we stopped at a fast-food restaurant; I handed him a ten dollar bill and explained the amount of change he would receive. I sat in the car while he went in to buy a hamburger and watched as he approached the cashier. As he reached for his change I saw the cashier pocket a bill. I ran in, raised a big fuss, and realized that we had a great deal of work to do. After all our effort over the years, however, the concept of money still eludes him. He has learned to write checks to compensate for this skill deficit.

Billy carries his checkbook with him everywhere. I made a card that he keeps in the back of the checkbook, listing numerals and corresponding words so he can fill out the amount. He also has a card listing frequently used payees, such as the church and his grocery store. In addition to his checkbook, two other items are vital to Billy's self-assurance—his ID card and his cell phone. They are symbols of his adulthood and citizen status.

When Billy applied for a job at Food City, he was required to obtain a picture ID. We went to the Division of Motor Vehicles, stood in line with persons applying for driver's licenses, and he received a card which closely resembles a driver's license. He grinned as he proudly slid the card into his wallet—it meant that he would not need to rely on my license to cash a check.

I felt Billy's need for a cell phone was unwarranted until I understood his reasoning that "everybody's got one." We chose an inexpensive minute-to-minute program, requiring a $20 "top-up" every ninety days. We programmed it with family phone numbers and he has not abused it, calling us only when necessary to reaffirm transportation or to ask, "You need anything from my store?"

Billy's understanding of time is an area that has required constant learning and re-learning. It is such an abstract concept—and such an important one—that we have tried to put time into concrete terms. One of the things that makes it difficult for many children is that we use ambiguous terms, such as quarter to, quarter till, twenty minutes past or after, and so on. In teaching children to tell time, we need to be consistent to avoid confusion. For example, one year Billy's grandmother promised him a watch for Christmas if he learned to tell time. He was proud of his accomplishment and rightly puzzled when she presented him with a watch that had Roman numerals.

Billy has adapted to the demands of time in his own way. He learned that he could put a potato into the oven at 5:30 and it would be done at 6:30. However, he would phone me to ask, "Mom, if I put my potato in at six o'clock, when it be done?" Although the concept was missing, he adapted.

One of his most critical needs is to be on time for work, to punch the time clock at the precise hour. He is always ready and waiting for his ride, a commendable trait for one who depends on others for transportation. When he had access to a transit bus he waited outside regardless of the weather until the van arrived, sometimes as much as thirty to forty minutes later. When this occurred, especially in bad weather, I urged him to come inside to wait, but he was determined to be in place when the driver got there.

There are a number of skills that don't appear on the adaptive behavior scale, tasks at which Billy excels. He learned to program and tape television shows before I did; he repairs table legs, cabinet doors, dripping faucets. He plays video games, CDs and DVDs. He will labor with any electronic equipment for hours and if it doesn't work for him, he calls his nephew Warren. It's always interesting to hear him explain the problem.

Billy, like his brothers and sister, loves music. When we are in a store, he might stop and say, "That's Eric Clapton playing Layla!" when I am unaware that music is playing. He remembers the titles and actors of past and present movies and television shows, challenging his siblings in the game. His long-term memory amazes me. If I mention Chattanooga, he immediately says, "That's where Mr. Pack lives." Mr. Pack was an associate of Bill's when Billy was a young boy. If we could tap that kind of associative memory, we could teach children anything.

Billy learns by paying attention and imitating. He acquired his remarkable social skills while growing up with his socially adept siblings and by noticing people's actions and reactions. He also learns from the feedback he gets from others. I once asked him, "Billy, why do all the ladies like you?"

He responded, "Because I tell them they're so pretty." In addition to wanting the ladies to like him, he is also sincere; he does think they're beautiful. Sometimes this takes an interesting turn. He once said to one of his "pretty ladies" at church, "Can I take you home with me?" She, going along with the joke, responded, "You'll have to ask my husband." Without missing a beat, Billy said, "He's not my type."

He has learned—or knows instinctively—how to play the social game. One day we stopped at the post office and I asked Billy to go inside and mail some letters. Sitting in the car, I saw him come back out while carrying on an animated conversation with a man who had greeted him—a man I did not know. When he got in the car I asked, "Billy, who was that man?" He responded, "I no idea."

Billy's social skills have grown as a result of his own sensitive and gregarious nature. Shortly before we moved to Kingsport, he spent the weekend with his sister and her family. They all attended a school play; afterwards Billy navigated through the crowd, extending his hand and offering "Hi, I'm Billy. I going to move here." A similar event occurred recently when he and I were in an airport, waiting at the luggage conveyor. He extended his hand to a young man also waiting for his suitcase, and said, "Hi, I'm Billy. What's your name?" Initially surprised, the man began talking with Billy and discussed with him the extent of their travels.

Billy is naturally friendly and uninhibited socially. When Tom lived in Asheville, he invited Billy to visit him for the weekend. Tom had been invited to a party and took Billy with him. The guests were sitting in the living room, and conversation had languished. After a while, Billy broke the silence: "Who wants to arm wrestle?" The ice was totally broken and the party revived.

So—how intelligent is Billy? How shall we identify him? And what is his label? Over the span of his life, Billy has been described as having Mongolism, Down's Syndrome, and Down syndrome. He was referred to as trainable mentally retarded, then for a brief time cognitively disadvantaged, and is now called developmentally disabled. Even The American Association on Mental Retardation, referred to earlier, has just adopted a new name: The American Association on Intellectual and Developmental Disabilities.

During the time frame of this book, designations have changed from being handicapped to having a disability, and from mainstreaming to inclusion. When I began reading in the field of mental retardation, terms such as idiot, moron, and imbecile had only recently been discarded. It was common to see "the retarded" in referring to people with low IQs. However, at the time the now-objectionable terms were in common parlance, they were useful for communicating in medical, social, and educational settings. This should be the purpose of all labels.

Certainly we are influenced by legislative terms such as The Law for Education of Handicapped Children and The American with Disabilities Act, but such measures cannot keep pace with changing ideas. Perhaps we need to look at the reason behind the constant changes.

When we consider labels objectionable, perhaps we are really talking about the conditions themselves as objectionable, or at least difficult for us to accept. By changing the label, we are easing the impact until the new label becomes objectionable. Since we are powerless to change the perceived problem, this is a temporary solution.

What is never objectionable is considering people with disabilities first as *people*.

I think we will just call him Billy.

When I see Steve?

I DON'T KNOW WHEN OR HOW it germinated, the idea for me to pursue a doctorate in education. Perhaps the seed was planted by Dr. Laura Newell, my model for teaching. She was a charming, quiet-mannered woman who immediately put her students at ease and made them eager to learn. She had a confident, engaging manner as she manipulated blocks on the overhead projector, transferring math concepts from complex ideas to understandable discoveries. I wanted to be like her.

I do know that the idea of the doctorate culminated in a remark by Dr. Coss, the somber, distinguished head of the Elementary Education Department, who—upon closer acquaintance—revealed himself as a warm, compassionate man. I had completed the summer session of the demonstration class and made an appointment with him to discuss the possibility of registering for a sixth-year certificate curriculum. He asked, "Why don't you go for the doctorate?"

I was floored. The idea had never occurred to me; I had not pictured myself at that level.

I loved school. Taking classes, developing projects and delving into new ideas were an enormously satisfying part of my life and I didn't want to stop. In addition, our family life needed change. Bill was totally out of the life-insurance business and was in what I now recognize as deep depression. Nothing had worked out for him; he was doing bookkeeping for small businesses and barely getting by. He was not motivated to find a more lucrative business and was at a standstill personally and professionally.

The family agreed that I should become a college professor and was willing to make the necessary move to Auburn where I was required to be in residence. I was strengthened by their support, which I perceived as a tremendous sacrifice for each of them.

The reality of the change surprised me. I recently asked Tom to tell me how he felt about the move and received the following response:

The move to Auburn actually came into my life at a very opportune time. Columbus was increasingly claustrophobic for me. As one of a handful of civilian kids at my high school, I found my conflict between my newly energized desire to be an artist and my perceived (and real) expectations to be an academic. I was making friends with officers' kids who had been (gasp) stationed in California and Europe and was infused with "new" liberal ideas about the culture and the war [Viet Nam]. I was feeling stuck. In adolescence, many of my childhood friends and I were parting ways philosophically.

Spiritually, I was beginning to formulate a personal world view that involves issues of empathy and fairness that became the foundation for the art that I continue to make today.

I had a lot of questions. And the world was in turmoil. In many ways our family dynamics mirrored that tension. I was as aware as a kid can be that my parents were questioning the trajectory of their lives. I was becoming very close to my older brother. He was in COLLEGE. He would give me books to read. I got a lot out of those books. I wanted to move.

I wanted my sister to move. I wanted her to experience change, so that perhaps she would not have to face some of the struggles that seemed so weighty to me. I wanted to be able to reinvent myself, and going somewhere new was a threshold that I was dying to cross. At first I was dismayed because the parental units bandied about living on a farm, and that seemed like a step backwards. It seemed like it would be full of work. And that type of work wasn't what I was looking for. When it turned out that we would live in a college town, and I ended up in a school that was integrated and full of professors' kids, I thought "Give me six months. I'm cutting loose."

I loved helping my mother with her statistics. I loved cultivating the idea that art and math and science and history could be connected.

Where was Billy in this for me? We learned together to be acolytes. We "pumped iron" together. I began to understand that other people saw him in a way that angered me. I wanted them to see him as he was in our house. As I saw him. I made the connection with how he was treated and how all "others" were being treated during those times: blacks, Hispanics, hippies.

And because of the move, I began to see my mother in a new light. A new kind of model. A woman with a focus and drive that wasn't about keeping the freezer frost-free.

But mostly I started to see that in our case, home was not about the hearth. It was about dynamics. And in fact, the largest point of discord (as I saw it) revolved around my father's difficulty with accepting this new paradigm of interests and power, even as he took his place in its creation.

To this day I credit this move with creating a shift so that I would come to know that change is not just good—it is essential to me. My model is that you can begin again and again. It set the mood that allowed me to get my MFA at the age of 48. It taught me to teach my own kids that we carry our homes with us, and that you can, you really can, dive into the murky backwaters of the unexpected.

We were like Columbus: sailing off the edge of the known world. In a "thanks vermillion" Maverick.

Mary, at seventh grade, was due to move into a different school and thought moving to Auburn sounded far more interesting. She had lived in the same house all her life and welcomed a change.

We did hate to take Billy out of Mrs. Sanders's class, but were sure that in this university town the resources for him would be exemplary—its special education program was considered one of the best. For Billy, living near his friend Steve from the demonstration class was the best thing that could happen.

John and Barbara had married and were teaching in Columbus. Their son, Paul, was an adorable baby and our first grandchild—I hated to move away from them. I knew Mother would miss us too, but considered all together the good seemed to outweigh the bad, and we knew we would only be as far away as my regular commute.

After I was accepted into the doctoral program, I began taking classes in the summer prior to our move. We put our house on the market, and Bill assumed responsibility for selling it. I knew that he was a good salesman but was amazed at the determination he revealed in this particular task. He came alive in a way I hadn't seen him for months: he had a mission. The last couple who looked at the house was about to decline when he displayed his true salesmanship; he would not allow them to leave until they agreed to buy! He was selling so hard that I was uncomfortable and had to leave the room, but he did it, and we were free to begin to find something in Auburn.

We couldn't find a place to rent in Auburn and, with the sale of our house in Columbus, were able to buy a new house—a first for us. I don't know how we thought we could pay for it, but somehow we did. We moved in time for the children to start to school, with a great deal of help from John and the rest of the family. Our house was clean and comfortable, although the yard was pure mud. Our little cocker spaniel, Honey, was confused and apparently thought the green carpet was the closest thing to grass that she could find.

During my summer course work, I overheard a conversation in the coffee shop that alarmed me. Two teachers were talking and one asked, "Where will you be teaching this year?" to which the other answered, "Oh, I'll be with a class of nuts at Samford Middle School."

That class was the one to which Billy had been assigned. I knew at that moment he would not have a good year. He was not in Steve's class, because Steve was considered EMR (educable mentally retarded), while Billy was TMR (trainable mentally retarded). Try telling *them* that.

Billy's class was in a trailer behind the school, standard special education at that time, and the teacher and students appeared unmotivated. During the year several of the students were suspended for behavior problems, and it was obvious that very little education was going on, special or otherwise. I talked with Mrs. Harris, Steve's teacher, and got Billy transferred to her class. Then he was in clover, going to school with his dear friend.

Billy and Steve were so close that they talked on the phone after school every day and visited with each other frequently. We went with Steve's parents to their home at the lake where the boys played in the water and Steve tried to teach Billy to swim. They put on concerts for each other, pretending to be their favorite singers. Billy made a microphone from a piece of wood, a rubber end cap, and a string; he didn't *imitate* Tom Jones—he *was* Tom Jones.

Billy had never had a real friend before. It was worth the less than perfect learning situation for him to have a best friend.

Surprisingly, in the short time that we lived in Auburn, Tom, Mary, Billy and I all formed strong friendships that have lasted over the years.

Tom found several friends who shared his interests in art, reading, and seeking adventures. Two of his friends assisted us later in our move to North Carolina, joined him in hiking the Appalachian Trail, and visited us frequently in the mountains.

Mary's friendship with Rebecca began in art class, where both of them developed their talents, leading to their separate but similar careers in graphic design. They were like sisters, their devotion extending into adulthood.

My friendship with Ann Turnbull began in Auburn. In one of our graduate classes, the poorly informed professor made such a ridiculous statement that we looked at each other in disbelief, rolling our eyes, forming a bond. Both of us moved to North Carolina, became fellow authors, and developed a close business as well as personal relationship.

Bill did not have the opportunities to meet people that the children and I had in school situations. He was always gregarious, however, and became friends with neighbors and a couple with whom we played bridge.

Some new educational developments had been instigated in the schools. One of them was open classrooms, another was individualized instruction. I was rather amused when Mary, who had been sick for several days, came home with an armload of papers. When I asked why she had so much work to do, she replied, "Oh, I got behind in my individualized instruction while I was absent."

Tom was in a new high school, where the trend was to eliminate windows from the building. I asked Tom, "How can you daydream when you have no windows to look out of?"

His answer was, "You have to be pretty creative."

He graduated from high school at the end of our two years in Auburn.

During the summer, I had heard of a grant available for the coming year, designed to help those pursuing advanced work in mental retardation. Because I had such a poor opinion of my major professor, and before I knew how important the game was, I bypassed him when I applied for the grant. Big mistake; I didn't get the grant and knew, from the smirk on his face, why I didn't get it.

Since I had to work to pay my tuition and expenses, I obtained a job in the reading clinic; this proved to be an excellent training ground. The purpose of the diagnostic service of the reading clinic was to "assess existing reading problems, investigate possible causes, and to recommend proper instructional procedures... The diagnostic service is provided throughout the year and includes screening for physical factors such as vision and hearing, an individual assessment of mental ability, and intensive analyses in all areas of reading."

On the strength of my background in intelligence testing and teaching reading, I was hired as a graduate assistant and, with another doctoral student, evaluated children who were having reading problems. Had I received the coveted grant, I would have missed this excellent opportunity to interact with children and their parents. In one memorable case, I was administering an intelligence test to a third-grade boy when he began to have a grand mal seizure. I immediately stopped, and when he had recovered, talked with the mother. Apparently she was unwilling to acknowledge his primary problem and was cloaking it in the more acceptable diagnosis of a reading problem.

The reading clinic was housed in the Haley Center, a new education building where most of my classes were held. Like Tom's school, the center had no windows, and after a day in the building I emerged to find sunshine, rain, or, on one occasion, snow. I felt cheated and isolated from the real world and could identify with Tom. It was, however, a convenient arrangement and saved valuable time.

During the second summer I had another amazing opportunity. Since there was a push to have children with mental retardation identified and placed in special classes, the state of Alabama was looking to hire psychometrists on a part-time basis. Identified from classes in psychological testing, teams were formed to travel throughout the state, administering tests and making recommendations. I was selected to be a leader for one of these teams, to send evaluators to identified areas of the state and to review their findings. It was a perfect situation for me: no traveling, as I arranged trips for my team by phone, and being compensated well for my time. That summer I made a good amount of much-needed family income.

The second year of my doctoral program I found a part-time job as coordinator of special education in Opelika, Alabama, a small town close to Auburn. It was my task to visit the classes, confer with the teachers, make recommendations for instruction, and administer tests when necessary. I loved being in contact with the real world of teachers, children, and schools and appreciated the opportunity to feature the children as subjects in my dissertation.

My working experience was so valuable and enjoyable that I became glad I hadn't been awarded the grant. Unfortunately, Bill's experience was less challenging and remunerative. He began keeping books for small businesses and, during tax time, worked for H & R Block. He set up an office in our garage, with a desk and an adding machine. The contrast in the trajectories of our careers was obvious, and although he had been in favor of my pursuits, he began to resent my successes. Nevertheless, the children and I were happy and we maintained a cheerful home environment. We began gathering after school hours to watch Dark Shadows and to share the day's activities.

I found most of my classes stimulating and exciting. I was particularly involved in my classes in behavior modification, partly because I saw the practicality of the principles and partly because of Dr. Turner, a particularly engaging professor. Of our projects, two were inspired by and developed for family members.

Bill, a heavy smoker, agreed to my project designed to help him quit. First I charted his smoking behavior, finding that he was smoking three cigarettes an hour regardless of other activity, such as eating and driving. I had come across a horribly apt picture: the skeleton of a hand holding a cigarette. Each time he reached for a cigarette, I held the picture in front of him. At one point I felt it was working, but found that he was simply leaving the house to smoke. Later, he reported that it wasn't so much the skeletal hand that bothered him as my expression while I waited for him to extinguish the cigarette.

My other project was with Billy. One of his major handicaps is his fear of heights. This crippling anxiety is traumatic for him and sometimes for us. In an attempt to modify this behavior, I conceived of a well-designed project, using the technique of systematic desensitization, providing increased degrees of exposure to fear in a relaxed environment. I combined this method with that of peer influence and social reinforcement. With his mother's approval, Steve agreed to help with the project. It took place at the Haley Center, a high-rise building with a balcony at each floor.

Billy was not afraid of riding in an elevator, only of being in high, open places. With Steve at his side, he rode the elevator to the second floor and came out onto the balcony, at which time I took a Polaroid picture of them from the ground. I showed it to them when they descended and we applauded Billy's performance. On succeeding days we had Billy and Steve go to increasing levels, repeating the procedure, until they achieved the height of the sixth-floor balcony. We were all pleased and excited and Billy was proud of himself; he was comfortable at Haley Center, and it was a good exercise for me.

A success in part, we learned over time that the acquired skill did not generalize to other situations and therefore was not entirely beneficial. The inability to transfer learned skills from one situation to another is a typical problem for persons with Down syndrome and other disabilities. Knowledge of this trait has helped reduce our frustration when Billy does not make the expected intellectual leap and reminds us that it is important to teach specific skills for particular situations.

For the most part my courses were interesting and rewarding. Being with other doctoral students provided good discussion situations and the means to learn what was going on in public schools at the time. Observing my own professors' methods and teaching styles, I had a growing mental list of what to do and what not to do in my future role as a professor.

As I approached the end of my course work, I saw students consistently arranging their schedules to avoid taking classes with Dr. Punké. I wondered why and, since he was approaching retirement, decided to register for his course. During the first class he asked me a question—I don't remember what—which I smugly answered. Then he questioned me about my answer, backing me into a corner with his queries and making me realize how shallow I had been. This great educator taught me the power of questioning in the educational process.

In addition to the course work and part-time work in Opelika, I was writing my dissertation. Typically, students complain about this process, but I loved it! For the first time in my life I had a place of my own to study: a carrel at the library. I gathered books, papers, and writing supplies into the tiny space that was mine. Each Sunday afternoon I retreated to the library and got lost in my searching and writing. I had chosen the weighty title, "A Study to Determine the Effects of an Individualized Art Program on the Perceptual-Motor Performance of Mentally Retarded Children." With the Opelika students as subjects, I gathered samples of their art, pre- and post-tested their perceptual-motor abilities, and did my research.

As I progressed with the dissertation, I dropped off the first chapter for my major professor's approval. When I didn't hear from him for several weeks, I stopped at his office to seek his opinion. He reached on the top shelf of his bookcase, pulled down the unopened envelope, and handed it to me. Since he had been assigned as chairman of my program, I had no recourse but to move on and leave it with other members of the committee. Fortunately, they read my material, made good suggestions, and approved the work.

When I came to the statistical portion of my dissertation study, I went to the newly designated computer center to analyze my data. Computers were new to the education world; then, a large computer filled a small room. I picked up the green cards used to enter data, signed up for help and an appointment, and found that the computer was scheduled for the next two months! I needed to move much more quickly if I was to graduate in a few months. Crushed and confused, I realized I had to change my statistical analysis to a simpler procedure and to analyze the data without the computer. I remember vividly sitting at Bill's desk in the garage, textbook and data before me, hands on the adding machine—totally lost. I worked until about 2:00 a.m., when Tom walked in from a late date and found me in tears, my head on the desk. He pulled up a chair and worked with me most of the night until we had the data interpreted. It is a turning point of motherhood when you realize your children can reverse the roles, rescue you, and become your heroes.

Upon completion of my dissertation, I was satisfied with its soundness, and was particularly pleased with photographs of the children's art. These images preserved the memory of working with some very special children for a year.

I still faced two more hurdles: the oral exam and the written exam. The oral exam took place in the conference room of the graduate school office, a place that was hallowed ground for me. Although I was nervous, as the exam progressed I felt comfortable with the knowledge I had acquired. The written exam was set for August 3, and since I was to graduate that month, the pressure was intense. I passed both tests and was ready to begin my new career.

CHAPTER 15

Destination

I miss my mom

IN THE SPRING prior to my graduation, I looked at openings for positions in the area of special education. Bill and I had agreed that we would seek a position for me and that he would find work wherever we went. One opening that looked promising was the position of county special education coordinator in Rome, Georgia, with a good salary. I applied and was granted an interview. Bill and I drove to Rome, where I met with several school superintendents and learned that the position entailed working with special education teachers in a large area, supervising placement of children and evaluating their progress. The people who interviewed me were cordial, interested in my background, and called later to offer me the position. For some reason I was not excited; on the drive back to Auburn, I knew this was a good opportunity for me and perhaps for Bill, but it just didn't feel right.

Another opening was at Western Carolina University, in Cullowhee, North Carolina. The position was that of assistant professor in special education, the role for which I felt prepared. After applying for and receiving an invitation for an interview, Bill and I went to Cullowhee for a few days, traveling from the lowlands of Alabama into the Appalachian mountains of North Carolina. Although a native of North Carolina, I had never heard of Cullowhee, nor could we find it on a map. It was a delightful trip, seeing the dogwood trees in bloom for the second time that spring, and enjoying a totally different landscape. We felt more hopeful and happier than we had felt for a long time.

The interview with the department head, Dr. Roy Cox, increased my interest in the position. He introduced me to members of the department, showed me the offices and classrooms, and he and his wife, Audrey, took us out to dinner that night. They expressed interest in our family and seemed to enjoy our company. The next day Dr. Cox and I met again, when he told me he had one more person to interview and would contact me soon.

Bill and I drove around the tiny town of Cullowhee and the slightly larger adjacent town of Sylva and realized that this was exactly where we wanted to live. We looked at schools and homes and decided that if the opportunity arose, we would like to live there.

When we returned home the next day, there was a call from Dr. Cox offering me the position; I accepted. When I phoned the people in Rome to decline their offer, they raised the salary considerably higher than the one Dr. Cox had offered, but my elation over moving to Cullowhee made that factor seem unimportant. We were going to North Carolina!

Several gigantic precursors to our moving arose. First, we had to sell our house in Auburn. Second, we had to find housing in Cullowhee. Third, at that time I still had my oral exam, two courses, and completion of the dissertation before graduation at the end of August.

During the break between the spring and summer quarters, we took the children to Cullowhee to look at possible housing and to show them the community. We stayed in a local motel which was sandwiched between a creek and the railroad line. The sign "No Trains at Night" amused us. We had decided that this was an opportunity for a real life change, that we didn't want to live in a development, and that we wanted to be close to the beautiful environment. After looking at several houses for sale, we discovered our home—it was on top of a mountain, several miles above the community of Tilley Creek, with the ethereal mail address of "Star Route 66."

We took the winding road past a little gathering of houses, several small homes, and a picturesque white frame church, to a brick-red house with a balcony across the front, facing the mountains. This house was built by a man short on building skill but long on appreciation of beauty. Entering from the back of the house, we found a living room and a dining room embracing a magnificent view of layers of mountains. It was so spectacular we gasped at the beauty and knew that this was our dream house. We agreed to purchase it and found that it was available immediately.

Since this was May and I wouldn't graduate until August, Bill set about selling our house and working toward the move. The day after he put a sign on a tree in the front yard, Bill sold the house! He worked with the buyers of our Auburn house and established a mortgage on the house in Cullowhee. At this point, we encountered another piece of discrimination—sex discrimination.

In 1971, banks were not inclined to grant mortgages to women. Since I was the one who had a job, it was necessary to base the purchase of the house on my employment. The bank did not want to allow us to borrow money based on my work, but, ever the persuasive salesman, Bill convinced them that I had a contract and that I wouldn't be having any babies. I also faced sex discrimination among people reluctant to recognize women as having terminal degrees. One night someone phoned, asking to speak with Dr. Schulz. I replied, "This is she."

"No," they responded, "I want *Doctor* Schulz." On several occasions, in groups where we were introduced as new people in the university community, greeters frequently approached me with the question, "And what department does your husband work in?"

After our house in Auburn sold, I still had to finish my course work and my dissertation. We decided that I would stay with Mother in Columbus, once again commuting to Auburn, and that Bill and the children would move to Cullowhee, returning for my graduation.

Loading the moving van was a family effort. Steve and Chris, Tom's friends, joined him in the heavy lifting. We added a small trailer to the van to convey the rest of our accumulated goods. As Bill drove around the corner, with Billy riding shotgun, I saw the trailer sway from side to side. This disturbing mental picture stayed with me, with Mary riding in Chris's little MG behind the van and trailer, in front of Tom and Steve driving the Maverick. The motley crew, accompanied by Honey and Chris's Irish setter, headed off for their adventure.

I stayed behind to clean the empty house, gather my materials for the dissertation, and drive my car to Columbus. How I longed to be in the caravan with my family! Once again I employed the Alabama bridge technique as I tried to concentrate on the job ahead.

Being in Auburn alone again brought forth many memories: the anxiety of driving there for the first time, the frustration of registration, the time away from my family. In walking about the campus for the last weeks I recognized that I would miss its beauty, the fragrance of the magnolia blossoms, and the excitement of classes. I would remember this as the place I had found my promise as a teacher, the joy of exploring new ideas, and the fulfillment of a dream.

At Mother's house, I put the dissertation together in a manner that would seem antiquated for today's students. I finished typing it, had copies made for all the committee members, and with the help of my niece Annie, pasted photographs of the children's art in place. Pages to be collated created a path throughout the house, and Mother was delighted to be part of the process.

I thought of my family constantly; my desire to be with them in our new home kept me motivated to finish. I was encouraged by letters from Bill; I could sense that he was coming out of his depression and he seemed enthusiastic about new opportunities. About the move itself he wrote:

> You knew I didn't want to leave Auburn, didn't think I could drive that trip in that overloaded truck. Gas mileage a fabulous 5 miles per gallon! We came up to the house from Franklin (short cut). The drive up from that way is just beautiful. One curve took over 5 minutes to navigate around, it was so sharp. I couldn't have done it without Tom, Chris and Steve. Today I had to get the TV going— couldn't take much more Tom Jones. Billy has taken this just great and at times we can even get him out on the balcony—a wonderful place to sit and meditate…you can sit and watch the clouds change the whole scene by the minute.

Bill was looking for work and found several people who wanted him to maintain their books. He also had an interview with the editor of the local newspaper about selling advertising. He wrote encouraging words to me: "It's almost over honey, then I'll greet you with open arms." I could feel his energy and optimism returning.

Mary's description of the move added to Bill's picture:

> I'm going to start from the beginning and hit all the highlights. All in all, the trip was a real success. We didn't have nearly as much trouble as we thought we would with the truck. We also got extremely good mileage with the Maverick and M. G. The only bad part about the trip up was that after lunch (about 2:00) I threw up all over Chris's car. (I thought in time to lean over the window!) We only had a few minor casualties besides that such as 6 headaches. The weather has been very cool because of rain. It poured last night and has drizzled a little late this afternoon.
>
> This morning I woke up with a smile on my face, a cool breeze on my shoulders, and with my whole body being aware. A rooster crowed a few times, then gradually birds, cows, and dogs joined in. (I slept downstairs with Honey, and everyone else slept upstairs.) I thought I heard them clunking around upstairs, but I went up and they were all sound asleep. I watched the fog roll off the slopes, and soon the sun showed through the clouds. It was so beautiful, I went up and woke Tom. He was so grumpy, though, he didn't even get up. He just held up the curtain and hardly looked. I ran back downstairs, and saw that the sun was all the way out. I ached for you, Mom! Then I finally went back to sleep. This morning the boys unloaded the rest of the truck.

Mary wrote frequently, usually including menus of meals she had prepared for the family. One day's menu made me laugh:

Breakfast—orange juice, bacon, eggs
Lunch—we had breakfast at 12:00
Dinner—baked chicken, beans, salad, milk
Our meals have been good, but they aren't nearly as good as yours.

In Billy's handwriting, the note on the outside of the envelope really made me long for my family:

Hi, Mom! PS Billy Love

I completed my dissertation, took the final doctoral examination, and finalized the course work. In line with the other graduates, I felt sure that someone would tap me on the shoulder and say, "You missed a course you should have taken. Step out of line." I marched with a thousand students and took my place for the graduation ceremony. My entire family—including John and Barbara who came over from Columbus—was there, watching with pride, having attended my three graduations. I felt my diploma belonged to them.

Although we had lived in Auburn for only two years, we had developed close friendships and regretted leaving people behind. Billy's dear friend Steve had a gift for me with a card I still have: "To Mrs schulz From: your second son from Steve." We left with promises to return and to expect visits from our friends, especially Steve.

Headed for the mountains, this time all of us got into the same car. Full of hope and anticipation, we felt our time had come.

WE WERE IN CAMELOT. Imagine driving seven miles to a height of 4,000 feet, watching the landscape change with each mile, curving around the mountain slowly enough to absorb the landmarks that would become so familiar. Around a horseshoe bend, you look up, and there it is: a brick-red house on top of the mountain, a porch circling the front and hugging its side, beside a huge maple tree with a swing dangling from a massive limb.

In my absence Bill and the children had arranged every-thing beautifully and function-ally. It was apparent that they had worked hard to please me and they certainly accomplished that goal. It was home.

Our home was a perfect fit, my work was exactly right for me, Bill had found a good job, the children were in school, and the view from our porch was spec-tacular! We could see the Blue Ridge Parkway, 25 miles distant from us; the sunrises and sunsets

I tole you!

were breathtaking. I was giddy with happiness.

Tom, Mary and I began taking a walk every evening after dinner, regardless of the weather. This became a cherished habit and contributed to our closeness as we shared our thoughts and experiences, walking past the bus turnaround to the witch's tree—named by us be-cause of the black shape on the trunk and bark. One night we were expecting John and Barbara to arrive for a visit; we walked to the witch's tree, sat beneath it on the bank, and waited for their car. As we sat in silence, appreciating the full moon, a motorcycle came roaring up the road. It came to a full stop in front of us, and the couple riding it disembarked to take in the spectacular view. From the darkness of the night, Tom pointed and said, "Look at the moon!" They turned and saw us, crouched in the dark, got on their bike without a word, and tore away down the road. We still laugh about that, imagining the story they told.

Chris had left Mollie, his Irish setter, with us and after our beloved cocker spaniel died, Tom brought home a German shepherd for Billy. He named her Friend and that's what she became for all of us. The two dogs always accompanied us on our walks and became part of the family.

I had about a month before starting my classes—a welcome period. I would need to get our children enrolled in school, assemble a wardrobe suitable for a college professor, and study the books Dr. Cox had given me for my classes.

I gratefully found time to walk with the kids, to enjoy the swing, and to cherish the peacefulness of being on top of a mountain. Each morning Bill, an early riser, brought coffee to me as I sat up in bed looking out the window at the marvelous view before us. Bill developed a habit of saying, "It changes every minute. "

We kept asking ourselves: "When will the vacation be over?" It was a slow, wonderful transition.

The children were as thrilled with our new environment as Bill and I were. We had been somewhat concerned about Billy's adjustment, especially being apart from Steve, and found that he had cleverly managed to keep in touch. When we opened our first phone bill, it was apparent that Billy and Steve had maintained their practice of talking with each other every day after school. As amazed as we were, we realized that we hadn't explained the difference between local and long-distance phone calls. We also acknowledged our surprise and delight that he had managed to make the calls. Wouldn't you like to have heard his exchange with the long-distance operator?

I had explored resources for Billy during our first trip to the area, and found that there was a TMR class in an annex to the building where I would be working. I met Carol Thomas, the teacher he would become so fond of, and felt secure knowing he would be near my office and classrooms. Billy and Mary had a new experience in riding the schoolbus that labored up the mountain and turned around at the county line just beyond our house. Billy loved the bus; Mary was less than excited.

As winter approached we were thrilled with snow and frequently had snow on the mountaintop when it was merely raining in Cullowhee. Since we were the last house on the bus route, the school officials began calling us to determine whether or not the snow would be hazardous for the buses and therefore require a snow day. One morning about 4:00 the school principal called to ask about the situation. Tom answered the phone and, tired of such intrusive calls, said that the snow was knee deep. At breakfast he said to Mary and Billy, "Guess what I did for you today?" They never called us for weather information again.

Billy carried a book with him on the bus—he had chosen *The Godfather* from our collection and carried it boldly. Carol, after learning to know me better, revealed that when she saw him carrying that book into her classroom she was intimidated by his supposed sophistication.

Mary attended the small high school in Cullowhee, near the university, and quickly made a place for herself as a good student, an aspiring musician, and a budding artist. She formed close and lasting friendships. Tom spent a year in college at Western but left the art program and worked at a Christmas tree farm and in construction.

Bill was selling ads for the weekly newspaper, getting to know the business people in the town of Sylva. He seemed contented for a while but decided to take a course in real estate and ultimately became a broker. This seemed a natural career for him, given his success in selling and buying our homes and his general interest in houses and land. He opened his own real-estate office in Sylva, thoroughly enjoying his work, driving clients through the countryside in his trusty Jeep.

We joined a beautiful, small Episcopal church in Cullowhee, pastored by the father of Mary's new friend, Sallie. When we went to Communion the first time, we noticed that Father Rivers was wearing hiking boots beneath his robes, a hint of his way of life. Mary and Tom began taking hiking and camping trips, frequently with groups from the church. Tom took hiking to a serious level when he decided to hike the Appalachian Trail.

On a dreary, rainy afternoon on the tail of winter, I drove Tom to the beginning of the Trail in Dahlonaga, Georgia. He stepped out in the fog with his minimal backpack and provisions; our goodbye was painful for both of us, excruciating for me. It was one of those times a parent faces in knowing that children's choices must be honored, yet fearing for undue hardships and danger. I cried all the way home. A letter we received from him didn't help my feelings:

> We are off the trail again—clean now—and ready to get back on probably tomorrow, content right now with eating and watching the girls stroll by in the sunshine.
>
> Soon we will be going to Maine walking some and hitch hiking some but every plan that we make, we alter, glad now to be free and foot loose, the road (the asphalt) calling to me as strongly as the trail. But sitting here, I feel a little tired already of wondering just where I will sleep at night.

He enclosed a letter to Billy, closing with:

> I will see you later old chump.
> P.S. love Tommy
> P.S. I miss you.

Bill and I had many opportunities for social involvement, joining a couples bridge club and participating in numerous university-sponsored events. The first year we lived in the mountains we were overwhelmed with visitors from Georgia and Alabama, all eager to see and enjoy our new surroundings. Steve's parents brought him to spend a week with us, a week of pure bliss for Billy.

Our favorite visitors were John, Barbara, and Paul. It was a unique place for family reunions, a place where we could walk to the top of a nearby hill on pretty days, play in the snow, or sit before the fire on winter days. They called coming to our house "going to North Carolina." Little Paul and I were walking down the road one brittle wintry day. His cheeks red from the wind, he faced me and pleaded, "Grandma, let's go back to North Carolina!"

Paul began spending vacations with us when he was quite young. One Sunday we stayed home from church to play ball in the cow pasture below us, near the Adams farm. Trying to catch the ball he had thrown, I stepped back and fell directly into a cow pile. As I got up, both of us laughing heartily, he exclaimed, "Grandma, that was because you skipped church!"

When John and Barbara were expecting their second child, Billy was curious about the approaching delivery. Because his adolescence, like other areas of his development, had been delayed, his interest in the reproductive process was newly awakened. As the time approached for John Robert's birth, Billy asked, "When they gonna cut that baby out of Barbara's stomach?"

I explained,"No, Billy, that isn't what happens. There is a special opening and when the baby is ready, Barbara and the doctor will work hard for the baby to come out of the opening."

"No, Mom, I'm right."

Barbara ultimately required a Caesarean delivery. Billy's reaction? "I tole you!"

Augmenting the company of our out-of-town family and friends, we began new relationships with our fascinating neighbors. Carol and Louise, two brilliant and lively retired women, lived next door, and McKinley Adams, a weathered mountain man, lived just below our house on a very old farm. McKinley referred to us as "the Alabams" and to Mary, "the girl."

Western Carolina University was the perfect place for me. At that time it served about 6000 students—small enough to be friendly and large enough to afford an excellent faculty and good support systems. My department head had faith in my ability and provided me with a number of opportunities to grow as a teacher.

I met my new best friend, Florence Sumner, soon after I arrived in Cullowhee. One Sunday afternoon she drove up the mountain to welcome me. Our lively conversation gave us the impression we would share good times together. Through the years, we shared the joys of our children's marriages and the births of our grandchildren. We also supported each other through blizzards, illnesses, and deaths. When I learned that my new office was adjacent to hers, I knew I would feel at ease.

In preparation for teaching my fall classes, I poured over the books I had been given and realized that I was teaching five courses! I had very little time left to compose my lectures, but found the work fascinating and compelling. I made copious notes and was eager to begin. I met my first class with some nervousness and a great deal of enthusiasm. Alas, in my zeal I ran through notes for about four lessons! I realized I had a lot to learn about timing. One thing I will never forget from that first day was the student who approached me saying, "Dr. Schulz, I'm a senior majoring in mental retardation and I have never seen a retarded child." The next day I brought Billy to class and introduced him to the students. Thus began our partnership, which was to become more structured and sophisticated as we reached out to students, parents, and professionals. I assured the students that we would provide them with many opportunities to see and work with children who had disabilities. Through agreement with Billy's teacher, his class became a valuable source for my students to learn things that were not in the textbooks and to provide friendship and assistance to the children they met.

I began to investigate programs and resources in the community and found that the university had a close connection with and obligation to serve schools and institutions in the western part of North Carolina. My goal became to establish long-term involvement between college students and schools, benefiting Billy, other children with disabilities, and the college students.

Billy and I participated in Special Olympics while we were in Auburn and were surprised that it had not been introduced at Western. I met with Helen Hartshorn, a professor in the department of physical education, and we planned to develop the program in our county. As we explored possibilities and planned for implementing Special Olympics, we found that surrounding counties were also interested in participating. The result was overwhelming, culminating in small events in individual counties, a huge district meet on our campus, and several busloads of children progressing to the state event.

These activities involved a number of students—including fraternity and sorority groups—to train, encourage and supervise the children. Many of the children who participated in Special Olympics had never been out of Jackson County. Their excitement and awe made the work rewarding. During this time my student, Lynn Causey, evolved as a leader and a dynamic organizer. We worked so closely together and enjoyed each other so much that she became a member of our family.

Billy, as well as the other children, benefited greatly from the training and involvement with college students. Joe Allen, a special education student, assumed the task of teaching Billy to swim. Under this strong leadership, Billy's skills and confidence developed swiftly, allowing him to earn medals in the swimming and broad jump events of Special Olympics.

Students showed their regard for me and for my family in many ways. One brought me "dahlia 'taters" from his grandmother's garden. One day I saw another student, Eddy Kieffer, stroll into my front yard with a tree in one hand, a shovel and a bag of manure in the other. When I joined him outside and asked what he was doing, he replied, "I never brought you an apple," and he planted the tree.

The summer after my first year, Dr. Cox proposed a venture designed to help certify teachers of TMR students from schools throughout the state of North Carolina. We met with representatives from the North Carolina State Department of Education to plan the program. Dr. Cox introduced me, advised the group that I would plan and develop the program, and proposed the salary I would receive. They were surprised, objecting, "We could get Bernice Bumgardner for that price." Ms. Bumgardner was a leader in the field.

Dr. Cox responded, "Then get her."

The representatives approved my appointment, based on Dr. Cox's confidence, and I realized how much responsibility I had assumed. With no experience in what to do, I implemented a program that I thought should work in the field because I knew it would work for Billy. We joined forces with a school system in Shelby, North Carolina, and developed a course that involved teachers and students working together.

Again I took Billy with me. We stayed in a hotel, to his delight, and through the graciousness of the manager, used the hotel swimming pool as part of our training program. Dr. Hartshorn, now affectionately dubbed "Hartsie," came over to direct the swimming, throwing coins in the water to encourage the children to dive in. Some of the children had never been swimming; it was alarming to see one little girl simply walk into the deep end of the pool with no concept of danger. Other facets of the program included working in the wood shop and cooking. Students and teachers alike pursued achievement during the program, and I realized that this combination would become my trademark. I still treasure the stool with a woven top that I made in our first workshop, remembering how many times I had to saw the legs to make them even.

During the three-week period in Shelby, I worked closely with Ann Hyde, a consultant with the North Carolina Department of Education, and we formed a lasting friendship and working relationship. Ann and I developed other summer programs, usually in Cullowhee, as part of the teacher training program at the university. When Paul visited, he was always included in summer programs with Billy. Attesting to my behavior modification techniques, I overheard Billy saying, "Now Paul, do your work an' when we get home you get ice cream."

My association with teachers through the Shelby project led to more consulting opportunities among schools serving exceptional children. Dr. Cox encouraged me to accept the offers to travel within the state and nationally. He believed my workshops promoted the university and provided me with broadening experiences. Bill also encouraged me and, with his management of the home, made the travel possible. I vividly remember when he surprised me with a new outfit before one presentation I was to make at a major conference: a white pleated skirt, a navy top, and a red jacket. My friend Elsie had sent me a red brief case for my birthday, and I felt smart enough speak to anywhere!

One interesting presentation was the result of an invitation from Ann Turnbull, my friend from our Auburn days. As it happened, both of us had accepted positions in North Carolina, she at the university at Chapel Hill and I at Western. When she asked me to do a sexuality training workshop at an institution near Chapel Hill, I welcomed the opportunity to work with her. At the end of the workshop, given a check for $75, I said to Ann, "I spent fifty dollars for the jacket I'm wearing!"

True to her spirit, she declared, "Well, that means you got a new jacket plus twenty-five dollars!"

This was the start of our working relationship and the continued development of one of my most fulfilling friendships. Our professional relationship would escalate with emerging educational trends.

THERE WERE MAJOR CHANGES taking place in special education during the 1970s, culminating in 1975 with passage of The Law for Education of Handicapped Children. This law dramatically affected practices in public schools and, therefore, in teacher training programs in colleges and universities. The most striking changes the law dictated included the education of all handicapped children—including those most severely impaired, the involvement of parents in planning for their children, individualized education plans for all exceptional children, and education of handicapped children in the least restrictive environment. This last concept was classically known as "mainstreaming."

My mom teach the little children.

The first mandate that affected my work was the education of severely handicapped children—children who had not previously been in school. Western Carolina University had been selected to work with the area mental health organization and the state department of public instruction to design a program to train teachers to work with severely handicapped children. Implementing this new program was difficult, challenging, and rewarding. The first step was to identify and select children to participate in the program, a monumental task. Many of the children lived with their parents in remote regions of the counties to be served. Some of the parents, raising their children to the best of their ability, were reluctant to admit them to a program led by strangers. Others welcomed the help and were totally cooperative. Finding the homes in secluded mountainous areas was an adventure. When I arrived at the homes, I found some families welcoming, and some hostile.

Although I was experienced in my field, there were many surprises. At Sam's house, receiving no answer to my knock, I looked through the door and saw a boy lying on a mat on the living room floor. He was about three feet long, with a large head and scrawny limbs. He looked up at me and, in a loud but high-pitched voice, asked, "What the hell are you doing here?"

Once the children were identified and the teachers selected for our three-week program, we packed up our materials and caravaned to "camp." Our accommodations were in a beautiful mansion, owned by Smoky Mountain Mental Health, perched on the peak of a mountain near the Cherokee Indian Reservation. The house was purchased for use in developing therapeutic camps and retreats and provided a beautiful setting for us. In keeping with my policy, each teacher was paired with a child, sleeping in the same room, devoting all of his or her instructional time to that particular child. Since there were no experts or real guidance in this area of education, such intimacy provided practical knowledge of the child's needs and abilities. We learned a great deal, especially how limited our knowledge was.

My child was Ben, a nonverbal, hyperactive boy. On his entrance into the program, we noticed many bruises on his body and wondered if he had been abused. After spending one sleepless night with him I could understand the bruises. He sat up, I pressed him back, he sat up, etc. The next day, the teachers asked me, "Well, do you think his parents have abused him?"

I responded, "If they did, I know why."

We developed empathy for parents of such developmentally delayed children; I was more grateful than ever for all the things Billy could do.

Based on the parents' wishes, our focus was on toilet training, made possible by the large number of bathrooms in the mansion. Thereafter, the program became known as "Tee Tee Camp."

We used a program requiring the children to stay on the toilet until they urinated, after which they were reinforced. We learned to delay their breakfast, feed them salty food which made them thirsty, have them drink large volumes of liquid, and remain in the bathroom for long periods of time. One could hear a trainer yell throughout the building, "Jenny peed!"

Of course there were other elements of the curriculum, depending on the needs of the child, self-feeding, dressing, etc. We, the teachers, did not go home during the three weeks, for fear of breaking the training process.

It was an extremely hard period, made more pleasant by the bonding of the teachers, excellent meals provided, and unparalleled learning. I have never experienced closer relationships. Culminating with a party at my home, the students presented me with one of my most cherished gifts, a hand-painted toilet seat.

The second mandate of the new legislation affecting my work was "least restrictive environment," the requirement that became my mission and that of my friend Ann Turnbull. While attending a state conference, Ann and I decided to write a textbook reflecting the new legislation and impending educational reform as well as strategies for teaching exceptional children. The result was a first book for both of us, *Mainstreaming Handicapped Children: A Guide for Classroom Teachers*. This was a landmark textbook, to be followed by several editions. Publication of the book would ultimately enhance our careers as well as provide a number of opportunities to speak on the topic. Writing it required us to meet, usually in Chapel Hill, and to work together. We had so much fun doing it that it was a joy as well as a mission.

In writing the book and exploring teaching methods for integrating children with disabilities into regular classrooms, I began to realize how little I knew about current practices in public schools and I desired to be part of that process again. Frank discussions with my family and heart-rending internal deliberations led me to leave the university and return to the public-school classroom. I followed through on the decision and wrote the following letter to Dr. Cox, my department head:

> Dear Roy,
>
> As you know, last month I applied to Jackson County Schools for a teaching position. This morning the Superintendent assured me that there would be an opening for me in the fall. I am, therefore, resigning my position as Associate Professor in your department.
>
> The decision to leave is based on my personal need to be involved with children and to reassure myself that I can do what I am teaching others to do. Special Education in the public schools has changed so drastically in the past few years that I feel this is a necessity for me at this time.
>
> The five years that I have worked with you have been challenging, exciting and rewarding to me. The confidence in me that you have demonstrated so freely has enabled me to grow both professionally and personally. Your own insight and creativity have encouraged me to "try my wings" in many directions. I think that we have done some outstanding things together.
>
> Since I will still be in the community, I certainly hope that our working relationship will continue. I will welcome any opportunity to be of service to you or to the University.
>
> Thank you, Roy, for your fine leadership and your irreplaceable friendship.

This mammoth decision proved to be one of the best I had ever made. It enabled me to continue working on the book, bringing in real-life experiences with children and developing a number of teaching techniques that I found advantageous. Furthermore, it gave me credibility with teachers when I continued to speak with them about the problems and solutions I had encountered in the classroom. But the most extraordinary benefit was the opportunity to know, learn from, and work with delightful children and dedicated teachers.

In August, I began my new work as a resource teacher. Children who were having particular problems would come to my small room for designated periods. I had been given authority to establish my own system and, decrying the use of labels to identify children, organized groups according to their needs, e.g. reading, math, and spelling. In this arrangement, children with various disabilities and from different grade levels came together for a common academic need. In my naiveté I felt this would eliminate the need for labels, such as retarded, learning disabled, etc. Soon, however, I received a memo from the main office asking me to list my students according to handicap, and I realized that labels were necessary for funding purposes and that we would continue to categorize children by disability. In classroom practice, though, my academic groups worked well. An excerpt from my letter to Mary, who was in college, describes my pleasure:

> The neatest thing happened today—one of those rare pictures of things actually working. David, the blind boy, is good in math and needs practice in braille. Ted and James need to learn the multiplication tables. Picture this: James is filling in a grid I had prepared; David is brailling the multiplication flash cards and giving them to Ted to solve and I'm checking his braille (by use of my chart). It's beautiful, and in walks the principal. I couldn't believe it, because the last time he came in I was pulling up my knee socks.

Several of the children are outstanding in my memory: David, who taught me so much and who is still my dear friend, and Tommy, who spent a large part of each day in the resource room and became my staunch advocate. I wrote the following incident in my journal:

> Keith is a disturbed child, given to tantrums. I was ineptly trying to deal with him today when he shouted, "Shut up, old lady!" Tommy grabbed him by the shirt, almost picking him up off the floor and said, "Don't you talk like that to her, you son of a bitch!"

In addition to getting to know children again, I also learned a great deal about the situations some of them came from. Another letter to Mary recorded the revelations and variety of my experiences:

> I had a real interesting week at school. I want to tell you about one afternoon. I had decided to take four kids (the spelling group) on a field trip, to view some vocational possibilities and to meet their parents when I took them home. We went

to a filling station (where Larry works; he was nine feet tall when he had to put air in tires and the other kids watched!) and then to Dad's plant store, where they all potted a plant to take home. Then we took Libby home; Anice [my student teacher] had wanted to talk with Libby's mother about helping with her grooming. Her mother was in the kitchen of a hovel. She was cleaning the stove; the 18-month-old baby was sitting on a table next to the stove, playing in a tub of water. The mother would wipe the greasy, black stove, then wring the rag out in the water the baby was playing in and go on cleaning. Anice went into shock and I had to initiate the conversation. Libby's " uncle" was sprawled out drunk in a chair in the living room; there was a pile of garbage in the middle of the kitchen floor. And we want Libby to come to school clean! Both of us wonder how she does so well.

Then we took James home. As we drove up, a woman rushed out to the car and shouted, "Dear God, please take me to the hospital; my daughter is dying; they just took her in the ambulance!" Naturally I told her to get in. She told me her daughter (mother of three) had leukemia and had had an attack. She was so upset I was afraid she was going to have a heart attack. We got to the hospital and the daughter had died.

There have been no dull days.

My belief that children should learn together—regardless of intellectual or emotional ability—grew stronger as I saw them interacting in all kinds of settings. David took his abacus into the fourth-grade classroom and taught the students the true meaning of place value. Edwin, identified as learning disabled, became a basketball star. Differences disappeared as teams worked cooperatively.

At the end of the year, I was presented with two options. The county school system wanted me to become coordinator of special education and the university wanted me to return to the teacher training program. Not wanting to be an administrator, and recognizing that teaching was my passion, I returned to the university—a far better teacher for my experience in the public schools.

I did fix the TV!

IT WAS IRONIC that during the time I was exploring mainstreaming as a viable educational practice, Billy continued to attend his TMR class in a room totally separated from a school. The students had no interaction with other students or their activities, living in their own little world.

Mrs. Thomas was devoted to the children, offering them unusual opportunities. Studying Thanksgiving, they baked pumpkin pies and put on a play, complete

with costumes and props. To this day, Billy remembers his lines as a Pilgrim:

> We came across the ocean, far across the sea. We came to America; we wanted to be free. Let's have a big big dinner, invite friends the Indians. God is good to us.

Dictated by Billy:

> I loved that class. One time Tom cut down a Christmas tree and brought it to us for our class. The whole class decorate the Christmas tree. Mrs. Thomas took me to her house for the weekend. I love her.

There was also a girl, Linda, whom Billy loved. She too had Down syndrome, and was a beautiful, well-mannered young lady who apparently felt the same way about Billy. He always chose a seat close to her in their activities. I asked him about her recently and he murmured, "She broke my heart."

As Billy got older, approaching the time he would be unable to stay in school (age 21 as defined by PL 94-142), Bill and I were concerned about vocational training for him. I attempted to have the class moved to the public school that Mary attended, even appealing to people I had come to know in the state department of education. The local administrators were unwilling or unable to move the class, and other parents were not enthusiastic about their children being moved from a cloistered, safe environment.

I wrote to the superintendent of the schools, asking if Billy could attend the high school in the town of Sylva; he replied that we could do that if we furnished his transportation. For one year, Bill took Billy to the large high school where he had a special education teacher, a young man who was supportive of Billy. One evening as I was doing laundry, I found a single piece of paper in Billy's pocket, a paper on which was written, in his teacher's hand, the word: "Ignore." What a world of hurt that unveiled.

Ultimately, I think to placate me, Billy was re-evaluated during the summer months and magically became EMR (educable mentally retarded), thus qualifying him for entrance into the smaller high school that Mary attended.

We had experimented on our own to provide Billy work experience during the summer. Tom was working in construction and offered to create a position for Billy as a helper during the summer months. Billy liked it at first, then suddenly refused to get up and go to work. Bill and I talked at length, trying to decide how to solve the problem. I suggested, "Probably the reason he wants to stay home is to watch his TV programs."

Bill agreed, adding "I can fix that. I will just take out the fuse leading to the television set."

He removed the fuse, closed the fuse box, and we went to work the next morning, leaving Billy at home. I was teaching summer school and when I returned to my office I had a message to call Billy.

"Hi, Billy. How's your morning?"

"Fine, Mom. I did fix the TV."

Again, Bill and I searched methods to motivate him to go to work. I told Bill I had an idea that might work if we had the whole family's cooperation. It was a desperate measure.

That evening Bill and I talked with Billy, telling him that—in our family—everyone worked, and if you didn't work you didn't eat. We further explained that on the next day if he didn't get up and go to work, he would not eat dinner. Then came the hard part: he did not get up the next morning, and when dinner was put on the table there was no place set for him. We thought we could handle that, but Billy's response surprised us; he came to the table, sat at his regular place, and watched us eat dinner.

Dinner was usually a sociable, enjoyable event for our family, but this was very difficult to bear. I don't think we ate much, but we stuck to the plan. He did not eat, nor did he ask for food. The next morning he got up and went to work with Tom. When I tell people this story, they think I am cruel, and it did feel horrible at the time. However, it worked and helped establish a work ethic which has remained with Billy.

Billy attended the high school with great success. His resource teacher, Mrs. Eddy, knew how to individualize instruction and was an excellent teacher and friend. He also attended shop, where he made a coffee table and a bookcase, items we still have in our home. He made friends with a high school student, Clarence Delforge, who became his advocate and protector, shielding him from insults and ridicule. Again, Billy was a pioneer.

In trying to continue Billy's vocational training and experience, we contacted the area mental health organization. Patty, who had worked with me in the summer program for severely handicapped children, found a work situation for him that would dovetail with his school schedule. She phoned one day to tell us, "Billy will begin working in Dodson Cafeteria—on the university campus—tomorrow. He will work pouring water and tea from 10:30 to 1:30 for $2.20 per hour."

We were so excited that we could hardly sleep that night. Billy was pleased but scared too; in the shower he talked nervously to himself. Patty said the job could develop into a full-time position in the summer, and we thought it could change his outlook for the future.

Billy took shop at school, walked the short distance to the cafeteria to fill glasses with tea and water for the lunch crowd, returned to school for language arts with Mrs. Eddy, and came home on the school bus. It was perfect for him. I went by one afternoon and sat at a table to watch him work. The rush hour was over and he was mopping the floor, something he had never done before. He was intent on the job and was doing it well. I was so proud of him I had to fight back the tears.

His school work seemed to be going well also. Mrs. Eddy called to ask if we had had Billy tutored during the summer, because he was reading on the third-grade level and just doing great in his work in the cafeteria. He seemed so happy at home and in school; needless to say we were delighted.

We relaxed somewhat until one day when he and Patty arrived at our home to announce that Billy had sneezed and was fired. I must admit that Billy's sneezes are uncontrolled and intense—an action you wouldn't want around food and drinks. However, we believed that if anyone else had sneezed the management would say, "Hey, wash those glasses and do the job over and don't ever let that happen again."

We were devastated and tempted to argue the point. The incident indicated, though, that they really didn't want him there. This made it an uncomfortable environment for him to work in, and would likely be a worse situation if we forced an issue of prejudice for his re-employment. This job was history, and even now, if anyone at our house sneezes, we say, "You're fired!"

After two years at the high school, Billy graduated: his greatest dream and ours. In the spring of his senior year, I had a phone call from him at school, proudly saying, "Mom, I need money for my class ring." These were words I never thought I would hear from him.

Billy's graduation was a major event in our family and circle of friends, as well as in the school community. One of the brightest spots was his preparation for the senior prom. He had saved his money and was ready to go downtown to Mr. Schulman's store, where we bought all of his odd-sized dress clothes. He chose

a bright coat to go with the dark pants and shiny patent-leather shoes. He was magnificent!

A major problem was finding a date for the prom. We called Linda and spoke with her mother, who would not allow Linda to go. Reconciled to that loss, Billy came home from the bus, exclaiming, "I have a date for the dance!" He had asked Sarah, a neighbor who also rode the bus, to go with him. Later in the afternoon, Sarah phoned to say she had thought he was asking for a dance and she unintentionally misled him. We talked long and hard to assure him that there would be others at the dance without a date. Finally consoled, he went to the dance, danced with many of his classmates, and had a wonderful time. When Bill went to pick him up at the end of the evening, he found Billy sound asleep in an easy chair, tired but fulfilled.

For Billy's graduation, friends and family came from Georgia and other parts of North Carolina. One former student of mine, Bill Moss, drove from Charlotte with his arm in a sling. We laughed and cried and nearly burst with pride as Billy marched with dignity across the stage in his cap and gown. We had a party to end all parties for we celebrated it as Billy's high-school and college graduation and his wedding reception.

There were many changes in our family during the years on Tilley Creek. Tom married Michelle in our little Episcopal church and moved to Memphis for a while. When they returned to North Carolina they lived in a remote rural area where Isaac, our third grandson, was born. Soon thereafter they decided to move to Sylva, much to our delight. Isaac was a beautiful, funny child; it was a joy to be part of his development.

Mary graduated from high school and went to Appalachian State University in Boone, just a three-hour drive from Cullowhee. I spent many weekends with her, meeting and enjoying her friends and watching her develop as an artist. She invited Billy to spend a weekend with her and she took him to a dance.

Getting her back to college after a Christmas break was sometimes a challenge,

but Bill loved to drive his Jeep in snow; at times, he brought Mary home through snow storms over treacherous mountain roads.

Mary always came home for the summer; we worked in the garden, sewed, and watched our soap opera with Billy. When the time came for her to return to school, it was always hard for me to see her go.

At the end of one summer, I wrote in my journal:

Mary went back to school; I'm going through all the motions of settling into a rut without her. She takes with her the life and the laughter—the vitality—of this house. She is light and a breeze and a song. That makes her sound flighty, which is an error. She is also deep and dark and sensitive.

The house is clean with her sewing scraps vacuumed and her room tidy and sterile. Can I cry now?

All of us were growing and doing well except for Bill. As he became engrossed in the real-estate business he dreamed of bigger profits, and began to build and sell spec houses. This venture failed abysmally. He spent beyond his means, overestimated the buying power of the community, began the projects during the years of highest prime-interest rate, and aligned himself with a dishonest contractor. I was not involved in the business transactions, but signed for loans when he asked me to. My trust was blind and foolish. I had no idea of the extent of his financial quandary. I knew that the spec houses were not selling, but I did not know the bank had threatened to foreclose on several of them.

Tom, who was working on some of the houses as a carpenter, confided in me that he was concerned about his dad's commitments and problems with the contractor. In retrospect I am appalled at my ignorance, inattention to past experiences, and sheer stupidity.

I had a rude awakening when, as I arrived home from work one evening, Bill announced, "Well, I sold the house today."

"What house?"

"This house."

"*Our* house?"

"Yes."

It took me a while to realize he meant our house: our lovely home high on a mountaintop, the place we moved to at the end of my struggle for an education, the house our family had dreamed of and worked for.

I was devastated, angry, frustrated with helplessness. Too late, I immediately rearranged our bank accounts and vowed that any future homes would be in my name. Our marriage was seriously marred; I felt I had been totally betrayed.

We would have to leave Camelot.

From the kind and healing distance of time, we remember our Tilley Creek days as a magic age. Never again would we live in a more beautiful place, a place where we experienced unrivaled family closeness, growth in many directions, and the realization of dreams we didn't even know we had.

CHAPTER 19

Downhill

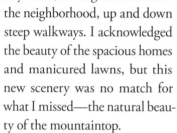

I jus don't know!

AFTER LOOKING at a number of houses, we bought a small house Bill had built in the town of Sylva, adjacent to Cullowhee. Bill called it the doll house; I called it the green house, not wanting to ascribe any special identity to it. Surrounded by a high wire fence, it had no welcoming air. It was comfortable enough but all of us hoped it was temporary. After Tilley Creek, no place looked good to me.

Accustomed to my daily walks, the dogs and I combed

the neighborhood, up and down steep walkways. I acknowledged the beauty of the spacious homes and manicured lawns, but this new scenery was no match for what I missed—the natural beauty of the mountaintop.

The year we lived in the green house seemed much longer, not only because of my disappointment at having to move, but also due to life situations we encountered while there. We navigated our deteriorating relationship, Billy's difficult work experiences, and, surprisingly, the escalation of my career. My work became my escape and my gratification.

I had returned to the university as an associate professor, working under a new dean of education and an unfilled department head position. Although I missed the life experiences of the children at Fairview, I found that the college students offered me similar opportunities for gratification. My year in a public school gave me many illustrations of the principles we discussed and credibility as a "real" teacher.

Many of our students were first-generation college attendants, eager to succeed and willing to work hard.

Some, as always, were poorly motivated and lazy. One student, in scheduling classes, asked for late morning classes since she commuted. Familiar with that concept, I asked where she traveled from. My sympathy evaporated when she replied, "from Sylva," which was about five miles from campus. Some students were insufficiently prepared for an institute of higher learning, as was one young woman who was transferring from a junior college. In selecting her courses, she informed me, "I've done took all my English." I couldn't resist replying, "No you ain't."

There were a number of humorous exchanges with students, but none that amused me more than the questions from a young man who had gone to school with my daughter. After our first class, he approached me and inquired, "Are you Mary Schulz's mother?"

I proudly responded, "Yes, I am."

He continued his query, asking, "Is she still so tall?"

Most of my students, majoring in special education, were vitally interested in learning and in exploring opportunities to work with children who had disabilities. We augmented their intellectual interest with activities such as Special Olympics, sheltered workshops, and summer programs.

At a time when federal money was available, I had the opportunity to take students to major conferences. Joe and George accompanied me to a national conference in Washington, D.C. Joe was sophisticated, made himself known in student groups, and even sent me a corsage for a major event. George, on the other hand, had never traveled and faced a number of surprises. On our return trip, although it was spring in Washington, we were informed that the airport in Asheville was snowed in. The announcement came over the loudspeaker: "We will give you a snack and try to land in Nashville."

As we approached Nashville, a similar announcement was made: "We will give you a snack and try to land in Atlanta."

In time we heard the proclamation: "We can now land in Asheville."

George sighed deeply and declared, "Good, I don't believe I could eat another snack!"

I became involved in organizations such as the Council for Exceptional Children, of which I was elected one year as state president. This gave me opportunities to meet faculty members from other colleges and to interact with personnel from the state department of education. A special advantage was the chance to meet with Ann Turnbull on many occasions, to share our family concerns and pleasures, and to enjoy some time together. We completed our textbook and interacted with our publisher, another new experience for both of us.

In the spring I worked in Cherokee, about half an hour's drive from Sylva. I had been asked to coordinate a project linking the university and the Cherokee Reservation in serving children who were severely disabled. Working with the local schools and social services, we identified five children and were asked to go into their homes to help their families take care of them. As part of the program, I was assigned a Cherokee aide, Flora, whose presence would ensure my entrance into the homes. Flora was a quiet, beautiful young woman, a born teacher, and a diplomat with the parents. Each Thursday I met Flora at an appointed place; together we entered the homes. We visited, talked, and taught the parents some techniques to stimulate motion, feeding, language, and other identified life skills.

Lining the road entering the reservation are rows of shops, restaurants, and trading posts. Many of them are housed in tee-pees, a false representation, since the Cherokees originally lived in dug-out mud homes. I had supervised student teaches and conducted workshops in the Cherokee schools, but this project was totally different. On a typical day, Flora and I left the populated area, parked our cars, climbed a mountain, and walked about a mile along a rushing stream toward a student's home. We saw impressive rock formations and even Native American men cutting stone out of the hills. One day I was alone; I stopped walking and realized that it was totally quiet except for the sound of the creek and I was deeply moved by the experience. Although their means and skills were primitive, the parents we encountered took loving care of their children and were reluctant to give them up to school situations. At the conclusion of the project, the parents presented me with gifts: an embroidered dresser scarf, a beaded belt, and a handsome piece of pottery created by a famous Cherokee potter—Amanda Swimmer, who was Flora's mother. For those few months, Thursdays were my glory days, weekly respites from the turbulence at home.

Bill was making every effort to get his business going again. He had stopped building spec houses and was concentrating on real-estate sales. He was a good salesman, met people with ease, and loved driving prospective buyers around the area in his Jeep. It became a family joke that every prospect wanted the impossible: two acres with a level lot for a house, a view, and a stream. Meanwhile we were trying to patch our relationship, but I still had open wounds of distrust. Our mutual focus was on Billy.

After graduating from high school, Billy had gone to work at a local lumber yard, helping to stack boards for delivery. The mental-health organization that had placed him in the dining-hall situation found the job, encouraged by a compassionate personnel manager at the lumber yard. It was a unique and gratifying experience to see him get up each morning, pack his lunch, and don his jumpsuit and hard hat. Bill, justifiably proud of him, took Billy to work each morning and picked him up at the end of the day. Billy made friends with other workers and was praised by his supervisor.

Billy had worked all summer. When I started teaching in the fall, I talked with a fellow professor and father of Billy's advocate, Clarence. He stopped me in the hall to tell me a story.

"Jane, I have something wonderful to tell you. Clarence and some friends who graduated with him and Billy had a party Saturday night. In discussing their summer jobs, they came to the conclusion that Billy had done better, and made more money, than any of them. Isn't that great?"

Later, into the fall, one day Billy refused to go to work. Nothing we said made any difference; he would not discuss it. We called Sandy, his personnel manager, who came to our house to talk with Billy, who could not, or would not, give him a reason for quitting. We were desperate, feeling certain that something had happened to cause his reaction. Our home life was painful, with Billy sullen and dejected, Bill and me puzzled and disappointed. We were at a standstill. I described the situation in a letter to Mary, who was at college:

> What a week! I had planned to wait to tell you about Billy because it's pretty complicated but I feel you need to know about it. We have really been sick except today I happened to think: everybody screws up once in a while. I think it was a combination of events: cold weather, working alone rather than with a partner, having to go up on a platform—all things he had done before but not all together.
>
> Your Dad handled the whole thing beautifully and has a Vocational Rehabilitation person coming in the morning. As you know, his counselor from Mental Health worked with him briefly but hasn't been near him for a couple of months. Perhaps someone else could be more objective and therefore helpful. Hopefully he will go back to work Monday. You know how important it is.

Billy stayed home for months while we wondered what to do. In desperation, we engaged a vocational counselor to talk with him and to try to unravel the mystery of his actions. Finally, after gaining confidence in the counselor, Billy confided in him. One of his co-workers had threatened to push him off a high place where the lumber was stacked and to beat him up if he told anyone. We never discovered who the co-worker was, but since we were familiar with Billy's fear of heights, we realized that this would be an impossible situation for him. Careful consideration led us to understand that Billy was not ready for competitive employment and that we needed to reexamine our goals for him.

Subsequent evaluation at a nearby sheltered workshop indicated that Billy "lacked the initiative to work an eight-hour day, found it difficult to communicate with his supervisors as well as other co-workers, and had not been given the opportunity to fully develop in the area of decision making." We began the journey of reevaluation and seeking alternatives for his training and employment, knowing it would take months to arrive at a solution.

In the fall I had been offered the opportunity to teach a three-week class in Jamaica, to begin in January. The university was developing a program to enable Jamaican teachers and counselors to complete degree programs, and one of the requirements was a course in special education. I was to teach the first class. I was excited about the opportunity to travel, to meet new people and to encounter a different culture. At first I was concerned about leaving Billy in his time of difficult transition, but believed that Bill was in control of the situation and hoped that a separation would be good for all of us.

In January Billy and Bill took me to the airport in a snowstorm; I took off my winter jacket, gave it to Bill, and left. The first entry in my travel journal indicated the benefits of taking a break from my everyday life:

> Yesterday I left Asheville in the snow and arrived in Kingston in 80 degree weather. Coming into Montego Bay was thrilling—the ocean was so green at the shores it would not be believed in a painting. Dr. Fox met my plane and was very gracious and comforting. He took me to the hotel and later to dinner. We had an elegant dinner—I had lobster!
>
> At the airport I bought *Passages*, a strangely appropriate book about the stages of adult development. I realize that this is the first time in my life that I could have made this trip. And while I'm looking forward tremendously to seeing the country and meeting many people, a big part of what I need is to be alone.

The journal continued:

> My days are full and my evenings are long. I have found that eating alone is no fun and I hesitate to venture beyond the hotel at night. I am adjusting, though, and doing enough during the day that I need long evenings. Actually I'm spending a lot of time in class preparation and it's paying off. Yesterday and today the class was great. What a good feeling anywhere!
>
> This morning I worked on the balcony of my room, then walked over to school. I happened to arrive at the kindergarten and felt at home immediately. One little black boy informed me in a clipped British accent, "My name is Zachary." Everything was out-of-doors: easels, sandbox, water pans, the whole bit. My student Michele is a teacher there. She is beautiful; is certified in mental retardation from a university in Vermont.

As I became involved with the students, they invited me to their homes and took me on excursions. I described a memorable one:

> Saturday was lovely. Pat, Mike, 20-month-old Mark and I went to Ocho Rios for the day. The drive was beautiful, through the mountains and Fern Gully—a

stretch of about a mile of dark, damp, cool growth with beautiful ferns all along the road. I could not believe Ocho Rios. Instead of the lack of green I expect at the beach, they have lovely grass, trees and bushes and the surprise: the beach and the "sea."

Later:

That night Joy and Larry took me to Explanitations, a Little Theatre production of Reggae, the Jamaican hard rock. Joy and Larry are Jamaican—a very handsome couple—and I enjoyed being with them. The concert was exciting! Six young men, all excellent musicians, presented a patriotic musical which, although mostly in dialect, was very clear in its message. The excitement of the audience was equally interesting. The whole thing really turned me on.

With Michele and her mother I went to the opening of a French tapestry collection and the sculptures of Mrs. Manly—a handsome woman in her seventies.

On school days my class and I explored institutions for children with disabilities, schools throughout the country, and many art and culture centers. I fell in love with the people—beautiful children from many countries, strong Jamaican women, and dedicated teachers. Of one school I wrote:

In a room which would normally accommodate 30 children, there were about 100. The grades were divided at the point where children were seated back to back. There were worn benches so close together the children had to climb over them to get out. Very few chalkboards, no supplies and beautiful, eager children! If you can teach here, you can teach anywhere.

One night as I was getting ready for bed, I heard a great deal of commotion outside my room. There were flashing lights and policemen, and I decided to stay in my room and find out the news in the morning. Headlines in the morning paper read:

COUPLE SLAIN BY HOLD-UP MEN

The hold-up took place in my hotel, not far from my room. My students wanted me to leave; one suggested I move in with her family. I reminded them that such things also happen in the United States and decided that I would stay in my room. When I returned from class, there was a soldier stationed outside my door; I believe one of my students arranged for him to be sent there to protect me. It felt odd to have someone sitting so close, a gun across his lap. Everyone was sad about the implications of the crime. As my taxi driver lamented, "It so bad when things happen to visitors because Jamaica needs them and it's too small a country for so much violence."

In addition to my regular teaching schedule, I was asked to speak on several occasions, to teachers and to parents. One presentation flyer stated that I would "talk about behaviour problems on an L.D. child at home and in the classroom and how to deal with them." There was a large crowd at the meeting. I began to feel I was not reaching my audience as I addressed cooperation between home and school. As I paused, one man asked, "Please, miss, how can the parents help when they cannot read or write?" A teacher from a downtown school said they are concerned about the sexual activity of the six-year-olds. I realized how little I knew of life in a third-world country, and how inadequate my knowledge was.

At the conclusion of the course, the class had a party for me with samples of sour-sop, avocado and papaya, little cakes, and limeade. The presented me with a hand-embroidered linen purse. I was touched by their generosity. Everyone expressed their thanks for the course, and one said that what they really appreciated was my interest in their problems. I felt very close to each of them and knew that I would do my best to return.

Back at the hotel I found the letter pictured to the right awaiting me.

My last journal entry:

> Billy's letter almost undid me. I'm ready to go home.

Bill and Billy were as glad to see me as I was to see them. They had enrolled in a pottery class, and Billy had made a gift for me:

lovely wind chimes. There was also promising news about Billy's situation. We discovered that—in a nearby town—a new program had been initiated to train and employ people who had disabilities. The appeal to Billy, and therefore to us, was that the work program was tied to a community college and would place trainees in a newly formed group home. From Billy's point of view, this was equivalent to going to college and living in a dormitory. It also sounded good to Bill and me as a step toward independence for Billy.

The three of us visited the workshop and the group home. The workshop was on the campus of the community college, the group home in a residential section of a town not too far from Sylva. In March we received a letter from the sheltered workshop:

This is to inform you that Bill has been formally admitted to the evaluation and training program of [our sheltered workshop]. His length of time in Evaluation will be determined on an individual basis, according to Bill's needs. At the end of that period, a comprehensive summary of Bill's abilities and work potential will be made; and, if indicated by the evaluation summary, he will either be placed in a competitive work situation or further training will take place.

Bill will receive a small wage during the training period. This amount will be paid by check once a week. His working hours will be 8:30 a.m. – 4:00 p.m., Monday through Friday.

Billy entered the evaluation program and worked each day, transported by Bill or me. His first check was $8.00 and he was really proud of himself, glad to be back at work. He applied for residence in the group home and we waited for his admission.

Bill had investigated the financial obligation to living in the group home and found that since Billy had worked in the lumber yard, a competitive work place, he would be eligible for the Social Security Disability Benefit to pay for his living situation. He was excited about living in the group home and eagerly awaited his admission. I must admit that as I thought about it I was excited, nervous, and scared for Billy, and anticipating loneliness for myself.

Both of us needed to grow up.

I not like to talk bout my group home.

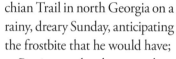

IN MY LIFE as a wife and mother, I have experienced a number of painful, heart-wrenching good-byes:

—Leaving Bill in a dark, cheerless nursing home, knowing that I would go back to a warm and friendly home;

—Saying good luck to my first born as he left for the Citadel, knowing that he didn't belong there any more than I had belonged in Milwaukee;

—Dropping Tom off at the beginning of the Appalachian Trail in north Georgia on a rainy, dreary Sunday, anticipating the frostbite that he would have;

—Putting my daughter on a plane for Holland, missing her already and thinking, "Good God, what if she decides to live there?"

—Seeing Billy walk up the steep stone stairs of the group home, his suitcase clutched in his hand, neither of us knowing what to expect, both of us afraid.

Billy had met his assigned roommate, had seen their room on a previous visit, and was looking forward to moving in. His sister had gone to college, living in a dormitory, and he pictured his move as a similar one. He did encounter a big surprise when he was not allowed to keep his radio or his record player for fear they would be stolen. Since music was such an important part of his life, this was a disorienting loss. Billy's loneliness was a reflection of my own as I received his phone call during that first week: "Mom, I had a dream 'bout you last night and I cry a lot."

"I'm sorry, Billy. What's wrong?"

"Little bit homesick. Have to stay here. Don said."

"Oh…"

"I love you, Mom."

"I love you too, Billy."

As the weeks passed, the group home seemed less and less like a dormitory. The staff had a difficult time getting Billy up in the morning and performing his chores. Things were no better at the workshop. Following his initial evaluation, his counselor wrote, "Client's very noticeable handicap and his manipulative behavior combined with an attitude of not having to stick to schedule and other poor work skills have made extended evaluation a necessity at this point."

I later chronicled the situation in the chapter of a book:

> During Billy's early rebellion against the group home and the sheltered workshop, we brought him home one weekend to make some decisions. I was angry and frustrated: I knew that he had no alternatives to the workshop and thus to the group home. He was unhappy and confused. As we talked, I realized that he was cornered; that he had no options. In desperation I resorted to a technique that had worked for us in many situations before—a contract. We discussed the terms. I went to my typewriter and drew up a document, which Billy and I signed and took to the group home directors.
>
> CONTRACT
> 1. I will work hard at the workshop—no goofing off—until Christmas time.
> 2. I will do my work at the group home.
> 3. I will come home one weekend each month:
>   September 15 (John and Barbara are coming)
>   October 13 (Dad's birthday)
>   November 23 (Thanksgiving)
> 4. At Christmas time if I don't want to return to the group home, I will stay home and work.[1]

The contract worked. In looking back, I think Billy must have felt abandoned, with no hope of change. He began to participate in the group activities, taking his turn at cooking and even finding a girl he liked at the group home. He asked to join a sexuality training program so he could "get a girl." One day Pete, the counselor, had asked me to help him with a client at the group home. After we talked, I waited to see Billy; he sat with me a while then said, "Well, Mom, you better go home and fix Dad's dinner." For the first time, I left and didn't feel sad.

His vocational goal at the workshop was to be an assembler of small parts, with his objectives to increase good work behavior, increase vocational exploration, and find successful employment. When presented with the goals and objectives of the program, Billy responded, "I will do everything so I can get ready to go on a job."

---

1   Schulz, J.B. (1985) "Growing Up Together" in Turnbull & Turnbull, *Parents Speak Out*, Merrill, p. 13.

As a step toward his independence, Billy was moved from the group home into a two bedroom apartment, with an older man, Johnny. They seemed to get along well, although they were dramatically different in their tastes and abilities. I noted a phone call from Billy when he called to make plans for Thanksgiving:
"Billy, is Johnny going home for Thanksgiving?"
"Mom, Johnny's parents got dead."
"Oh—would you like to bring him home for Thanksgiving?"
"Oh Mom, could I?"
"Of course."
"I put him on the phone and you can 'vite him."
"Hello, Mrs. Schulz. I understand you have a doctor's degree in special education."
"Yes, I do…"
"Then we have a lot to talk about. I'm an opera buff myself."
During Johnny's visit, we found him to be very strange; Mary in particular felt his stares at her were "creepy." Ultimately, the group home manager felt Billy needed to move into an apartment by himself. We were somewhat relieved and went with him to see the new apartment.

I understand the problems group home directors face. They need housing that is accessible to shopping, affordable, and within the group home supervisory radius. Frequently, this means the residences are old and in poor repair—this was certainly true of Billy's apartment. It was near a shopping area and close to a church, both important to him, but it was certainly not a place we would have chosen for him. The one positive factor was that one of the supervisors lived in the same building and would be available should he need her. He settled in, once again had his music, a refrigerator and a stove, and enjoyed living alone.

One night as Billy was lying in bed, someone broke into his apartment. I can only imagine his terror when he told me he stayed in bed and didn't move. The person stole his cherished high-school class ring and his collection of records, and ransacked his refrigerator. Billy was moved immediately into a more secure situation.

The Association for Retarded Citizens had purchased a tourist court that had been condemned. There were several units of one-room cabins, each with a bathroom and small kitchen, in a cluster that had probably been considered attractive at one time. When I first saw the apartment with boxes in the floor, food out on tables, and dirty Venetian blinds, I was sick. I spent one Sunday afternoon helping Billy get settled. We put up draperies from home, installed plant hangers, discarded unnecessary items, and brought things home that he didn't currently need. The chief drawback was that he would eat in front of the television and then lie down on the bed and watch it. I began to think he needed to come back home and find a job, but we were trying to leave it up to him.

The positive factor for Billy was that he made friends with a young married couple, Jimmy and Mildred (who had helped him in a medical crisis). He was happy in his apartment. He had an excellent counselor, Russell, who made a tremendous difference in the whole endeavor. A retired man, he seemed genuinely interested in the clients. He took Billy out for dinner with his family and had dinner with him at his apartment. Russell obtained food stamps and opened a savings account for him. Billy seemed genuinely happy and that, of course, pleased us. His stove was sparkling and he had food in the refrigerator.

Sometimes when I went to pick him up for the weekend I found him at Jimmy and Mildred's or with another neighbor, concluding that he appeared to have companionship and adequate assistance.

Bill and I went to see him on the weekends when he didn't come home, and one night he phoned to ask: "Mom, why don't you and Dad come for dinner tomorrow night?"

"We'd love to! What are you having?"

"Beef stroganoff."

"Wow! Do you know how to make it?"

"No, but you can show me."

"Well, okay...do you have all the stuff?"

"I've got the noodles."

In the meantime things were not going well at the workshop. We went to the workshop for a conference to find out what Billy was doing and what his future position would be. We discovered that he was not in a degree program (as we had initially been informed), and when we told them he wanted to graduate, they didn't know what to say. Everyone there liked him and was interested in his goals. We told them that they needed to level with him since he expected to graduate from the technical institution.

Several months later Billy's supervisor at the workshop phoned me and we talked for a long time. She said he was not working, he fell asleep on the job, and during the past week had made less than a dollar a day. She also said she thought he was drinking a lot of beer and never leaving his apartment after he got home from work, just eating, lying on his bed, and watching television. You can imagine how I felt, and that evening when Billy called to tell me that his friend E. P. was crying because his brother had died, I cried too.

A few days later Bill and I went for another conference at the workshop. There were about six people involved; all of us watched Billy do his work, so monotonous that I almost fell asleep watching. We decided that with nothing going on at work or at home, he was sleeping as an escape. The supervisor selected several jobs which required more skill and attention and also some after-hours activities. We talked about several alternatives, and all of us agreed that in his spot we would be sleeping too.

We called Billy in and his supervisor gave him the job alternatives. He chose one immediately. She said he would be required to go swimming once a week and to a craft class one night a week; he agreed and added, "and Social Club once a month." We drew up a contract, and before he signed it he said, "for one month." We had not stipulated a time limit! The whole operation was Billy asking for help; had he done his work, no one would have noticed or made any positive changes.

When Russell left and a new employee supervised his living situation, Billy regressed in his household maintenance and eating habits. He had already gained a lot of weight, and when I saw his new, overweight supervisor, I knew the food shopping would not be properly monitored. In response to an invitation from the new group home director, Bill and I went over for an interview. She told us that she thought Billy had been put in an apartment before he had proper skills and that the new policy was to put people in the apartment alone only if they could operate independently. I wondered whom she would put there, since such persons would not need the agency. Bill and I had agreed to listen, so we did. At that time they agreed to try Billy for a month to see if he could stay in the apartment with some help. The suggested alternatives would be to return to the group home or to return to Sylva.

I found myself in a frustrating position. As a special education professional, supposedly knowledgeable in the field, I was expected to know what to do; I did not have a clue. As parents, Bill and I felt Billy's wishes should be primary, but we deplored many aspects of his present life.

Watching Billy's living and working situations deteriorate, we began to talk about bringing him home. However, he still wanted to stay in his apartment. Just as we were wondering about a job for him if he should come home, a significant incident occurred. My office adjoined that of my department head, Larry Grantham. One day Mr. Kirwin, director of the university library, called on Larry, describing an opening at the library. He said, "Larry, I think this is a job that a handicapped person could do. We can't use students because it is a security measure. Do you know of anyone we could consider?"

I waited for Larry's reply, which was, "No, I don't have anyone in mind."

I jumped up, ran into his office, and exclaimed "I do!" Both of them, who knew Billy, agreed that he would be a possible candidate. Mr. Kirwin pointed out to me that he didn't know when the job would be available but that he would keep me posted. He indicated that it would be approached through the newly founded Jackson County Sheltered Workshop for training purposes. This sounded like a good reason for Billy to consider returning to Sylva.

In September a notice appeared in the library publication of a staff position vacancy:

> Apply at the Personnel Office...within 5 working days from the date of this publication.
> HOURLY BOOK HANDLERS, Hunter Library; $3.10 per hour; process books for the Library. Job involves receiving books and periodicals from various library units at a central location, performing a processing operation, replacing books and periodicals on book carts, notification of departments when books and periodicals are ready to be picked up. Job training will be provided by the Jackson County Sheltered Workshop.

We kept Billy home on Monday to take care of applying for the job. I took him to Personnel and we filled out an application. He was calm and poised. As we passed through my office, an associate said, "I hope you get it, Billy."

He said, very assured, "I will!"

After completion of the application process, I took Billy to the workshop and asked my friend there to show him around. I also presented Billy with a choice: "Even if you don't get the library job, do you want to move back and go to this workshop?"

At the end of the day, he decided he did want to come back someday, to get a trailer and be near his family. It was good to know that there would be an alternative in the future.

I kept thinking that the reason Billy moved into the group home and workshop program was because he couldn't get along with the workers at the lumberyard. Here he was living in a community of disabled persons, working with disabled people, and I couldn't see that his situation was solving the initial problem. He was living in substandard accommodations, receiving little and spasmodic support, and acquiring no employable skills.

Billy's living situation was deplorable. Receiving no support from the group home supervisor, I outlined my concerns in the following letter to his landlord:

> I have made numerous attempts to reach you by phone. Since you have not returned my calls, I am writing to let you know the concerns I have about the apartment which my son Billy rents from you.
>
> In addition to charging exorbitant rent for substandard housing, you have failed to provide services which were included as utilities. The following items are examples:
>
> 1. Although cable TV was included as a feature to be provided, Billy has had to pay an additional fee for it.
> 2. During most of the winter, Billy had no heat. He used a small electric heater which we provided.
> 3. Billy's stove has been out of order since May; he has requested that you repair it many times. Since May he has been using a small electric grill which we provided. Because good nutrition is one of his goals, it is important that he be able to prepare meals other than fried hot dogs and hamburgers.
>
> Living alone is supposed to be a learning experience for Billy. He has learned many things: how to eat and gain weight without a stove; how to fight roaches and live in inadequate housing; how to live with the fact that there are unscrupulous people who will take advantage of retarded people.
>
> Since there are agencies working with Billy, I have tried to stay out of the situation; I can no longer live with it. I expect you to repair his stove immediately and feel you should compensate him for services which were promised and not delivered.
>
> I will appreciate hearing from you.

I sent copies of the letter to all the agencies working with the program as well as to the Better Business Bureau and the Chamber of Commerce. I soon received a frantic call from a member of the mental health organization asking if I would come for a conference. I responded that I would be glad to, but I never heard from him again. I didn't hear from anyone else.

Several months later, on a cold November Sunday afternoon, Bill and I went to see Billy at his apartment. He had no heat, his stove was still out of order, and he had no food in the refrigerator. Bill and I looked at each other in agreement and told Billy we were taking him home. He began packing the few things he had needed there into the car and with our help emptied the apartment.

During the two years that Billy was in the group home and sheltered workshop, he gained 35 pounds, lost many of his grooming skills, and could not talk about his experiences. We had tried to use the existing system and found it didn't fit. I had actually relinquished my parental and professional judgment in consenting to the continuation of a program that did not serve Billy well.

As parents and members of parent organizations, we had been aggressive in securing rights for our school-aged children with disabilities; it is natural to expect that the same emphasis on program quality would be present in work environments. The reality pointed out by researchers is that adult service agencies typically compete for inadequate resources; employ staff that is underpaid and poorly trained; provide placements that are not designed to facilitate progression into less restrictive, more normalized environments; and operate without the guarantees and guidance of public law. It is no wonder, then, that many adults with disabilities either stay at home or are automatically placed in fast-food restaurants or sheltered workshops.

I made notes of the conversations, letters, and other communications that took place during those two years. In writing about it, I had hoped for input from Billy, but he says to me, "I can't talk about it." Perhaps the most meaningful comment was the one he made on returning to our home. One night as we sat on the sofa, he reached over, touched my knee, and said, "I not be lonely anymore."

CHAPTER 21

Home Again

Mom, trol yourself!

WE HAD BEEN SO CONCERNED about Billy's situation that we had stopped looking for a different house until one day Bill phoned to say, "Come over to Locust Creek Road, there's a place I want to show you." Mary, home for the summer and ready to go back to Boone, accompanied me down the old Sylva-Cullowhee road. Beside the Tuckaseigee River, we turned onto Locust Creek Road, and in a mile and a half we saw the log house that Bill had mentioned. We pulled into the driveway,

got out of the car, and stopped short. There was our house—sitting solidly on a hill—tin roof, lightning rods, ancient trees and established shrubbery, looking as if it had always been there. We walked up roughly placed stone steps to the back yard, past the house and a large vegetable garden. There, shielded from the road, we discovered the small pond with ducks lazily drifting on the water. Up the hill behind the house were a barn, a wooden tool shed, and a grape arbor.

Already in love with the pond and the yard, Mary and I entered the house to find a large family room, two bedrooms, two bathrooms, and a galley kitchen. The adjacent living and dining rooms were separated by a white brick, two-sided fireplace. A steep, wooden ladder led to a loft which the owners had fashioned into a long, low-ceilinged bedroom. There was a front porch off the living room with, to my delight, a swing. With one accord, Mary and I said, "This is it!"

Our Locust Creek home was the balm to my injuries. I felt that I could live there forever and we approached it as if we would. Each summer I used my summer-school check, always our extra income, for additions and renovations. Bill had always had good ideas about home improvements, and we had fun planning the changes. Tom had his construction business at that time and wrought many miracles to reflect our tastes and increase convenience. We added a deck facing the pond, a more attractive and practical back entrance, and safer steps. I couldn't decide what to do with the white fireplace because it was distinctive but impractical and occupied valuable space. When we chose to replace the carpeting with hardwood floors, a decision had to be made. One day I came home for lunch and saw bricks flying out of the dining-room window. Tom had made the decision for me.

The loft developed a history of its own. Through the years it housed a newly married couple and later a student. It provided space for many visitors, including guests from Holland, Jamaica, and Lithuania. It was a playroom for the grandchildren and me; it held a studio for Tom's drawing and an office for my writing. And ultimately it was my refuge.

Where was Billy in all this? We had moved into the house shortly before he left for the group home, so that although he had a bedroom there, I'm sure it never felt like home to him. During his two years' absence he spent weekends and holidays with us but would return to his own place of residence. When he moved out of the group home, even as unsatisfactory as it had been, he wanted to reclaim his independence. I suggested we could put a trailer on our lot but he said, "That's too close."

In a college town with many trailer parks, we chose one near us for convenience, emergencies, and companionship. When the owner, who was a neighbor, agreed to rent a trailer to Billy, we actually ran to see it, and I was so excited that Billy said, "Mom, 'trol yourself!" We came home, discussed it with Bill, and Billy called to tell Mr. Blanton, "I take it." The trailer was clean and attractive, about a city block from us. I wrote to Mary, "He has really grown up a lot, and I'm enjoying him so much I think he needs to leave before I get dependent."

Mr. Blanton brought over a contract for Billy to sign, labeled "Park Agreement for Single Men." There were 15 items listed under terms and conditions. One stated, "There is to be no women in the Mobile Home after 11:00 P.M." and another requiring no group disturbances, loud parties, or noise. Billy would be in a student environment, treated like everyone else. I loved it.

Ecstatic about moving into his trailer, Billy began to move his belongings, but it took him a few days to decide to sleep there. Once we made it attractive and comfortable, he trembled with excitement, exclaiming, "I love my trailer." I had not seen him so happy for a long time.

As Billy adjusted to his new surroundings, we encountered a few conflicts. One area that bothered me was his lack of housekeeping skills. He knew how to clean; he had been the one at our Tilly Creek home who vacuumed while Mary and I worked in the garden. I supposed he became careless while living in his poorly supervised apartments. At any rate, I walked into the trailer one day to find utter chaos, with unwashed dishes in the sink and clutter everywhere. I started yelling about it, and when he could no longer stand my tirade, he stood with his arms crossed and screamed, "It's MY house!" He helped me realize that my values were not his values, and that while he needed encouragement to take care of his place, it was indeed his.

We also faced a problem when he began to enter our home and take food from our refrigerator—one example was a cheesecake I had made. We then made it clear that he could ask for anything but could not take it without our permission, or we would take away his key to our home.

With his own space, Billy began to collect things compulsively. While he had always been a "pack rat," this characteristic has continued to be problematic. Billy's "stuff" grows to fill his environment, just like the discarded goldfish that grew into a large carp in our pond.

Billy interacted with the students in the trailer park and joined in some of their parties and celebrations. They responded to his friendly overtures, and he blossomed under the attention. The friendships were short-lived, as the students moved frequently, but were nevertheless stimulating. Our warm and social Billy was back!

It was wonderful to have Billy living close by, able to join us for family visits and celebrations, and for meals on occasion. We shopped for groceries together, went to church together, and took short trips. We visited John and his family in Georgia, enjoying the trip as much as the destination. To keep him alert and attentive, I gave him a list of highway signs to look for along the way. He would say, "There's 76," or "There's Ellijay!" At one point I asked him to watch for 53 to Fairmont. He said, noting the speed limit signs, "Well, Mom, we getting close—I see lotsa 55s!"

During this period of change in Billy's living arrangement, Bill was proactive in finding the benefits to which Billy was entitled. He found that, in addition to his Social Security disability compensation, he qualified for HUD (the Federal Department of Housing and Urban Development) support for his rent. We elected not to apply for food stamps. There was no one to assist us with these benefits and I wondered, as I had in the past, what happens to people who have no advocates.

Billy enrolled in the sheltered workshop and made friends there, too. His need for friends was as great as his need for a job. He became friendly with an older client, whom he especially liked and whose company he enjoyed. They talked frequently on the phone, and when Billy wanted to invite her to lunch one Saturday, he phoned her at home and invited her. I obtained directions to her home from her mother, but when we got there, she refused to come to the car. Perhaps she or her mother was afraid for her to venture out. I had encountered similar reticence in other families who would not even let their daughters with disabilities ride the bus to the workshop if there were also men passengers.

Being new, the workshop had not yet acquired enough contracts to keep the clients working full time. However, it was a necessary step for Billy to be enrolled in the workshop should the job at the library open up.

As Billy adjusted to his new home, we were enjoying ours. The previous owners had left a bountiful garden, full of vegetables to be harvested. When Mother came to visit, we chatted happily while gathering and freezing food for the winter. We shelled and cooked black-eyed peas in great quantities. I told the family, "Eat all you want, I will freeze the left-overs." The peas were so good we never had any left to freeze. Green beans, corn, and tomatoes were proudly borne from the garden to the table. We fed the ducks, planted flowers, and began to feel whole and wholesome again. At last I, like Billy, was back home.

Our new house became a warm, comfortable place to welcome children and grandchildren. They enjoyed fishing in the pond, trying to catch a turtle that was eating the ducklings, running up to the old barn, and sleeping in the loft. During this period of settling, Bill had restructured his real-estate office and obtained a broker's license, and was optimistic about his business. In this setting, with Billy's situation resolved, I hoped Bill and I could return to a peaceful relationship.

After we had been in our Locust Creek home for a year, Mary graduated from college. When our family traveled to Boone for her graduation, we discovered Billy's fear of heights posed a problem. The graduation ceremony was in a large gymnasium and we, the audience, were seated in the balcony. Our grandson Isaac, seated between his parents who had recently taken him to the circus, yelled down to Mary, "Watch out for the tigers!" But Billy freaked out, hugging the central partition and refusing to advance to his seat. People stared at him as we pleaded with him to sit down. He could not (as opposed to would not) do it.

I did not yet understand the depth of his fear; I still viewed it as a behavior problem. I became angry with him, furious that he could spoil this special day for all of us. With time, however, I have come to realize that he cannot control this angst. I regret my reaction in this and other situations. We now try to anticipate the possibility of a traumatic situation by arranging for seats on lower levels, but we still experience some surprises in his responses.

After graduation, Mary completed her portfolio and arranged to go to Europe to work. While at Appalachian, she had met a young man from Holland who, along with the excitement of experiencing a new country, made this decision appealing. We honored her quest for adventure but we missed her sorely. Again I sought solace in my work.

Ann Turnbull and I were reaping the benefits of our book, *Mainstreaming Handicapped Children*. Both of us were asked to speak at conferences and universities to help with implementation of the concepts determined by Public Law 94-142. Schools of Education, working through their deans, were offered a special opportunity in the availability of Federal funds designed to promote the mainstreaming concept. Referred to as deans' grants, their purpose was to inform and indoctrinate faculties about practices to include all children in the general education classes of public schools. Following Ann's lead, I applied for and was awarded such a grant. The grant included money for travel, clerical help, and other expenses necessary to implement the project. My task was to work with our own faculty members to raise awareness of the law and its implications for teacher education. Following that, I was asked to meet with faculty in other universities for the same purpose. It was an enriching opportunity for me, providing experiences in speaking to groups in places I had not dreamed of visiting and of meeting stimulating, energetic people.

The initial efforts of the dean's grants focused on interacting with other coordinators and deans, working out strategies to involve their faculty members and, ultimately, students and teachers in university and public-school settings. It was a daunting task. For years teachers and administrators had placed children with disabilities in special classes, believing it to be the best setting. The current research showed that children learn more readily in a mainstream situation, and that separating them from other children constituted discrimination. Now schools, in accord with current legislation, would be required to accommodate all children in the least-restrictive environment. In speaking to people involved in this mandate, I could use many of my experiences with Billy to promote the rationality and humanity of this concept. In highlighting the success of the grant, I wrote, "The Dean's Grant at Western Carolina University has provided the opportunity for growth in awareness, understanding, and education of children who have special needs. We think it will help us cooperate and plan better to meet the needs of all children."

Bill encouraged me to travel, although one time he remarked, "You keep that suitcase packed and ready to go, don't you?" Certainly, having him at home to supervise and transport Billy made it possible for me to go. I began bringing a tee shirt to Billy from each place I visited. While I was still teaching a full load, I was making a trip about once a month, talking about my dream. What could be more fulfilling?

Only one thing. Billy phoned me from the workshop to say, "Mom, I got the job at the liberry!"

CHAPTER 22

The Library

This my liberry, an I work there 21 years.

Hunter's Clarion
November 1981 Western Carolina University
BILLY WORKS HERE

He presents a beautiful rose to Brenda Wheatley to adorn her desk…those who lunch beneath the dogwood in front of the library expect his black lunch box and lively company… he is known to sing while he works and a portable radio is one of his many friends…he displays with pride a new WCU T-shirt and is apt to hug you and tell you how much he likes you…his name is Billy Schulz.

Billy was hired last September to do a tedious book processing job for three days a week. It's the kind of job very few of us could do, repetitive work, confining, and offering little variation in daily routine. This Billy Schulz, however, does the job well and takes pride in his work. He looks forward to coming to work and he sees in his work features to be envied by many people, happiness and fulfillment. In short, Billy is an asset to Hunter Library. Tribute should be paid to Billy for performing so well a task which demands his care and attention. Gratitude should be expressed to those who diligently and patiently molded Billy and his job into one productive unit composed of books, spirit and flesh. The people who should be commended as playing major roles in this achievement are members of the Jackson County Sheltered Workshop and Brenda Wheatley in the library administrative office.

A university is an appropriate place to learn something and we have learned something through our experience with Billy. As a candidate for the job and as a trainee last fall, we knew Billy as being mentally retarded and thought about all the things he could not do. Now, we have learned that he is Billy Schulz and we know the things he *can* do. The roses, the T-shirts, the lunch box and radio, and those smiles and hugs of friendship, they are now a part of the library because Billy works here.   —Joe Sanders

BILLY STARTED WORKING for fifteen hours a week at the library and
continued at the workshop several more hours. I wrote to Mary, "we don't know
what the structure will be, but at minimum wage the library job will buy his food
and the Social Security will pay his rent, so I think he's in good shape. Most of all,
I am glad he will be out of the workshop for part of the time. If he does well, this
is a permanent position. He will be inserting tape in the back binding of books
so they are bugged when people try to lift them."

The first day Billy went to work at the library was unforgettable. At the correct
time he was waiting by the road, wearing his Nebraska tee shirt tucked into his
new jeans, belt tight around his ample middle. With his lunchbox in hand, he was
ready and anxious. I was so proud of him and eager for him to find satisfaction in
his work and in his life. His training proceeded well, and soon his only supervisor
was Brenda, whom he adored. She confided in me that Billy was doing well but
was asking for help from her when it was not necessary. She suggested that he call
on her only in cases of emergency. After she told Billy this, he asked me, "Mom,
what's a 'mergency?" We identified a number of things such as losing a book or
catching on fire, on and on until finally I said, "Billy, just don't have one!" It was
obvious that he just wanted to be near her.

Sometimes when I returned from teaching I would find a note on my desk that
someone from the library had called. One day the message was from Joe Sanders,
Billy's supervisor. I always got a lump in my stomach when he called, but it was
just to change Billy's schedule to Tuesday, Wednesday, and Thursday. He said it
was really a compliment, because Billy was working so hard they needed a day to
get the books ready for him.

On another day Joe called to say, "I'm not concerned about Billy's production;
I'm concerned about Billy." Joe expressed concern that Billy was depressed and in
love with Brenda. Brenda explained to Billy that she was his friend but was engaged to be married. I told Joe it was the same when Tom got married. Billy faces,
each time, the fact of his retardation. I remembered so well the walk we took on
Tilley Creek when Billy asked, "Mom, will I get married?" "Probably not," I said.
He wanted to know why. Wondering what to tell him, I first considered, "Because
you can't afford it," then remembered John, Tom, and even Bill and me. None
of us could really afford to marry at the time, yet we did anyway. Finally I said,
"Because you have Down syndrome." It's not a good reason but it's the reason.

Joe's concern reflected the acceptance and caring of the library personnel. It
was obvious that although knowing Billy was a new experience for most of them,
they genuinely liked him and wanted him to succeed. Although he was a part-
time worker, they began to include him in their social activities. They asked him

to join them for a covered-dish dinner, and his friend David invited him to a party at his home. He accepted every invitation and always had a great time. He and I went to Brenda's wedding together.

In addition to the library staff, Billy met many students who worked there as well as those who were making use of the materials and assistance. Soon, as he and I walked about campus, we were greeted with, "Hi, Billy! How's it goin'?" and I acknowledged my new status as Billy's mom.

When Billy's training was completed and he was working at the library four days a week, he asked me if he could quit at the workshop. I asked why and he responded, "I tired of playing Bingo." That sentence sparked a rage in me that had been brewing for several years. I had been on the board of directors at a workshop in an adjoining county, and had also had experience with the one where Billy had worked. I was familiar with the stated goals of sheltered workshops: to prepare clients for competitive employment if possible, and to provide work for those not able to fill positions in community settings.

While I was grateful for the training that Billy had received to fill the library position, I was angry that more clients were not trained for community placement and were languishing in a holding position with not enough work and no training. I knew a number of the clients from my work in the public schools, knew that they had untapped gifts and potential for developing skills. Many of them had wasted years in school and were now wasting more time in workshops, with little hope of moving on. Forget Bingo!

Later, serving on the board of directors of this particular workshop, I understood that the problem was systemic. The workshop's funding was tied to the number of clients being served at the workshop rather than those being placed in the community. Added to this ill-considered arrangement, personnel were underpaid and, in many cases, poorly trained. The situation was a prime example of our society's lack of concern for adults who have disabilities. The same people who fought for rights of children with disabilities in public schools dropped the ball when these children reached adulthood.

Billy's schedule was set for him to work from 8:00 a.m. until 1:00 p.m. Monday through Thursday. This was perfect! He could ride with me to work and I could bring him home during my lunch time, or if that didn't work, Bill would pick him up. Billy loved it too; he got home in time to watch "All My Children" on television and didn't go to work on Friday. He would tell people, "I don't work on Fridays," and that became a motto that all of us envied.

Billy continued to work twenty hours a week. There were two practical reasons for limiting the hours of his employment. From the employer's point of view, it meant that he was not eligible for employee benefits. To his advantage, it would not jeopardize his disability compensation.

When Billy's workday was over, he would walk over to my office to wait for me, interacting with the people there and sometimes helping me and others with sorting papers, making copies and the like. One day I came to the office from class to find him in my office with tears running down his face. He told me of a problem that had occurred, a serious problem.

A dedicated movie-star fan, Billy particularly admired Jane Fonda. When he was not busy at the library, he perused the movie magazines and looked for her picture. As he sobbed, he told me that he had cut pages out of books with his pocket knife— pictures of Jane Fonda. Brenda had caught him and threatened that he would lose his job if it happened again. I talked with him, stressing the magnitude of this offense; he promised me and Brenda that he would never do this again. I don't believe he did.

Thereafter he made photo copies of the pictures in his spare time at the library—a more acceptable solution to his hobby. Collecting pictures of pretty women had always been a practice of his; as a young boy he drew cigarettes in the mouths of models. I think he thought that was sexy. The present collection grew until he had boxes full of pictures. I never understood this compulsion or many of his other idiosyncrasies.

A further example of the importance of his stuff was the bag full of video- tapes, magazines, and books that Billy carried to work each day. He had a series of bags, gradually larger as the contents required; he brought back the same bag and contents each day. His friends at the library teased him about it but lovingly gave him a leather bag, similar to one a physician would carry. There was no way, in the few hours that he worked, that he could use the contents of the bag. I talked with him about this, reminding him that other people, while they may carry briefcases, do not carry bags to work each day. As he had learned to do, he listened to me and then did as he chose. His doctor told him that carrying such a heavy bag was not good for his back. Nevertheless, each day he waited by the side of the road with the bag at his side. One day I said to him, "Billy, put the bag back in your trailer or I won't take you to work." Without a word, he went back into his trailer, bag in hand, and didn't return. I backed up and said, "Okay, if you must take it, get in the car." I don't know if it was a battle or a war, but I know who won.

From time to time I found phone messages from the library on my desk. One read: "Ruby from the library wants to know what kind of cake Billy would like for his birthday." This began a practice that continued throughout Billy's career at the library. Billy's birthday has always sparked a major event, and I knew from the note that he had advertised it widely. Ruby, a member of the maintenance crew,

was particularly fond of Billy and instigated the annual birthday parties, to which I was always invited. The first party included Ruby, Brenda, Joe, Billy, and me. We enjoyed a cake, cards, and soft drinks.

Gradually more of the library personnel pitched in to celebrate this affair, increasing each year in size and abundance. People brought cards, gifts, and always food. The cake and soft drinks evolved into a vast presentation of sandwiches, chips and dips, and even crock pots with little sausages. Billy was lord of the occasion, presiding graciously and appreciatively. At one party, I asked a member of the staff, "How many of these parties do you have each year?"

She replied with a smile, "Just one."

IT BEGAN SIMPLY, in the way many things do, as the solution to a single problem. Jim Watson, a former student of mine and principal of a school for children with special needs, had invited me to do a two-day workshop with his teachers. At the conclusion of the second day we talked about training needs of his staff and he said, "Jane, what I really need is for you to talk with the parents of our children. While we're trying to teach life skills, the parents are afraid to give their kids the opportunity to try things on their own. I need you to tell them what Billy is doing and help them to let go a little."

It dawned on me, "The person you need is Billy."

Jim was thrilled with the idea and said that he would schedule a date for Billy and me to meet with the parents.

During the long drive home, I asked myself, How are you going to pull that off? Granted, Billy was living in a semi-independent fashion, doing his own cooking and housekeeping. But I never considered Billy's verbal skills to be his prime asset. I thought of the way I prepare for a presentation, gathering information, jotting down ideas and notes and compiling the parts into a folder. Since Billy's reading skills were minimal, perhaps there was another way to prompt his remarks. Suddenly the thought occurred to me: we could use slides as prompts for his comments.

We shot slides of Billy's trailer and the library where he worked, and action photos of him cooking a meal and cleaning his place, filling my car with gas, bringing in the mail, and so on. He quickly learned to operate

An you got any questions?

the slide projector we had borrowed from my department, and after a great deal of practice, we were ready to do what became "our thing."

In November of 1982 we drove to the Center for Developmental Resources and saw our names on the program: Dr. Jane Schulz and Mr. Billy Schulz. Although hesitant at first, Billy gave his presentation following my remarks, fielded questions from the parents in the small audience:

"Have you ever been burned on your stove?"

"How do you get to work?"

"Who buys your groceries?"

At the conclusion of the program Jim presented me with a corsage and Billy with a check. He really liked getting the check and said, "Mom, let's do this again!"

I realized that my role as Billy's mom brought credibility to my remarks. With this particular group of parents I shared my own misgivings as Billy moved toward independence. I urged them to allow their children to take risks and to explore possibilities. But my message acquired reality as Billy portrayed his own life and revealed his pride in living alone.

I began taking Billy to my classes, with his slides, and was thrilled to see him develop confidence and poise. At the end of his presentations he frequently followed my example and asked, "An' you got any questions?" It was a new and valuable experience for the students to realize his accomplishments and to know him beyond the identity of a person with a disability.

Our first break into the professional circle came when Larry Grantham, my department head, asked us to be keynote speakers at the Southeastern Division of the American Association on Mental Deficiency [later retitled Mental Retardation]. This was to be a major conference composed of professionals in the field of mental retardation. I was particularly pleased to participate in this conference because the focus was on adults with mental retardation as opposed to the usual emphasis on children with mental retardation. The topic I developed was "Family Supervised Community Living," a new concept in 1985. I felt uniquely capable to address this subject because of our experiences in Billy's difficult years after high school and how we resolved some of the problems we had encountered. Billy was excited about going to Atlanta and invited my mother, Tom, and our friend Bev to join us for the presentation.

Although I had made a number of presentations on my own, this was the first major event for Billy and me as a team. With this group I expressed the anxiety that Bill and I had felt in seeking services for Billy when he left school and related some of our unhappy experiences. I suggested that many parents were capable of helping their children with disabilities achieve some degree of independence if they had assistance from professionals in the field.

When I introduced Billy, he rose slowly and stood hesitatingly before the microphone. I think his practice with his pretend mic, playing Tom Jones, gave him some stability, but he was obviously nervous. Everyone in this audience of speakers identified with him and waited patiently for him to begin. He followed my example by introducing Tom, Memi, and Bev, then got into his mode and performed like an old hand. My theory was made believable by Billy, whose commentary and rapport engaged the audience. The evaluations reported that we were the hit of the conference. Tom later quipped, "Let's take this show on the road!"

Several months after the Atlanta conference I had a call from David Mills, my friend in the North Carolina Division for Exceptional Children at the Department of Public Instruction. David and I had worked together in a number of situations related to teacher education and exceptional children's needs. On this occasion David asked Billy and me to be keynote speakers at the 37th Annual Conference on Exceptional Children in Charlotte. David followed my acceptance with a letter to Billy and enclosed his very first contract. Teachers and administrators from all over the state attended the conference; it was by far the largest group we had ever addressed.

Our presentation was entitled "Teachers and Parents Preparing Handicapped Learners for the Future." It was described as "A unique presentation by a mother and university professor, along with her handicapped son, presenting information about ways in which the school and the home can work together to help children move into independent and semi-independent places in society."

Billy and I were on a stage in a large auditorium, standing at a podium, facing an ocean of people. As was our custom, I addressed the group and then introduced him. The slide projector was properly positioned, the remote control on the podium, the microphone in place. He looked at me and whispered "Mom, I can't do it." I understood his panic and said, "O. K. Billy, I will do it for you," and picked up the remote control. He immediately stood up, took the remote control from me, and said, "These are my slides." As he gathered momentum, he performed beautifully to a cheering audience. Mary and Jos, who had driven from Chapel Hill in a blinding rain storm to hear us, shared his anguish and ultimate victory with me.

With each presentation, Billy gained poise, strength, and force; I was aware of a new dimension in my career. I had always felt that my work was important. I could see students listening and learning, opening to new ideas and approaches, with different levels of acceptance. Now, watching Billy relate his life to the audience, I saw respect for him and appreciation of his accomplishments; I saw hope and encouragement.

We were partners and we had a mission.

As we received invitations to speak, our presentations fell into several categories. Although my focus in the past had been on the mainstreaming—or inclusion—concept, we were more recently being sought by groups focusing on Down syndrome. The Blick Clinic of Akron, Ohio issued an invitation to participate in a national interdisciplinary seminar on Down syndrome. This two-day seminar involved a number of well-known and erudite professionals, including the director of Children's Brain Research Clinic in Washington, D.C., a pediatric neurologist from the Institute for Basic Research in Developmental Disabilities in New York, and a number of people whose names I had seen in professional journals. On the program, among this distinguished list, was I, listed as Professor, Special Education, followed by Billy, Book Handler, Hunter Library. Inclusion on another level was taking place; professionals were acknowledging the benefits of involving families in discussions of services for people with Down syndrome.

Several incidents during this symposium demonstrated Billy's social and professional growth resulting from our presentations. The evening before the seminar opened, we were included in a dinner at an exclusive restaurant. A gentleman in the party related an amusing exchange with Billy that he had had in the men's restroom. The man had apparently spilled something on his trousers and was wiping it off when Billy emerged and asked with concern, "Oh, did you have an accident?"

The seminar took place at Quaker Square in Akron, a redevelopment of the Quaker Oats Company's factory and silos. I found the tall, tubular hotel difficult to navigate, so on the morning the seminar opened, I suggested to Billy that he wait in the room until I came for him. After several speeches, I left the auditorium to get Billy to join me for the break, but as I headed out, I saw him at the refreshment center, coffee in hand, talking with a group of people gathered around him. I realized then that his sense of direction is better than mine, and that he was already playing the audience.

We were the last presenters of the conference, closing with a topic we had developed called "Growing Together," describing ways we had grown as individuals and as members of a strong organization. I made several points that became part of my message to parent groups:

—We are the kind of group that brought trainable classes from churches to schools;

—Our children have gone from the institution to the marketplace;

—Our families have grown from passive recipients to respected experts; and

—Our groups have progressed from small voices in the wilderness to power in high places.

Billy's slides and comments underscored my points. At the conclusion of the program, as Billy later told his dad, "They stood up and 'plauded!'"

We were invited to participate in a number of conferences related to the National Association for Down Syndrome, groups in which we felt very much at home. The feedback we received made me realize that this was a special niche for us. One letter from the executive director in Chicago expressed her point of view:

> You made a significant impact on our parents—the beauty was not only in what you said, but in how you said it and in who you are. I know you touched the professionals too and several teachers told me how much they liked your presentation. It's no easy task to be a hit when you have such an act to precede—Billy is such a charmer and I know how proud you must feel to see him doing such a great job. I believe presenters are successful when they touch people's minds and teach them something, but when they also touch hearts it's even more powerful. You and Billy were such presenters. Thank you!

She added in a letter to Billy: "I hope my son can grow up to be a fine guy like you."

Comments from parents at a similar conference in St. Louis were also encouraging and rewarding. Another letter to Billy stated:

> Even though my daughter is much younger than you, it was very helpful for me to see how you have been able to succeed in your work and living environments. It gives me a goal as a parent to help my daughter achieve when she gets older.

Billy had asked one of the fathers to videotape his presentation and later, when we received the tape, this note was enclosed:

> Dear Billy,
> Do you remember me? I am the little girl who waved to you and blew you a kiss at the end of the day. I am too little to know what you said to the big people. My mom and dad just said you were great! They said they were not so worried

about when I get big now. Only you could do that they said so I am so glad you came here to talk to them.

My dad felt really happy to make this tape for you and your mom. You said you wanted to show it to your dad too. I hope that you and your mom and dad can be happier too with the tape. Thank you for helping as only you can.

Mom and dad helped me with this note, but I made the picture on back myself.

As we mingled with the parents in these and similar groups, I realized that many of them had not been introduced to adults with Down syndrome. It occurred to me that they had not even dared to imagine their own children as adults. National Down Syndrome Congress Conventions are now featuring adults with Down syndrome as speakers and printing their stories in the Congress newsletter, but I have not seen anyone featured who is Billy's age or older. I truly believe that presenting a positive picture of his adulthood is our mission.

Another avenue opened for us about that time. Laura Dinkins, a student of mine, introduced me to her mother, who was employed by the Florida Diagnostic and Learning Resources System. As a coordinator for the resources system, Mrs. Dinkins recommended us to people throughout the state of Florida, resulting in a number of opportunities to participate in programs. Topics ranged from developing coping strategies for parents to parent-professional communication, which became my favorite topic. I had become aware of the need for increased communication between families and professionals a number of years ago. In addition to my own difficulties in this area, a specific incident made me aware that it was a common issue.

During my first year at Western, Dr. Cox asked me to accompany him to a residential school in Knoxville, Tennessee, to speak with parents and teachers. My role at that meeting was to facilitate communication between the two groups, who were seated in separate sections of a large auditorium. I began by asking the parents: "What would you like for your child to be learning?" Immediately one of the parents exclaimed, "I want my child to be toilet trained!" One of the teachers replied, "But your child *is* toilet trained!" It amazed me that a child who was severely retarded could distinguish between the expectations of home and school.

As I researched topics for my book, *Parents and Professionals in Special Education*, I found that many parents and teachers were, for a number of reasons, unable or reluctant to communicate effectively with each other. The Knoxville experience revealed that when the two groups stopped thinking of themselves as opposing sides, they were able to work together for the good of the child.

In addition to our targeted audience, Billy's influence was seen in other relationships. During our first presentation in the Florida consortium, Billy noticed a young man who was working with the media equipment. He introduced himself to Frank Cosby, a media specialist, and helped him move and set up gear. They became friends as we worked together in various meetings. One time when Frank took Billy to lunch, I thanked him for his kindness. He replied, "Oh no, don't thank me. Until I met Billy I was afraid of people with disabilities. Now I know how much fun they can be."

Among our exciting and invigorating trips, we especially looked forward to presenting at the Parent and Professional Training Conference at the University of Alabama. I admired the work of Robert and Martha Perske, authors of *Circles of Friends*, and was looking forward to meeting them.

Moreover, we eagerly anticipated our reunion with Billy's dearest childhood friend, Steve Hinton. Steve and his parents had moved from Auburn to Tuscaloosa and had planned to meet us at the conference. The reunion, however, brought sorrow to Billy and to me. Margie had warned us that Steve has Alzheimer's disease, which appears to occur more frequently and at an earlier age in people with Down syndrome than in the general population. Although we knew that Steve's behavior would be unpredictable, we hoped that he and Billy would retain some degree of their relationship. Billy was devastated when Steve neither recognized nor spoke to us. He could not understand, as none of us can, how a deep relationship can disappear from someone's mind. Billy still recalls with sadness, "Steve not know me."

Apart from this personally tragic trip, our excursions to conferences and conventions heightened the importance of Billy's role in my own career and his positive effect on others. While other people might develop an inflated ego from these experiences, Billy continued to go about life in his understated way. He did his work, carried on with his life, and went on trips with me when they were scheduled. He talked very little about our adventures, although the people at the library called him their "star." Billy was such a gentleman to travel with: he carried our luggage, retrieving it at the airports, made friends wherever we went, and performed with assurance. He learned to deal with his fear of heights related to air travel by taking an aisle seat and asking me to close the shade at the window. Once we were airborne he relaxed.

Billy gained so much confidence from his travel experience that he decided he would like to fly to Boston to visit Tom. We made the arrangements, and I asked him, "Aren't you a little bit afraid to fly by yourself?"

With his newfound assurance, he replied,

"No, someone help me."

On his return trip, I met him at the airport and watched him disembark from the plane, on the arm of an attractive flight attendant, an exuberant smile on his face, calling out, "Hi, Mom!"

Our travels have accommodated visits with friends and relatives and have rewarded us with new friends whose courage and determination have inspired us. We believe we have reciprocated in our presentation of a model, a challenge, and encouragement to families of persons with disabilities. Our message expands as we continue to acknowledge the changing landscape of our own personal challenges.

SEVERAL YEARS AGO there was a television show called "Life Goes On." It was the story of a family, including one member who had Down syndrome. It was a sensitive program, enlightening the public about Down syndrome and illustrating the challenges and victories experienced by Corky, the protagonist. The thing I liked best about the story was that it chronicled the life of the family, highlighting events that included each member and the family as a whole. This is the way it was with Billy and the rest of us. He changed and each of us changed; sometimes the events appeared to be apart from his life but ultimately affected all of us.

I loss 30 pounds!

During our first ten years on Locust Creek Road we experienced a wedding, two divorces, a failed business, the birth of a fifth grandchild, and my husband's stroke. I continued to teach, to write textbooks, and to make presentations—frequently with Billy.

Some of these events were negative, some positive, and some fit both categories. The most obvious conclusion is that during this time Billy contributed less stress to the family than did other members. In fact, during some of the troubling times he became my most valuable and practical support. In discussing coping strategies I explained this shift:

> During the past decade, the problems associated with Billy's transition into adulthood, the difficulties in finding suitable housing and work for him, and the lack of resources to assist us with these problems created tremendous stress for our family. It was interesting and revealing to find that his problems were no longer our chief focus, and that his contributions far

outweighed his demands. However, there is a more subtle problem concerning Billy than is apparent on the surface.

In family system theory, we frequently state that what happens to a person with a disability happens to the entire family. What we fail to mention is that what happens to the family also happens to the person with a disability. Explaining the changes that have taken place in the last 5 years and helping Billy to understand and deal with them has been difficult.[1]

Mary's marriage springs to the forefront as an example of the effect of family members on each other. Jos asked Billy to be his best man at their wedding, a choice that moved us and thrilled him; this was the incentive that led him to Weight Watchers and gave him the motivation to lose weight.

Preparations for the wedding began before Mary and Jos arrived from Holland and continued with frenzy. We had had very little rain during the summer, and since we were using a well for our water, were greatly concerned about our supply running low while we entertained so many guests. Sure enough, the morning of the wedding our well was dry. Billy invited Mary to his trailer to take a shower for her wedding.

At the church, Billy remembered to put the rings in the pocket of his new, smaller suit and performed his duties with dignity. John and Tom took charge of arrangements for the reception in our yard. John, who had landscaped the yard to have the look of an old established flower garden, declared it would not rain. Tom, an experienced realist, rented a tent "case instead," as Billy would say. The rains began as we were finishing the hors d'oeuvres, driving the cautious guests to the house, while the champagne and another gathering of revelers remained under the tent during the downpour. Periodically, the edges of the tent would sag with the weight of collected water and the guests teamed up to push it over the sides, drenching our feet, making our long gowns heavy and our faces light with laughter.

Following their honeymoon, Mary and Jos moved into our home, claiming the loft as their space. Friends tried to find apartments for them, and at first they explored the possibilities of moving, but we soon found that the arrangement suited all of us. Jos enrolled at Western to complete his degree in chemistry. He adopted what we called the "smokehouse" for his study, trudging up the hill before dawn to prepare for his classes. When breakfast was ready one of us rang an old cowbell and he joined us, ready for his informal English lessons at the table. Mary and Jos brought the life and fun into our home that had been missing, and we valued the opportunity to get to know each other well.

---

1   Schulz, J.B.(1993) "Heroes in Disguise," in Turnbull, A.P., Patterson, J.M., Behr, S.K., Murphy, D.L., Marquis, J.G., Blue-Banning, M.J., *Cognitive Coping, Families, & Disability*. Baltimore: Paul H. Brookes, p. 31.

Mary worked at the Mountain Heritage Center, which housed the office sponsoring the World's Fair in Knoxville. (She joked that she was tempted to answer the phone with "World's not fair!") We accommodated guests from far and wide that summer, as we were not far from Knoxville. We frequently accompanied our guests to the Fair but one trip stands out in the annals of the family. When John and his family came up from Georgia, we drove two cars in caravan style. J.R. rode with Jos and Mary in their little Colt, and as they honked and passed, he flashed us with a moon! Billy shook with uncontrollable laughter and still finds it a hilarious moment after all these years.

Our house was a great party place. The favorite gathering spot was the deck that overlooked the pond, close enough to the ground that it was nonthreatening for Billy. With John's advice and help we created a yard full of flowers for each season, the setting becoming more beautiful each year. Tom built a dock for the fishermen and all of us struggled with securing the minnow tank, from which spring water overflowed into the pond. Our ducks amused us and offered opportunities for education. Seeing the enamored male almost drown the female, little Isaac exclaimed, "Look, Grandma, they're playing boat!"

When it rained, we enjoyed the front porch, which Bill had screened. There we had a swing and several rocking chairs, plus a cabinet to hold toys for the children. The front porch constituted a large play pen. When Daniel was a toddler, we were all relaxing on the porch when he went inside, brought John's guitar to him and said, "Sing blow up the TV." Those were my favorite times.

When Tom asked to build a home for his family on our property, we felt this would ease the loneliness that ensued when Mary and Jos moved to Chapel Hill. He and his crew removed the useless old barn on the upper part of the two-and-a-half acre lot and built a charming house. Watching Isaac and Carrie grow up nearby was a true blessing.

As all of us settled in, the loft took on a new use. Tom constructed a desk for me from a door and two filing cabinets; John sent me a new, supportive office chair. At the other end of the room Tom placed his drawing table. This proximity allowed us many hours of communication and the opportunity to vent our concerns. Late one night as I was working on my book, I looked up and saw him climbing in the window at the small balcony—one of my favorite mental pictures.

Once Tom and his family moved into their new home, Billy approached Bill and me, saying, "I'd like a new place too." Although he had once said our backyard was "too close," following Tom's lead that a grown man could choose to live near his parents made it acceptable to Billy as well. Billy, Bill, and I went shopping for a trailer and found a nice one that met his needs. Billy could hardly wait as we laid the foundation on a hill between our house and Tom's, installed the hook-ups, and brought the trailer in. It was on a hill between our house and Tom's. Memi had it landscaped for Billy, and he was genuinely thrilled. He lived there for almost twenty years, gradually adding his own touches—and stacks of his stuff—and making it his home.

Although Billy didn't really have a social life outside of the family and library staff, most of the time he was content. His favorite pastime, other than watching television, was going to concerts frequently staged at the university. We saw some famous groups, such as Chicago, at our beautiful new stadium. But the concerts I remember most fondly were held in the old gym, where everyone sat on the floor listening to the songs of Linda Ronstadt, Loggins and Messina, and Seals and Crofts. Describing one concert to us, a friend remarked, "You walk into the room and get high." Billy responded, "I'm 'fraid of heights."

All of us appreciated the concerts in Asheville, just an hour's drive from Sylva. Billy especially enjoyed Kenny Rogers, John Denver, and his all-time favorite, Tom Jones, whom he had seen several years ago in Charlotte. The friend who went with us commented on Tom Jones' tight pants, and both of us wondered where he put his shirt tail. Billy later told his father, "Dad you not believe this: the ladies throw padded bras at Tom Jones!"

My students also included Billy in some of their parties and invited him into their homes. One young man asked Billy, "Would you like to go to Fuddrucker's for lunch?" Billy's vehement reply: "I can't say that word, my momma kill me."

Still, his greatest pleasure was in family gatherings such as birthdays and holidays. Billy grieved when the divorces occurred, changing the order and composition of these events. In a family as close as ours, divorce was difficult to absorb. Billy loved his sisters-in-law and has never been able to understand what happened. For years he asked, "When they get back together?" and none of us could answer his questions. The pain he saw did, however, make a deep impression on him. Sometime later, not connecting my question to the divorces, I asked, "Billy, do you still think about getting married?"

Without pause he responded, "No, I can't handle it."

Although he was reluctant (or unable) to share his questions and concerns with us, we realized Billy needed someone, perhaps out of the family, to talk with. I approached Michael Dougherty, a counselor in our department, to see if he would work with Billy. His response was immediate and positive; they began weekly sessions in Michael's office. I'm not sure what they talked about, but I do know that Billy could raise questions with Michael that he hesitated to pursue with his family.

They formed a bond that became a lasting friendship. The sessions were beneficial to both of them—Billy was able to communicate more freely, and Michael gained new skills in counseling that he could share with his college students.

Many changes in the family were quiet, and we acknowledged them slowly. I'm not sure that Billy was aware of his father's problems and distress. They maintained their relationship, with Bill sharing transportation needs and continuing the patterns he and Billy had established. The rest of us, however, were aware that Bill was in trouble.

For more than five years Bill's real-estate business had been declining while his indebtedness was climbing. Until the day we lost our home on Tilley Creek, I had had no idea of the extent to which he had borrowed, mortgaged, and promised all

of our assets. When Bill began to reveal our financial picture at that time, I was stunned by his mismanagement and dishonesty. Here in our log house on Locust Creek, we continued to struggle through the maze of deceit: a struggle that seriously damaged our relationship and my respect for him. I stayed in the marriage because I wanted to keep our family together, to maintain some shred of decency and because, in my misplaced sympathy, I didn't think he could support himself. I talked about divorce but never followed through with it. Although the years after we moved into our new home were strained, we established a working relationship and concentrated on giving Billy the help he needed to move into adulthood.

Bill was struggling to make a living, planning to make a fortune, believing every day that his ship was about to come in. His yellow pad, on which he daily wrote the sums of his expected sales, was a fixture at the breakfast table. When he was forced to close his real-estate office, he began working with a nearby firm dealing with time-share sales. At one point, even though the firm had asked him to leave, he kept going to the office. He was a desperate man.

In addition to his business failure, Bill was emotionally and physically fragile: smoking heavily, drinking steadily, and flying off the handle at the slightest provocation. Although he hadn't been to a doctor in years, I felt sure his blood pressure was extremely high. I said to Tom, "I feel as if I'm sitting on a powder keg."

Tom replied, "No, Mom, you're holding the fuse."

NONE OF US WAS SURPRISED that day in March. Several weeks before, I had predicted to Mary, "Your dad is going to have a stroke."

Bill had a cold, and had stayed home from the time-share office. I came home from my office at noon to check on him, and found him sitting in his red leather chair, smoking and silently looking out the window. I gave him some medicine for his cold, fixed his lunch, and sat down to eat with him before returning to work.

On Friday afternoons, the halls were deserted and the office was quiet; it was my favorite time to accomplish tasks I had postponed during the week. Although Bill's condition was in the back of my mind, I worked late. I put my papers into labeled file folders, dropped them into my tote, and locked the office door behind me. At home I walked from the wintry chill through the airlock into the stuffy den and saw that Bill was not all right. He was slouched in his chair; his

I be right there!

mouth twisted and drooped, and he had a vacant and confused look in his eyes. He tried to speak, and his speech was slurred and unintelligible.

Tom was coming down the hill from his house just as I was about to call him. We looked at each other and said in unison, "He's had a stroke."

Bill could still walk, so with Tom's help I got him into the car and took him to the emergency room, where the doctor on duty confirmed my suspicion and hospitalized him. Within a few hours Bill was unconscious and partially paralyzed. It became apparent that his left side was affected, and because he was left-handed, the implications were serious. I met with the radiologist on duty, a friend of ours, who showed me Bill's X-ray. He pointed out the affected areas and indicated that the damage was probably irreversible. Devastated, I returned to Bill's room to find him working a crossword puzzle.

I came home from the hospital in a daze. Looking about the house, I found cigarette butts all around the floor, a number of burns in the red leather chair, and food scattered about the rug. We later reconstructed the scene with him and realized what a nightmare the afternoon had been for him. Covered with bruises from falling, he had been unable to use the phone.

The ensuing week was an ordeal of watching, waiting, and wondering. I was furious when a nurse gave him a cigarette, incensed that he was left in a wheelchair with nothing on but a short, open nightshirt. Although treatment was in progress, there was a total lack of feeling for Bill's dignity as a person.

As he began to respond, Bill's personality changed. The irritability and anger of the past few years gradually disappeared. He regained a sweetness that we hadn't seen for a long time. I began to think that perhaps I could love him again.

Toward the end of the week, our doctor referred Bill to a rehabilitation hospital in Asheville, about fifty miles away. On Friday, I rode in the ambulance with Bill while Mary and Jos, who had traveled from Chapel Hill to help, followed in their car. Then the real story began.

As we entered Bill's assigned room, we encountered another patient in the four-bed room. I introduced myself and asked, "How long have you been here?" He looked around the room for a moment, then looked at me and responded slowly and with great puzzlement, "I really don't know." Mary and I looked at each other and silently communicated our dismay. Thereafter, we answered many of the questions asked of us with, "I really don't know."

As part of the admission process, Mary and I met with the hospital social worker, a gentle, empathetic woman who seemed to be quite knowledgeable about stroke patients. Our exchange of facts about Bill was mostly rote and dreary, but when she asked if Bill had undergone a personality change, both of us smiled and said together, "Yes, for the better!"

She responded, "Don't count on it—it may not last." I filed that warning away for later retrieval.

After getting Bill settled, I returned home to piece my life together. I realized that our family dynamics had changed drastically and that now, instead of having help from my husband, I would have two family members with disabilities. Bill had dealt almost entirely with Billy's transportation needs, a major concern in a semi-rural area. Although Bill had seemed unable to view Billy as an adult, they were devoted to each other, and had developed a relationship filled with rituals and clichés. Now, seeing his father helpless and noncommunicative was difficult for Billy, but with repeated visits and increased communication, the two of them fell into some of the comforting rituals of the past.

Billy frequently accompanied me on visits to the rehabilitation center. As he became accustomed to the environment, he tried to cheer his dad with remembered jokes so we could all laugh together. We also began to acknowledge humor and irony in some of the situations that we encountered.

One Sunday afternoon Billy and I met Mary in Asheville to share in a picnic with Bill. We arrived as the church service was ending. Billy and I were on one side of the auditorium, waving to Mary as she entered on the other side. The unfortunate text chosen for the rehab patients, most of whom were in wheelchairs, some with amputations, was from the 37th chapter of Ezekiel, including "Dry bones, hear the word of the Lord...our bones are dried up and our hope is gone; we are cut off." I met Mary's eyes across the room and with one accord we mouthed the words to the old spiritual song:

"Them bones, them bones gonna rise agin,

Now hear the word of the Lord!"

Both of us convulsed with repressed laughter. What a text to choose as a sermon for that congregation!

Bill was in the rehabilitation center for six weeks. Mornings were occupied with training and visitors were not allowed to visit until late in the afternoon. I was teaching in Asheville one night a week, so I would stop by to see him before class as well as on the week-ends. With the help of occupational and physical therapists, Bill was making progress. They taught him to use the washing machine, which he had never done before, and the oven, which he had not used for many years. Therapists visited our home to determine if it would be feasible for Bill to come home; they felt it would work out well. I must admit that I wasn't so optimistic.

Billy seemed to change before my eyes, or perhaps my perception of him changed with my need. He realized how much I needed him and became my reliable helper and primary comforter.

Billy's real strength, physical and emotional, became apparent when Bill returned from the rehabilitation center. Although he had shown initial improvement, Bill slowly deteriorated physically. I could not lift him when he fell and frequently had to phone Billy to help me. He always replied, "I be right there." I could not have managed without him.

The grandchildren were deeply affected by the changes in their grandfather. Because Tom and Michelle's children, Carrie and Isaac, grew up so near to us, they saw us on a daily basis. After the stroke, while Bill was still ambulatory, Isaac ran in one day and reported hysterically, "Grandma, I saw Grandpa walking down the road smoking a cigarette."

One of the most touching, and telling, examples of the children's consternation was a poem written by Carrie, our only granddaughter:

YOU WERE ALWAYS THERE

Why did you leave?
You left us all—
At least that's what it seems like.
You didn't have to,
But you did.
Why?
I can remember
Running down to see you
You were always there,
Smoking.
But one day,
You couldn't talk
Or walk
You just sat there, staring.
You are still alive,
But I don't really know you
Because I never got the chance to know you.
Grandpa, why?

Smoking was an issue for all of us. Bill's physician had said that refraining from smoking would be more beneficial to him than all the medication he was taking, but Bill was completely addicted. In our daily walks around the track, he would pretend to take a detour and I would see him smoking. During Mountain Heritage Day he sneaked behind the booths to have a cigarette. He had been blessed with a second chance and literally blew it.

I refused to buy cigarettes, but Bill had his friends bring them and continued to smoke surreptitiously. I made it clear that he was not to smoke in the house because of the danger of fire, so he continued to smoke on the front porch, sitting in his rocking chair. Eventually Bill stopped sneaking and I stopped pretending he would ever quit.

While caring for Bill, I was still teaching at the university and trying desperately to maintain a reasonably normal life. John, Tom, and Mary gave me strong and loving support, coming to relieve me for short trips, planting flowers in my yard, and helping me with Bill's physical needs. However, they had families of their own and were unable to help with the daily business of my life. Then Bill began having seizures, frightening for him and for all of us. I described one event in a letter to my mother:

> Saturday we went to Mountain Heritage Day and then to the grocery store. While Bill was sitting in the car he had a seizure. There's nothing to be done about it, so I just brought him home. His left leg went completely out, and Billy and I couldn't get him out of the car. I called a neighbor from across the street and we finally got him in bed; he was zonked for two days. Then Monday morning as Billy and I were leaving, we heard a loud crash, and found Bill flat on the floor. I had to go to my classes and called Florence to stop by and to call if I needed to come home. Bless her heart, she brought muffins and coffee and stayed with Bill a while. I simply asked him not to get up unless I was there. Tuesday I took him to the doctor and we are checking his blood for all sorts of things, including his seizure medication level. The doctor said that we have to expect this once in a while, and that it will take him several days to recover.

Billy and I tried to incorporate Bill into our daily lives, taking him with us on shopping trips and several times to visit family members. We went to Rome, Georgia, to visit John and his family; while we were there Bill had a seizure and we decided to come home. John followed us all the way in his car, making sure we arrived home safely.

A healthy diversion for Bill was his regular Wednesday lunch with the "boys," Dick, Jimmy, and Jim Ballard. They called for Bill each Wednesday and took him to a restaurant for lunch. All of them were in pretty bad shape, and as I watched Bill stagger down the walkway with tiny, hesitant steps and the three of them help him into the car, I wondered which one would bring the others home. Bill looked forward to his Wednesdays as to nothing else and it was a wonderful social experience, his only one outside of the family. Surprisingly, Bill outlived the other three men.

In the midst of our difficulties we experienced some distinct joys. Jos graduated from the University of North Carolina and was offered a position with Eastman Chemical Company in Kingsport, Tennessee. Billy and I, as well as Tom and his family, went to his graduation and marveled as Mary, nine months pregnant, negotiated the stone steps and crowds to take pictures of the event.

Daniel had the good judgment to be born during my summer break, enabling me to bring Mary and Daniel home with me while Jos moved their belongings into their new home. Bill was almost as thrilled with the new grandson as I was.

The last time we managed a trip with Bill was to visit Mary and Jos for Thanksgiving; Bill was eager to see their new home. Only twenty miles out of Sylva, Bill wanted to stop at a rest area. Billy went in to help him, as usual, and for some reason the procedure took about an hour. This delay caused us to be traveling in the dark. As we drove the steep, winding, deserted road through Sam's Gap, it began to snow and soon I could hardly see the road. Our progress was slow; all three of us were frightened, and we knew that Mary would worry. Once we arrived, Bill was distraught and disoriented in their new home; it was such a difficult trip that we decided it would be our last out-of-town venture. Thereafter I arranged for someone to stay with Bill when I was away.

As I continued to work, Bill frequently called me out of class. I would rush home not knowing what to expect. En route to or from work, if I saw an ambulance I would turn around and follow it. I was so torn between duties that I felt I wasn't doing anything well. Although my career had been a fascinating and fulfilling part of my life, it could no longer be my primary concern. While not ready to give up the intellectual stimulation and satisfaction of my work, it became clear to me that I could not continue being torn between work and responsibility. I decided to retire earlier than I had planned.

My retirement was a heartwarming celebration. The students planned a beautiful reception in the Hospitality Room of the new, large activity center. University friends, peers, and students from near and far came to honor me. My family was there, including Bill, who sat at a table with his friends. I hadn't seen some of the students for years and eagerly heard stories about their families and their teaching experiences.

The evening celebration, dinner at a country inn, was planned for my family and close friends. My children and I were seated at the head table with invited guests surrounding us. We laughed and reminisced, sharing moments dear to all of us. After dinner we gathered for a slide show and good-natured roasting. The videotape of the event reveals a close-knit and affectionate group. I knew that I would miss my peers and my students.

Mary compiled a scrapbook of the letters I received from students. In reading them I became convinced of two things: the importance of teaching and the magnitude of the rewards. Many letters referred to personal encounters, such as: "I remember the day I was so discouraged and we took a walk on the trail." One student commented that my sharing Billy with her enabled her to look at her brother, who has a disability, in a different way and to think of him as an asset rather than a burden. My friend Eddy, who had been teaching for twelve years, concluded his letter with the following thoughts:

Adding to my skills, giving me clearer insight and exposing me to realities previously unknown to me was a big part of your job. Talking with people with such love, your family you share, dealing with your life challenges with such skill, courage and joy: thanks for showing me that too.

I have not read these letters for a long time. Rereading them now, I am grateful for having found my mission, for experiencing the joy of watching young people mature, and for belonging to such a noble profession.

As I close the retirement keepsake book, two full brown envelopes fall to the floor. One is labeled "Second Retirement" and the other "Third Retirement."

My dad not know me!

FOLLOWING MY RETIREMENT, my department head asked me to teach a course in summer school. This seemed like a good situation; I could leave home after helping Bill dress, preparing his breakfast, and administering his medications, then return in time for lunch. I welcomed the diversion and opportunity to stay in touch with peers and students. To my disappointment, Bill still called me out of class frequently, and I realized I would have to devote my time to caring for him.

We settled into a fairly comfortable routine, with our little jokes and rituals. I was still transporting Billy to work and decided to indulge myself with short courses in piano lessons and weight training while I was on campus. I played the piano badly, but Bill loved to hear it, and it was a solace to me. The weight training helped with my ability to lift Bill and relieved my physical and mental stress.

Billy and I cared for Bill at home for almost five years. During that time we tried to maintain a degree of normalcy in our lives, collecting a list of people we could call on if we wanted to go on short trips or make our presentations.

I began teaching a night class just once a week and working on another book. However, Bill's general health and mobility were failing; Billy and I were under constant tension. I wrote to a friend:

> Bill has fallen twice this week and it's getting so hard to handle him, big as he is. Our doctor here told me that there is nothing more she can do. We are seeing a neurologist next week and from there I don't

know what to expect. The doctor thinks I should look into nursing homes. There is a new home here that is very good, but I haven't mentioned it to Bill. At this point the children are more worried about me than about Bill, because I know the strain is showing.

No longer able to manage care for Bill at home, and with no rooms available in the new nursing home in Jackson County, we had to place Bill in a facility about thirty miles away. The day I took him to the nursing home may have been the most heart rending day of my life. Mary, realizing how much support I would need, brought her baby and drove down from Tennessee to help me with the transition. The night before we went, we sat and sewed name tags into Bill's clothes, reminding me of sewing name tags when the children went to camp. But this was no trip to camp for any of us. The next morning, Mary and Daniel followed me and Bill in their car, helped unpack Bill's meager belongings, and stayed with him while I kept a doctor's appointment in Asheville to investigate some medical problems of my own.

When I returned to the nursing home and went to Bill's room, I saw a poignant picture I will never forget. Mary was helping her dad put his clothes away in the shabby dresser assigned to him, while Daniel, happy in his newfound game, arranged coat hangers in a row on the metal bar of an adjoining bed. It was a somber but peaceful scene.

The nursing home was old, shabby, and crowded; it smelled terrible. I immediately saw features that made me wonder if this was the right move for us. A line of patients in wheelchairs waited to use the bathroom and the "living room" was dark and dreary, with one small television set in the corner. Most of the patients sat around with their heads drooping in sleep and hands folded in their laps. The staff members were kind and competent, but the atmosphere was totally depressing. I promised Bill that we would transfer him soon, but it broke my heart to leave him. I returned to my charming, comfortable home, filled with unbearable sadness, torturing myself with the unanswerable question: How can I live in this lovely place while Bill is in a hellhole?

That summer was very difficult for me as I visited Bill, trying to pacify him, and dealing with my gathering despair whenever I came home. I woke up one morning to hear myself declare, "I can't handle any more!"

I sought help for depression. I took the prescribed medication and it induced me to sleep for three days. I knew I didn't want to live that way. I slowly gathered strength and energy for the difficult time ahead.

Billy and I gradually adjusted to our new lives, becoming closer and more dependent on each other. We visited Bill frequently, and after a seemingly interminable time—over a year—managed to get him into the newer, nicer nursing home in our town. He said he thought everyone should live in the other nursing home first to fully appreciate the one in Jackson County with its indoor and outdoor gardens, lovely dining rooms, and places to host family members and friends.

The new nursing home also made it more pleasant for family members to visit. Soon after Bill moved there, our new grandson, Warren, was born. I went to Kingsport for his birth and shared Daniel's delight in his tiny brother. Soon he joined Daniel in coming to the nursing home; Warren especially enjoyed riding the wheelchair on Grandpa's lap. Visits from Mary with her two sons were Bill's chief sources of joy. For Bingo prizes the patients received quarters, and Bill always saved them for the boys in a little pouch. When the children arrived, they went directly to the particular drawer, withdrew the quarters, and headed for the vending machines. They called the nursing home "Grandpa's house."

Bill was peaceful in his new home for a while but soon began to be depressed and resentful. When John, Tom and Jos were there to help bring him and his wheelchair up the steep bank, we brought him home for visits. The unaccustomed commotion of the family visits confused and tired him, though, and he was usually ready to return to what was now his home.

Billy and I took his dad out to lunch frequently, and Billy learned to fold up the wheelchair and toss it into the trunk of the car. I could do it when necessary, but it was easier for Billy. I was always so grateful that Billy could take his dad to the men's room, because it was awkward for me to negotiate Bill and his wheelchair while trying to avoid other men. These many years later, when we drive past the rest area we used on that difficult trip to Kingsport with Bill, Billy usually reminds me, "Me and Dad had a hard time there."

Learning how to manage the wheelchair required skill and foresight gained through trial and error. Bill's holiday delight had always been the selection of our Christmas tree, so Billy and I took him with us on this excursion. After choosing the perfect tree, we put Bill in the front seat, the wheelchair in the trunk, and then realized that if we put the tree in the back seat, there was no place for Billy!

Once our lives became involved with the nursing-home staff and patients, we found that there were good times still to be had. Bill, always a romantic, managed even in a nursing home to plan celebrations for our anniversaries. After one of these parties I took him to his favorite restaurant for lunch, where we had a nice visit and delicious meal. Concluding the anniversary celebration, I asked him if there was anything else he wanted to do. I watched this frail man—his face distorted into a half-charming grin, his voice slurred and uneven—as he responded, "We could go to a motel." Some things never change.

The nursing-home environment is a world of its own. People wander around, sometimes talking to themselves, sometimes talking to unseen images, sometimes friendly and lucid, sometimes engaged in peculiar behavior. One day as I entered Bill's room, I noticed a pair of ladies' bedroom slippers next to his bed; we laughed at the implications of that scene. When his roommate's dentures disappeared from the usual resting place on the night table, the nurses initiated a search and found that one of the women patients had stolen them.

The employees were also characters, some kind and helpful, a few curt and ill-tempered, others as funny as the residents. One kitchen employee regaled me with her nighttime exploits of dancing and meeting men, talking with a slow, monotonous beat. She saw me at the back door once, gathering empty boxes for packing books, and asked, "What's the matter, did your rent come due?"

Bill's responses were often more humorous than he intended. When I asked him, "What's wrong with Richard?" he replied, "He's from Florida."

Sometimes there was abuse in the institution. We hear stories about staff abuse but rarely about patient abuse. Bill's first roommate was so abusive to him I tried to get one of them moved, to no avail—it turned out they had the same doctor, who advocated for both of them. I began to take notes, trying to build a case for Frank's removal from Bill's room, or a new room for Bill. The following notes built a good case:

JUNE 10

Bill: When they wheeled Frank by me, he said, "You damn Jew."

JUNE 12

Bill: I entered my room to shave. The nurses were hoisting Frank up; he saw me and asked, "What's that bastard doing here?" Nurses replied, "He lives here."

Frank: "That s.o.b., hell."

Bill: When he got outside the room, he was still swearing. His language to the aides is terrible.

JUNE 15

Bill: They brought him in to the lunch room, saw me sitting at a table, said, "That bastard Jew." It makes me so angry I want to hit him. He has no respect for the aides. When they come in to dress him he says, "Leave me alone, sons of bitches."

This is a morning ritual.

JUNE 21

Bill: This morning was a rerun of the normal get up. The nurse's aide checked him and said, "Let go of my tit." More bad language to the aide.

Billy: Mr. M. called me retarded son of bitch.

JULY 4

Bill: While I was dressing myself, he was lying on his back, looking out the rail. I was standing, pulling up my pants. He said, "I hope you fall." That was my good morning, then, "You bastard Jew." How can an old man act like that?

Once in the middle of the night, Bill heard the good-natured nurse's exchange:

Nurse: "Mr. M., did you wet your pants?"

M: "No, I did not."

Nurse: "Then we'd better get a guard in here—somebody peed all over you!"

The only way we finally got Bill away from Frank: Bill had surgery and was put in a more intensive care unit.

Bill had several surgeries for bladder cancer and occluded arteries. I always called Mary, who came to be with me during the crises. Each time we thought he would not live through the surgery, but he consistently came through. After several such trips, she declared, "I'm going to stop bringing my black dress."

As people must, we adjusted to family changes and soon faced another pressing situation. Billy had worked for a number of years at the university library for twenty hours a week, just about right for his stamina and preference. In a budget crunch, his hours were cut in half, a tremendous blow to him and to me. He loved his job, and ten hours a week allowed him far too much time on his hands.

Calls to friends, trips to Vocational Rehabilitation, and routine job searches brought only openings at fast-food restaurants. Billy was hired at Burger King and began with great success. He made friends with employees and became a good worker. He enjoyed seeing friends from the community and appeared happy in the new job. After a few months, the manager phoned me to say that Billy was slowing down and seemed unable to perform his duties.

I tried to analyze the problem and came up with no clues to the change in his performance and attitude. An outbreak of hepatitis required the restaurant to close down temporarily; Billy was never rehired. When I asked Billy if he wanted to return to the job, he said, "No, I not like Linda." I had never heard Billy say that before; he liked everyone or politely said nothing about them. On inquiry, I found that Linda, a supervisor, was constantly yelling at him to hurry, which conversely caused Billy to panic and slow down.

After trying two different fast-food places over several years, it became apparent that the pressure of the job and the speed required were too difficult for Billy, and we knew we had to seek another, creative, solution.

Visiting his dad frequently, Billy had become quite familiar with nursing-home procedures and was at ease with the patients. I became active in the organization for families and was on good terms with administrative personnel. I saw that there were jobs suitable for Billy and pursued the idea with staff members. After training with a job coach, Billy was employed as Interagency Assistant, taking water to patients, helping in the kitchen, and, ultimately, his preferred task: calling Bingo. Although he had hated playing Bingo at the sheltered workshop, he liked calling it and being in charge of the game. This task particularly endeared him to the staff; they hated the tedium and pace of Bingo, but it was just right for Billy and the nursing home clients.

Soon after he began his new job, Billy came home in tears, inconsolable because a patient he had grown to love had died. He never got used to the idea that this was a place where people died. Neither did I.

Ten years after his initial stroke, it became apparent that Bill was reaching the end of his life. Billy had seen many patients die at the nursing home, but watching his father fade away was a totally different experience. As Bill ceased to recognize people, Billy lamented, "My Dad not know me!" and it was obvious that his heart, too, was breaking.

When Bill's death became imminent, I tried to explain to Billy what would happen to his dad. I said, "Billy, Dad won't be with us much longer."

"Where my dad going, Mom?"

"He will go to be with God, and he won't suffer any more."

After a long silence, Billy asked, "Will Murray Jackson be there?"

Caught off guard, I stammered, "Yes, I suppose so."

"How about Jim Ballard?"

"Yes, he will be there too."

"And Jimmy Lane?"

"Yes."

With a broad smile lighting his wonderful face, Billy declared, "Well, they can all have lunch together."

I thought to myself, You know, he may be right. And I felt comforted.

When Bill didn't want a cigarette, I knew it was over. The last week of his life was peaceful for both of us as I sat by his bed. Although he didn't speak, he listened while I talked about our good times, particularly when the children were young. My anger was gone.

My dear friend Lynn and I had planned a trip that week; instead, she came and sat with me. Billy came in occasionally but was crushed when his dad didn't talk to him. Billy still says, "My dad not know me!" and relives his experience with Steve.

As my family gathered around me, I was aware that for all of us, and for Bill, the ten-year ordeal was over. His memorial service was one of remembrance and acceptance. Tom described his father as "unencumbered by reality" and acknowledged his legacy. He said,

> I understand more the testimony to the raising up of four children who have been secure enough in love to go forth and be different and weird and to go on and have kids of their own. For love is our family totem, the sacred fire carted with care from camp to camp. Passed on, now it is our responsibility to maintain it.

Mary recounted some of her fondest memories of her dad: his stories, his singing, his optimism, his joy in surprising the family at Christmas time. She closed with:

> One family joke was to ask Dad what he wanted for Christmas. He always said, "I just want my children to be happy." And that was his greatest gift to us.

Daniel, at age seven, stood by the pulpit in his white communion suit and read his tribute:

> Grandpa was always nice to us. He was always redy for a visit with quarters in his drawer. He was always redy for a hug too. At Christmas he gave us sweat sherts. He put liter around all the animals in the slae. Warren (my little brother) used to ride on his wheelchair. Sometimes on easter we found eggs in the garden by the nurseing home.

When I emptied Bill's dresser drawers, there was his little pouch, full of quarters Bill had saved for the boys' next visit. Warren's drawing of his Grandpa in a wheel chair depicts his memory.

I was overwhelmed by the support and kindness of my friends and family; I was particularly touched by the presence at the service of students from the class I was teaching. The church and our home were filled with flowers and plants, the kitchen loaded with delicious food. I was in a daze, but mostly, I was just exhausted.

A year later, I wrote to my children:

It seems like yesterday and like twenty years ago. I used to get so tired of my widowed friends who changed their husbands into saints after death. I haven't done that, but I do find myself remembering the good things about our life together. I often think about our last week together—I can't tell you how sweet it was. The past was past, there was no future, and we simply were together, with no need for any spoken communication—only assurance that we were there. And of course, your being attests to the miracle of our marriage. There were many good times, and the rest just doesn't matter.

Sorry, you have to wait.

MY LIFE SETTLED into a comfortable pace. I rejoined the bridge club, became a board member of the Smoky Mountain Mental Health Association, taught one or two classes each semester, and remodeled my kitchen. My yard pleasured me with the expanding growth of lilies, spring bulbs, and shrubbery. I kept a small garden of tomatoes, beans, squash, and asparagus, just enough to provide Billy and me with some good vegetables.

One feature that made my life much easier was

discovery of a new transit system in Sylva, relieving me of transporting Billy four times a day. Designed for persons with disabilities or illness, the system operated on an ability-to-pay scale and transported Billy three times a day. The only time I needed to pick him up was at the end of his day at the nursing home. Sometimes I went in to visit with some of the patients there but felt less and less inclined to do that.

The summer after Bill died I planned a trip I had wanted to make for several years.

It wasn't the usual European trek I was after—the art museums of Italy, the tulips of Holland. I wanted to go to Lithuania. Myra Goodwin, a friend and former student, had traveled to Lithuania with a group known as APPLE (American Professional Partnership for Lithuanian Education) for six years and each year had urged me to accompany the group. It seemed an opportunity similar to my experiences in Jamaica, with the added interest of its distance and mystery. And I would be teaching—the way I enjoyed learning about people and their cultures.

With minimum arrangements for Billy's needs in place, I could finally see the opportunity for this unique experience. I decided to go.

Following Myra's coaching, I met administrators at the Sylva hospital who donated a host of medical supplies, collected from my friends all the cosmetic samples they could muster, and gathered the materials I would need for teaching over thirty people. After classes were over, each day our plan was to engage in leisure and craft activities for fun and to promote interaction among students and teachers.

When I met Myra at the Asheville airport, she had what resembled a body bag containing toys for children and medical supplies among her pile of luggage. I presented two enormous suitcases, which Billy had helped me pack and close. In Newark we met a number of people from APPLE, most with Lithuanian backgrounds. The congestion at the Newark airport was phenomenal, but I found that there were so many aggressive people in our group that the confusion about our passports was quickly resolved. I thought these people seemed pushy until I heard some of their stories.

Aldoona sat next to me on the flight to Copenhagen. She wanted the aisle seat because she's claustrophic and explained why. When she was ten years old she, her parents, and her brother fled Lithuania just ahead of the Soviet occupation. As they reached the train to Germany and freedom, the train was pulling out. Her parents thrust her into a window and a German soldier held her tight so she wouldn't fall. There was no place to stand and she didn't know where her family was. She had no way of knowing how long she endured this restriction and fear before she heard her mother's voice: "Aldoona, Aldoona," and she knew she would be safe.

Many stories were shared during our stay about the Russian atrocities and the Lithuanians' acts of bravery as they fought for their freedom. In one dramatic event, courageous Lithuanians held hands and encircled a communications building to prevent the Russians from destroying it. As we toured the capital city of Vilnius we saw many churches, almost destroyed during the Soviet occupation, in the process of reconstruction. Vilnius was a lovely old city, full of history and mystery.

About forty of us were in Lithuania to teach for the three-week session. Many disciplines were represented, including special education. All of us, however, were assigned to teach one class of English language, which I thoroughly enjoyed. Without an interpreter, we pantomimed English and Lithuanian words, humor and creativity being the most engaging teachers.

I had over twenty Lithuanian students, mostly teachers, in my special education class, including mothers of children with disabilities. I brought a videotape of Billy's trailer, his working place, and his involvement in the community. One young mother told me that she had a son who had Down syndrome and wanted to bring him to class. Even though we communicated through an interpreter in this class, we shared our concerns and our pleasure in meeting each other. She brought Domenykas, a beautiful five-year-old boy, to class several times, and we demonstrated a number of assessment and training techniques with him. As I worked with him, I thought of Billy, so far away in space and time.

During our stay, we became aware of many social issues prevalent in Lithuania. In counseling sessions, the women in particular related their problems with alcoholic and abusive husbands. They were concerned with the widespread use of abortion as a method of birth control, and uncomfortable in their living arrangements. The Soviets had built high-rise apartment buildings, with small and limited rooms. Frequently, several families lived in the confining spaces; we were sympathetic but powerless to advise or help them.

On weekends we crowded onto obsolete busses and toured the countryside, visiting parks and beautiful landmarks. On Sunday we attended church and heard formal sermons in the Lithuanian language. Again I thought of Billy as he sat in church every week trying to decipher the message of the sermon. Was it as difficult for him to understand as the Lithuanian language was for me?

We were housed in a rural vocational school, empty for the summer. Although the facilities were antiquated, our meals were delicious—fresh vegetables and the best yogurt I ever tasted. I found that there were showers on a lower floor and gathered my clothes and toiletries, eager for a nice hot shower. As I entered the shower stall, anticipating the steaming treat, I stepped on a slippery, live frog. Others in adjacent stalls laughed heartily when they heard my exclamation of surprise and I knew they had shared the same experience.

The people we met were thrilled to have us there and appreciated everything we did. During our afternoon leisure times we distributed the cosmetics we had collected, items almost unattainable for most of the young women. One American teacher brought scarves and demonstrated different styles of tying them; Myra taught them to line-dance. I had brought materials to make books, and kits for making earrings. The books, with cloth covers, were intended for their students to write stories in.

Making earrings became a favorite activity; by the end of the course everyone was wearing them. The girls who worked in the kitchen asked to be included in this activity and we arranged an evening session for them. I was happy to have a way to express my gratitude for their efforts in preparing such good meals. It's amazing how much fun you can have and how well you can communicate without a common language.

Every evening we were entertained as people from surrounding villages came in with balalaikas and accordions. They accompanied their songs and played while we learned their traditional folk dances. We smiled incessantly, rotated partners, and danced for hours.

At the conclusion of our three-week class, the students brought such gifts as beautiful hand-embroidered linens and pieces of amber. They prepared elaborate refreshments, including champagne. I was deeply touched that these people, coming out of bondage, having little in the way of material goods, shared so generously with us.

I compared teaching in Lithuania with my previous experiences in Jamaica. I had taught a total of four times in Jamaica, each time in a different location, and each time I had encountered children with disabilities and their parents and teachers. In both countries, seeing them, talking with them, gave me a feeling of connection that was unparalleled. It was not just the features of Domenykas, or those of a little boy with Down syndrome who smiled at me from the street as I sat on a bus in Jamaica. It was the universality of disability and of parents and teachers who wanted to improve the lives of their children. Living with Billy, experiencing his difficulties and victories, had enabled me to feel a kinship with the world. This realization brought a poignant desire to go back home.

Billy fared well in my absence, enjoying his work at the library and getting acquainted with the transit drivers and passengers. However, as he gradually opened up to me, I realized that things were not right with Billy at the nursing home. He told me that he was not delivering ice to the patients' rooms anymore, and that Linda, his supervisor, was trying to find other things for him to do in addition to calling Bingo. When I asked him what he would be doing tomorrow, he frowned and said, "I just don't know!" The next day when I picked him up in the afternoon, I spoke with Linda, who had been his constant advocate.

Linda had been informed by the director of nursing that Billy was to be relieved of setting up the cart and putting ice in the residents' rooms; neither she nor Billy was given a reason. Billy was very disappointed in the change, since he enjoyed the task and interaction with the residents and felt he was performing an important service. Linda had tried, without success, to have him reinstated in this position. She told me that she and others had tried to find other tasks for him to do and that he had done whatever was required of him.

In talking with Billy I found that he no longer felt secure in his job, since he didn't know what he would do when he arrived at work. Most of all he didn't understand why he had been relieved of a job that he felt he did well; neither did I.

I spoke with the new director of the nursing home about the situation and asked that he review Billy's position. He told me that he was unaware of the particulars and would investigate and get back to me. I didn't hear from him, so after a month I wrote a letter to this same man. I had thought I was through writing letters; the difference was that this time I knew our rights. In my letter I reviewed the situation and concluded with the following paragraphs:

> If Billy was doing something inappropriate, he should have been corrected. Linda will agree with me that he responds well to constructive criticism and correction. If he needs further training, the sheltered workshop will provide it. If he was taken off the job because of prejudice towards his Down syndrome, there is a much larger issue that we need to discuss with hospital administration.
>
> I respectfully request that Billy be reinstated as ice distributor, where he was efficient, appreciated, and content. I would appreciate hearing from you very soon.

Within a week I had a reply from the director, apologizing for the delayed response. He outlined the facts he had assembled, suggesting that we employ a job coach as I had suggested, and concluding with this paragraph:

> Billy is a valuable member of the team at our nursing center, and Billy's employment here stands on its own merit. Hence, Billy's job satisfaction and success is important to us as it is with all of our team members. Billy requires and receives no more or no less consideration or treatment than any other employee. The mistakes made in the original occurrence were solely related to the overall functional problems of the center at the time of the event. Our center is, always has been, and will remain an Equal Opportunity Employer.

Problem solved; back to normal. Billy worked at the nursing home for seven years. He participated in classes regularly required for all employees, usually related to safety issues. At one point he was awarded the title of Employee of the Month and had regular raises in his pay.

Billy's favorite job at the nursing home continued to be calling Bingo. Sometimes I sat in to watch the game and enjoyed the pleasant banter between Billy and the residents.

"Come on, Billy, call out B-3!"

"Sorry, you have to wait."

I HAVE NEVER LIVED ALONE and, for the most part, that has been my choice. Even after Bill's stroke, there were others who shared my home, by mutual need and consent. My oldest grandson, Paul, moved into the versatile loft while attending college at Western. I welcomed his humor, his affection, and his kindness to his grandpa and to Billy. About the same time my mother moved to Sylva.

Mother had lived in Georgia for many years, in later years depending on her friend Miss Bea for assistance. In her nineties it became obvious that she needed to be near me, a possibility we had always recognized. Since she wanted to maintain her independence, we decided that the house behind mine, which Tom and his family had previously occupied, would be suitable and desirable. Her moving goal was Labor Day, and we had a lot to do! I sent out a cry for help to my children and described the results in a letter to my brother:

> But Memi, I am a grown man!

> We had a work day on July 6, and you can't imagine the work we got done. All my kids came, and it was wonderful. They tore down the shed behind Billy's trailer, and Tom built a lovely fence facing Mother's house. They hauled off trash, cut down dead trees, and did everything possible outside of the house. Mary and I cooked, of course, and we really had a good time together.

> John is coming up August 3rd to trim trees, bushes, and spray out some weeds, and then we will have the house painted. I want it to look great, because I know this will be a very difficult move for Mother.

Mother had lived in Columbus for over thirty years, building a broad social network. She participated in church activities, civic organizations, and played bridge frequently. I'm sure she was lonely in Sylva, and all of us attempted to help her build a new life. My friends invited her to bridge parties, our church welcomed her, and family members assisted her in every way possible. Somehow, she felt it was never enough.

Billy was particularly attentive to his Memi, bringing her mail and newspaper to her, taking out her trash, and fulfilling any chores she asked him to do. She returned his affection but continued to treat him like a child; that bothered him.

I began writing about Mother in my journal and described her as an "amazing woman." In unflattering terms I stated my feelings.

> She drives me crazy: I admire her, resent her, dislike her, love her. Her vanity is the quality I most dislike and it is what has kept her going.

As an example I described a particular event:

> Monday night we were invited to an open house. She was so weak all day I had to wait on her constantly—she didn't think she could go; neither did I. I got ready to go and looked in on her.
> "Will you button my blouse? These buttons are ridiculous." She looked lovely. We went to the party. I asked, "May I get you a plate?"
> "Of course not; I can do it." She smiled and held court.

Another day we got an invitation to a shower, addressed to Jane Schulz and Tommie Bolton. Hours later, Mother said, "I've been thinking about that invitation. Wouldn't you put the mother first? And Bolton even comes before Schulz alphabetically."

My silent comment: "Good grief!"

When she wasn't focused on what others thought of her, my mother was charming and fascinating. Our best experiences were when we got away from home, and I enjoyed taking her on business trips with me. During these times she reminisced about her childhood and her early life with my father.

Her favorite childhood memory was the year her mother told her she could pick turnip greens from the garden, sell them, and keep the money. In a family with five girls, this was a ripe opportunity. That autumn, her earnings enabled her to buy her first hat, developing a style that became her trademark. At church she was known as "the lady who wears a hat." One friend commented, "You look so nice; I think I will get out some of my old hats."

Mother responded, "I don't wear *old* hats!"

Her vanity became her own imprisonment in later years. Previously an active church member, she refused to attend with Billy and me once she needed a walker. We had pushed Bill in a wheelchair for years and were willing to do so for her, as well. She was unable to show signs of weakness or disability in public, a sad and alienating situation for her, and difficult for us as well.

Mother looked young for her age and did not tell people how old she was. She said that "a woman who tells her age will tell anything." One time my brother John brought a girl home from college. At dinner the young woman looked at Mother and said, "I hope I look as good as you do when I'm your age."

Mother rejoined, "You don't look that good now."

We thought that remark was funny until Fred, who was there, said that the girl was crushed; she was trying to be nice. Later Tom commented that Mother was parsimonious even in her humor: it was always at someone else's expense.

Although Mother was difficult and demanding much of the time, she always rose to an occasion. During the second winter in her new home near us, we had a blizzard, which left us without electricity and therefore unable to use any of our appliances. With our driveway deep in snow, our good neighbor Lee, who lived just above Mother's house, lifted her into his truck and brought her to my house for the duration of the storm and its aftermath. Billy joined us, and we spent a week without heat except for the fireplace in the family room. We heated water and food on a small gas burner, and slept in two rooms, with Billy on the sofa. Billy saved the day with his battery-operated boom box and music. He brought in wood for the fireplace, and helped me haul water from the pond to pour into the toilet. I kept bottled water to drink in case of emergencies, but the toilet would not flush without the electricity that powered the well. Depending on the need, Billy would ask, "Need one bucket or two?" This difficult situation brought us closer as we struggled to survive. Mother told us stories of her childhood, read from the Bible, and led us in old-timey songs.

A few years after her move to Sylva, it became apparent that Mother needed more routine help and we agreed that she would move in with me. Reluctant to lose her beloved independence, she kept delaying the change. One Sunday when she was in church and my children were visiting, we moved her bedroom furniture into my guest room. When she returned from church she was surprised but pleased, and that evening as she was going to bed, she whispered, "I didn't know it would be so nice."

Mother and I had always had an amicable relationship, as long as I did exactly what she wanted me to do. Our biggest problem existed in the animosity between her and Bill. All my married life I was constantly pulled between them, each complaining to me about the other, each determined to direct my life. Now that Bill was gone, I believed that Mother and I could live together peacefully.

We settled into a manageable routine. We went to church and Bible studies as long as she was willing, and she continued to play bridge. Mentally acute, she attributed her alertness to her lifelong pastime of bridge. We found a group of retirees who played every week, and she joined them, giving her an outlet and me a respite. This group welcomed her and became her good friends. As she aged, they nonchalantly shuffled the cards for her and helped her without hurting her pride.

I realized that Mother was experiencing dementia when she began to hear people singing in the road beyond her bedroom window. She would call me in, saying, "Listen to them, isn't the music beautiful? And there is one young man who is quite tall and handsome. Don't you hear them?" When I responded that I did not, she declared, "Then you're stupid!"

As we settled into a routine, other issues came to my attention. I became concerned about Billy's bulging trailer. I described it in my journal:

> Billy's orderly disorder makes me crazy. He has never thrown away a TV Guide, has magazines 5 years old, 8 track tapes, cassettes and, most valued, Xerox copies of Jane Fonda and others…And videos—oh my!
> John told Billy that he would build shelves for the videos and magazines if Billy would empty his study, where most of the stuff resides. We have been working on it for weeks and I am overwhelmed at how hard it is for him to discard things. But after 17 years, a trailer has its limits.

It seemed that Billy was ready to clean up; as usual the incentive did not come from me. With John's promise, he discarded things I never thought he could part with. He had a bookcase he wanted to take to the library for his "office," so we went to the library and met his supervisor. I was amazed at the space his co-workers had created for him. They had made Billy an office by blocking off a section with boxes, which they planned to cover. In the corner was a table bearing a nice lamp and his coffeepot; over his desk was room for a poster. The bookcase was perfect, and he was delighted with the overall effect.

As he had promised, John and his helper came for the weekend to build shelves for Billy's "media center." We had worked for weeks to empty this tiny room and had taken his discarded things to the public dump. As John had pre-cut the shelves, the room took shape quickly. Billy helped with staining the wood and later thoroughly enjoyed putting his things in order.

Billy's personal sense of order extends to time and routine, also important to Mother. Both of them were completely reliant on television for their entertainment. Billy has his favorite programs and frequently tapes them for later review, a habit which heavily increases his accumulation of stuff. Mother watched her soap operas, the news, and two programs that were essential to her well-being: *Larry*

King Live, which played each weeknight, and the weekend sermons of Charles Stanley.

A neighborhood event interfered with the sacrosanct schedule. The cable company was installing a new system and needed to bring their wires across a neighbor's yard to reach our section of the community. The neighbor refused to let them pass and even threatened to pull a gun if necessary; obviously, this halted the progress, so that we were without television for several days—several devastating days.

Mother wailed to Billy, "I don't know what's going on without the news!" Billy responded, "Memi, I can get you some news!" He went to his trailer and came back with a videotape. He plugged it into our receiver and there was instant news— about two weeks old. Mother commented on a train wreck in Japan and was amazed at the devastation. Then, as old political news played, she asked, "Are they still rehashing that old stuff? I'm tired of hearing about it!" Entertainment and equanimity were restored. I had to go outside to laugh with true abandonment.

In 1999, Mother had her one-hundredth birthday. She was still reluctant to share her age with anyone outside the family, but conversely loved the limelight, and did allow us to celebrate the event. Fred and I planned a luncheon at a charming, old-fashioned inn. The menu included salad, baked mountain trout (a favorite of Mother's), vegetables, and a beautiful birthday cake. But the main feature was the family represented at the event: children, grandchildren and great-grandchildren. Family members traveled from New York, Maryland, Georgia, Tennessee, and Iowa. We read excerpts from letters Mother had written over the years, and she maintained her dignity and composure throughout. Some of the family stayed for several days, prolonging the party atmosphere. The day after the party, Jane and Terry (my niece and her husband) took Mother to lunch at a family restaurant near Sylva. I asked Mother what she had for lunch and she answered, "Trout."

I said, "Again? You had trout at the party yesterday."

She complained, "Yes, but it wasn't fried."

Our neighbor, who was a columnist for the local newspaper, called Mother to see if she could write an article about celebrating the one-hundreth birthday. Mother told her, "I know where you live and if you put that in the paper I will set fire to your house."

I wrote in the journal: I'm glad the birthday party was a success because it's been hell to pay ever since.

For my own mental health, I had to get away from time to time. Although Mother resisted the idea that she would need help in my absence, I asked a young couple, students of mine, to stay with her. For short trips, such as visiting Mary and her family in Tennessee for weekends, this worked well, but for longer trips, other arrangements were necessary. When I went to Alaska, Mother went to visit Fred in Maryland. When Tom and Sheila invited me to visit them in Boston, I took Mother to Mary's for a week and Billy went to Georgia to visit John.

My trip to Boston centered around Carrie's graduation from high school, and I reveled in the gift of quality time with Tom and Sheila. Taking the entire week off from work, Tom escorted me along the Freedom Walk. Carrie and Isaac joined us for a spectacular day of whale watching. The salt spray and tender loving care refreshed me and renewed my ability to face whatever situation would come my way.

After picking Mother up at Mary's I came home and wrote in my journal:

> Mary and Jos have their house plans in order and will start building in July. I will probably end up in Kingsport.

AS BILLY, MOTHER, AND I sat on the deck, overlooking the pond and blooming crabapple trees, enjoying the sunshine and gentle breeze, I wondered if the people now touring my house would buy it. I also wondered why I was selling it.

For some time Mary and Jos had invited me, urged me, to move to Kingsport. They were building a beautiful house on the lake and thought it would be a good time for Billy, Mother, and me to consider joining them.

I had said to Jos, "If I moved on Monday, you would be transferred on Tuesday!"

I gon to like it here!

Over time, he convinced me that he had no intentions of leaving the home of his dreams.

I responded, "Well, at least we will wait until Mother is no longer with us."

Resisting change, I continued to delay the decision until Mary challenged, "Mom, you are putting your own life on hold."

Several factors caused me to

hesitate. I thought a move would be difficult for Mother and that surely, now that she was over 100 years old, she would not live much longer. In addition, Billy was firmly entrenched in his lifestyle with two secure jobs, his own trailer, and many good friends. I knew I would miss my friends in the community, my connections to the university, and the home I had thought I would never leave.

There were also valid arguments pointing to the advantages of living near family members. Mother, though still in fairly good health, was becoming more difficult to live with and I really needed the kind of help I could only get from loved ones. As for Billy, I felt more and more uneasy about aspects of his continuing to live alone. In addition to the problem with his strictured esophagus, I worried about his eating habits and food handling. Frequently when I went to his trailer in the evening, I saw food left out of the refrigerator, dirty dishes in the sink, and a disregard for cleanliness. The order that had been achieved earlier was already gone again. In considering my personal situation, it seemed better to move while I still had the energy to adjust to a new environment, and the idea of seeing my grandsons and being part of their lives certainly was very appealing.

And then there was the real reason. Like other families who have children with disabilities, I was concerned about Billy's future. In the event of my death, he would have two situations to deal with: his grief and the necessity to relocate. Mary and Jos volunteered to supervise his living arrangements if my death preceded his, and moving to Kingsport seemed the logical thing to do to insure his stability and their convenience.

As the idea of leaving Sylva germinated, I began looking at house plans. For nearly a year I pored over issues of *Southern Living*, tearing out plans that would suit our needs and provide some privacy for Billy. This search became my escape, sending me to the loft—my retreat—as in the past.

One weekend, as I was visiting Mary and Jos, we looked at some houses in their neighborhood. There was a house for sale in the cul-de-sac where their home was under construction. I went to look at it and for the first time realized that I was actually considering a move. Although this house was not perfectly suited to our needs, it was available. I thought it was time to raise the possibility with Mother and Billy. On the drive home, I anticipated the resistance that I would receive from Mother. I walked in and asked, "How would you like to live in Kingsport?"

She surprised me with her answer, "I'll go where you go."

Billy's response would be another matter. Change was always difficult for him, and this was one he had never imagined. By this time, however, I was convinced that it was the best decision for all of us.

I put my house on the market and began the mammoth task of showing it to prospective buyers. I had thought it would sell immediately, but months would pass before the right buyer came along. As luck would have it, I needed this time to convince Billy that we were indeed moving and that it would be a good thing. For a long time, as we drove through Sylva, he would say, "But Mom, I like it here!" Moving was a torturous idea to him.

Before making any concrete plans, I needed to investigate what resources in the Kingsport area would be available to Billy. Having worked with numerous agencies in North Carolina, I knew the system pretty well but had no knowledge of Tennessee services and funding for persons with disabilities. I met with a friend at the mental health agency I was working with, who directed me to the proper sources. Mary made the appropriate contacts, and I made a trip to investigate them with her.

We went to nearby Johnson City, met with personnel at the Tennessee Division on Mental Retardation for the Tri-Cities area (Kingsport, Johnson City, and Bristol), and learned of the range of services available. I enrolled Billy in the system, and his category of need was, and still is, listed as "active," defined as "requesting services immediately but not having intensive needs that meet urgent or crisis levels." With that step accomplished, I could concentrate on housing.

In a series of visits, Mary and I followed newspaper ads, open-house events, and real-estate magazines. Her chief criterion was to have us within walking distance of her new home; that sounded good to me. The layout of the house in her cul-de-sac would not work for us, although it was close to her and Jos. Our extensive search delivered nothing to suit us.

In the meantime, Billy was still unwilling to accept the fact that we would be moving. I took him to Kingsport frequently; Mary, Jos, Daniel, and Warren made every effort to make him feel comfortable and secure. After many months of their efforts, one Sunday we joined them for a ride on their pontoon boat, cruising along the lake on which their home was located. Jos turned the steering wheel over to Billy, and that was the turning point. With his hands on the wheel, the breeze blowing his hair, and a big grin on his face, Billy said, "I gon' to like it here!" We learned of a house for sale at the end of the road near Mary and Jos, and while it would have needed a great deal of work, it had one attractive feature. Situated on a hill, the house had an apartment under the back side, an ideal situation for Billy. That week Mary made an offer on the house; it was rejected. Just as we were becoming discouraged, Mary's friend Sue Shuler, who daily walks the distance from her home to a turning place beyond Mary's cul-de-sac, phoned Mary to say she had noticed an empty lot nearby. She inquired and found it was available. I went to Kingsport to look at the lot; it was perfect, even with a slope to accommodate Billy's apartment.

We had a place to build!

Mary and Jos employed a skillful contractor who would be available to build for me on completion of their own house. Tom adapted the plan I had chosen from my collection to accommodate an apartment for Billy on the lower slope of the lot, and we were ready to start.

I was amazed at the way things worked out—far better than anything I had imagined. I went to Kingsport as often as I could to make decisions about our new home, and, in my absence, Mary worked with the contractor on the details. We involved Billy in the planning and decorating, particularly of his apartment. He wanted it to look just like his trailer, so we chose natural wood finishes, bookshelves and cupboards, and helped him choose wallpaper. The only thing that didn't meet with his approval was the absence of a kitchen in his apartment. To compromise, we put in a wet bar, with a small refrigerator, sink, and cabinets in his living room. His place contains a living room, large bedroom, laundry area, and bathroom, with an outside door and deck. Stairs lead to a hallway in the main part of the house—next to the kitchen we would share.

The plan I had chosen was open, sunny, and spacious. A front porch accommodated my swing and rocking chairs; a deck led to the back yard, which I could envision filled with flowers and a few vegetables.

Mother said, "You don't need to plan a room for me; the law of averages says I won't be there."

"Mother," I responded, "You beat the law of averages a long time ago." Of course she had a room.

As we progressed with our relocation, we decided it was time for Billy to resign from his jobs at the library and at the nursing home. His employers were not surprised, since he had talked about it from the beginning, but setting a date made it real for him and for his co-workers. Once we set a moving date, his friends at the library immediately planned a party at his favorite Mexican restaurant.

There were about thirty people present at this party to end all parties. There were testimonies and accolades, jokes, gifts, and the presentation of a marvelous scrapbook. We still enjoy perusing the pictures of Billy's work environment and the snapshots of his friends. Personal notes referred to his cheerfulness, punctuality, and conscientious work habits and remind us of the unique position he held at the library. The director of the library sent a note to be read that touched all of us:

> I regret that I cannot be at the luncheon today. I do want to tell you something publicly because I know others at the luncheon have had the same experience. That something is this: in twenty years of exchanging "Good Mornings" with you, your greeting or response has never been matter-of-fact. Your "good morning" has always had a zest that lets me know that you DO wish me a good day! Exchanging greetings with you has always put a smile on my face no matter how I may have felt. Thank you Billy for so many good mornings.

Billy's friends at the nursing home also took him to lunch and presented him with gifts. The residents there lamented that Bingo wouldn't be nearly as much fun without him. Even the drivers of the transit bus had a present for his new apartment.

Another beautiful and tearful moment occurred when, on our last Sunday, our minister presented Billy with a plaque in appreciation of his service as an usher for many years.

Billy's importance in the community was evidenced by an article printed in the local newspaper, commenting on his twenty-one years at the library and his impact on the community as a whole. I smiled as I read one letter Billy received from a friend, "I hate to see you move but I know you have to look after your mama."

My bridge club honored me with a unique party planned to avoid parting on a sad note. These were loving friends of long standing who had shared good and bad times with me. They understood my reasons for moving but knew they would miss me; I knew I could never re-place them. The party was in the theme of a Tennessee hoe-down, complete with straw hats, overalls, and pigtails. My friends' efforts at lighthearted fun helped us cele-brate our history and change, and we really tried not to cry.

I continued to show my house in Sylva, now a little edgy at the prospect of owning two homes. When the real-estate ads had not borne fruit, Mary made an ad for the Sylva newspaper and the re-sponse was immediate. A woman who was visiting a relative on our road saw the ad and made an offer. As my new home neared completion, I could at last begin packing and making arrangements to move.

Mary had offered to help me pack, but I asked her to have Mother and Billy stay with her instead while I did the packing. Two of my former students, now enduring friends, showed up to help in any way they could. Lynn was especially adept at in dealing with Billy's stuff. She backed her car into his yard and filled it with magazines, eight-track tapes, and stacks of photo-copies of movie stars into the back seat, all headed for the dump. Eddy joined us in cleaning out the storage house, filling his truck and heading for the same destination. There was no way or good reason to move it all. I had to tell Billy that some things were lost in the move.

On the day the papers were signed on my old house, the new house was completed. I spent the day packing my car and directing the young woman who had come to clean. My dear friend Florence phoned to say she was bringing lunch. We sat on the front steps, drinking the thick milkshakes she and I called a perfect lunch. It was bittersweet; I knew I would miss her and that she, too, would soon be moving to live near her daughter.

As I got into the car to drive to my new home, lamps filling the back seat, the cat on a pile of clothes in the front seat, my neighbor, Sherry, ran down the hill with a bunch of balloons in her hand. With no room in the car, we tied them to the door handle, blowing like flags announcing my departure, and I drove to my new life, another new beginning.

I ARRIVED IN KINGSPORT in time for Daniel's thirteenth birthday dinner. I drove to my beautiful new home, the house with the turquoise door, and broke into a smile. The movers had arrived, and Mary and Jos had supervised placement of the furniture. It was perfect.

In no time I got busy unpacking boxes, hanging pictures, and putting things away. Mary and Jos helped at every step, and I was beginning to feel at home. Daniel and Warren came over frequently, we shared meals, and I discovered the beauty of living close to them. Billy was occupied with filling his empty shelves and pinning up his Marilyn Monroe posters. Sometimes he sat on his deck, but never on mine. It was too high.

I love my partment!

Mother, Billy, and I were enjoying having meals together, and I think Billy was actually relieved to have help with cooking and cleaning the kitchen. After we put the washer and dryer in his laundry room, he informed me, "Mom, you can use my washer an' dryer anytime you want to!"

Mother was less pleased with her room and bath; they were a bit smaller than mine, and she did not like the arrangement of her reclining rocker and television. We put another recliner in the living room and agreed that we would watch television together. Because her hearing was impaired, the TV was unbearably loud, and I found I could hear Charles Stanley up on the street.

Within a few weeks John had brought his crew from Rome, Georgia, and completely landscaped our yard. We had impatiens along the walkway, shrubbery along the road, rocks placed in strategic places, and a Japanese maple in front of the porch. When I told neighbors where I lived, they said, "Oh, you're the one with the pretty yard!"

Investigating the larger neighborhood, I drove down Ft. Henry Road, past the exit to Sylva, and discovered three buildings in a row: Gold Star Gym, Hair Flair, and Holston Medical Group. We were in business.

During the summer, we invited many of our friends from Sylva to visit and to see our new home. My bridge club gathered here for lunch and to play cards. I wanted them to know that although I missed them, I was happy to be here.

From Billy's point of view, the most welcome guests were his friends from the library. Several of his coworkers came up for the day and Mary took us all for a ride on the pontoon boat. Billy drove the boat long enough to impress them. He showed them around his apartment, pointing out, "This my living room, this my bedroom, this my deck and my grill." He loved showing off; I think their visit eased the loneliness he felt.

On the occasions that we returned to Sylva, Billy always wanted to drive down Locust Creek Road and look at his trailer. Although he liked his new apartment, his trailer had been home for a long time. However, the last time we were there the new owner had painted the trailer blue. Billy was indignant, stating, "Trailers don't be blue!" He never asked to go there again.

Some of Mother's friends also came to see her, admiring the home and her quarters. Although she missed her bridge group at the senior center she wasn't interested in making new friends in Kingsport.

The boys helped lighten the mood around the house and provided us with some distractions. One evening, when Jos was away on business, Mary, Daniel, and Warren came for dinner. Daniel was working on social studies, and Billy was looking over his shoulder. He saw a picture of Stonehenge in the book and remarked, "That's in the Bible."

Daniel replied emphatically that it was not.

Billy said, "Wanna bet?"

Knowing a sure thing, Daniel said, "Sure, how about fifty cents?"

The bet was on, and Billy got a thick Bible picture book we used when they were kids and started from the front, looking at each page. Daniel began to feel bad about the bet and photocopied the Stonehenge picture on my printer, cut it out, and, asking me to call Billy away on a ruse, pasted it in Billy's book. Billy went back, opened the book, found the picture, and said, "See, you owe me fifty cents!"

Daniel gladly gave it to him. Billy showed it to Memi who said, "Of course it's in the Bible."

Mother enjoyed being near Mary and her family. Most of the time, however, her back hurt and she was not happy about anything. As her needs and dependency increased, she resented the assistance that Mary and I tried to give her, particularly in bathing and dressing. Always very proper about her hygiene, dress, and accessories, she found it insulting that we did not think her own efforts were sufficient. Our daily routine was so time-consuming and difficult that I became totally stressed and sought help from my empathetic nurse practioner. When I dissolved into a puddle of tears in her office, she said, "You need help." After she connected me with a home health agency, our lives improved in many ways. We had a physical therapist who worked with Mother on walking, practical nurses to assist her in personal needs, and a nurse to check her physical condition on a weekly basis. She was delighted on the days the physical therapist came to stroll with her—she was coquettish and enjoyed the company of a man at any age. However, she sent a few practical nurses away in tears—that is, until Shamrock entered the picture. Shamrock, petite and strong, asserted her authority, put Mother in the shower, shampooed and styled her hair, and accepted no complaints. They became good friends, and I felt that we had been truly blessed.

Now that I had professional assistance, I was able to return to the gym and found that, as I had discovered in the past, exercise was a physical and mental outlet. I also became more active in our new church.

Soon after our move, Billy and I had visited various churches. I had anticipated that we would join a neighborhood church, but when no one there spoke to us, we continued our search. We attended a church closer to downtown and still did not feel at home. I looked in the newspaper and noticed that one church listed a program designed for persons with disabilities. I thought that was an indication that the church would be responsive to Billy's presence.

On the Sunday morning that we approached First Broad Street United Methodist Church, I was amazed at the size of the building and wondered if we would feel at ease there. We were warmly greeted, enjoyed the service, and returned home to report to Mother that we had found a good church. That afternoon my first new friend, Irene Osborne, came to our home to welcome us with a loaf of homemade bread. We discovered that there were more activities at this church than we could possibly attend. We joined a Sunday School class together and were greeted with open arms by Max Hill, who became Billy's loyal friend. Billy circled the class, shaking hands and proclaiming, "Hi, I'm Billy. I live here now." Max asked Billy to turn out the lights in the room to signal that the social hour was over and the lesson about to begin.

One day when Billy was not there, Max asked me, in Billy talk, "Who gonna turn out the lights?"

Billy asked the minister if he could be an usher and was immediately placed on the list. If I contemplate missing a Sunday, Billy always informs me, "I have to go. I be a usher."

Seeking an outlet for myself, I found that the church had ongoing Bible studies. I joined a class that met one morning a week and found that—in addition to the intellectual and spiritual stimulation—I made a number of friends. It also provided solace for much of my frustration. In looking back at my notes in the workbooks we used, I find daily references to my anger and resentment toward Mother and prayers for patience. I wondered my whole life why I never had Mother's full ap-

proval, why I was still trying to earn it and why I couldn't just acknowledge that it would not happen. I never found answers to those questions but was comforted in the knowledge that I was doing the best that I could.

I know Billy wrestled silently with some of the same feelings. On a number of occasions he said, "Memi give me a hard time," always adding, "but I do love her." One incident made me realize that her treatment of him was sometimes verbally abusive.

Because raccoons were eating our birdseed at night, I began to bring the feeders in at dusk, placing them in a storage container at the door leading to the upstairs deck. One night when I returned home from a meeting, Mother, who was sitting in her recliner near the door, said petulantly, "Billy wouldn't bring in the bird feeders." I responded, with irritation,

"You know he can't handle the height of the deck!"

I immediately went down to Billy's apartment and found him in tears. I asked him to tell me about the encounter, but he could only say, "Memi call me a bad name!" There have been many times when Billy's loyalty and sense of justice caused him to stay silent or to understate his trauma. I will never know how many of these incidents occurred, but Billy remained kind in his words and actions towards his grandmother.

In the midst of my caretaking turmoil, Billy lent his support with kindness, patience, and empathy. It is difficult to explain to others who haven't experienced the frustrations of helping an invalid—the last-minute change of plans, the realization that you must allow this person to manage any possible task with independence even at an agonizingly slow pace, the determination to maintain cheerfulness, and the internal dialog that you must forgive irritation and hurt. Billy and I both know that this is, as Mother would have said, "a tough row to hoe." I had no idea that Billy would offer to me such saving grace as when he helped Mother tie her shoes, lifted her out of her chair, opened doors for her, and walked her slowly to the car or to the table for a meal. Along with the home health professionals, I consider Billy one of the angels that helped Mother and me through those years.

When Mother died, she was almost 105 years old; she had lived in three centuries. In her last week she expressed her gratitude constantly, and I think she meant it. My brother Fred and his wife Marie came down during her final days; their son and my children were also here. We had a small but meaningful memorial service in our beautiful church's chapel, with friends, neighbors, and Sunday School classmates in attendance. As we reflected on Mother's life, all of us were reminded of her intelligence and courage in difficult times and of her influence on our lives—her model of hard work and achievement and her legacy of humor.

The whole family helped me settle Mother's belongings and rearrange the atmosphere of our home. Their efforts ranged from cleaning the refrigerator to designing an office to replace our spare bedroom. Everyone stayed long enough to ensure my comfort and peace.

The morning after they left, Billy came upstairs, brought me a cup of coffee, and said, "Well, Mom, just you and me."

CHAPTER 31

One Thing

That's where I going!

IT WAS THE FIRST WEDNESDAY NIGHT SERVICE we had attended in our newfound church; it seemed a good way to meet people and begin to build our lives in a different community. I had planned to find a challenging program and, hopefully, something that would appeal to Billy. As we approached the door of the main building, Billy stopped short, hearing music coming from an adjacent building. He said, "That's where I going." I went with him to find the source of the mu-

sic and found a group of people gathered together singing with a young man, Russ Brogden, playing the guitar. Billy went to the front row, took a seat, and I left. Billy had discovered *One Thing*, one of the most positive elements in his adjustment to our new home. I just recently discovered that the first night Billy attended *One Thing* was also the night it began.

The church has always been an important part of our family life. We took the children to church early in their lives and entertained very few excuses for them to miss a Sunday. As they became old enough to take in the sermon, we expected them to listen to the sermon and to retain at least part of it. John developed a response that has been a running joke in the family. When asked what the minister had said in his sermon, John routinely reported, "God and Jesus and be good."

Billy loved to go to church and frequently imitated the minister, occasionally in the church and frequently at home. Several times we found him kneeling before a table, sink, or chest of drawers, a towel over his shoulders, a little plastic Nyquil cup in his hand, pretending to take communion.

When we were living in Georgia, Billy attended Sunday School class with Mary, but it wasn't appropriate for him. I wanted to provide for Billy's spiritual needs and also realized that many of the parents I had come to know were unable to attend church at all because of their children who exhibited distracting behaviors. So I started a Sunday School class for exceptional children at our church. Our minister was very supportive and assigned us a classroom at the end of the building convenient to the parking area for parents. We sent notices to all the local churches, and the local newspaper ran an article which read in part:

> …eight children have been enrolled so far in an exceptional children's Sunday School class to begin June 1. [The minister] commented that applications are still being accepted and that letters have been written to those parents who are known to have exceptional children in the Columbus area. He also noted that the Sunday School class, which will be non-denominational, will be held Sundays from 11 a.m. to 12 noon in the white frame house next to the church.
>
> "While children are attending Sunday School class, parents will have the opportunity to attend their own church," he said.
>
> Mrs. Jane B. Schulz will teach the special classes and the children currently enrolled in the program range from 7 to 13 years old…Mrs. Schulz will receive a bachelor of science degree from Auburn University in June…she has done practice teaching with exceptional children.

One of the reporters at the newspaper seemed to take a particular interest in the class and wrote several articles concerning its progress. What the newspaper could not report was the traumatic opening of the class. As you would expect, I had decorated the room with many pictures, books, and objects which would attract children. And then entered Danny.

Danny came to the class accompanied by his mother, who turned him over to me and left. He had a spoon in his hand and seemed to have characteristics of autism. I took him by the hand and led him into our classroom. He immediately pulled away from my hand, jumped onto the center table, pulled down his pants, and began to masturbate. I realized then why his mother had given him a spoon, which I immediately put into his hand as I lifted him off the table. Not exactly what I had expected for the first day.

Danny continued to be my greatest challenge and offered my most valuable learning experience. I was determined to get his eye contact, to no avail. One day by chance I hummed the song "Shenandoah" and he immediately looked me straight in the eyes. Thereafter when I wanted his attention, I hummed that song and he looked at me.

Several years later, when I was a graduate student in psychology, I was required to administer a number of IQ tests and chose to use Danny for one of the subjects. I had seen him reading the newspaper and knew that he was intelligent. As I administered, or attempted to administer the test, he repeatedly failed the questions, not responding at all. Finally he was as exhausted as I was, took the card I was holding from my hand, and looking at the bottom credit line, read in a clear voice, "Copyrighted by Charles Merrill Company, 1956" and handed it back to me. In talking with my professor about the test, I admitted a failed attempt, to which he replied, "This is probably your most successful test experience; you have learned that some children cannot be tested."

In that Sunday School class Billy assumed the role of class leader, helping me with materials and ensuring that each member had a place to sit and behaved properly. It was a class of characters, each contributing his or her unique talents. There was Carol who informed us that she was born in "Fran Sanfrisco," Bobbie who was in Billy's class at school, Mary Jane who had some interesting behaviors, Billy, and Danny.

A major event was our participation in the church Christmas program, also chronicled by our faithful reporter, Lisa Battle:

> The drums were coffee cans, the castanets were bells-and-paper plates, the maracas were light bulbs in papier-maché and the sound was not bad at all. The kids who played and the kids who listened loved it.

Staff Photo by Stan King

RHYTHM BAND AT ST. MATTHEW'S CHURCH WAS HIT AT PARTY
Children Made Own Instruments in Special Sunday School Class

The place was St. Matthew's Lutheran Church and the occasion was the annual Sunday School Christmas program. The rhythm players were exceptional children from a class taught by Mrs. Jane Schulz.

This week Mrs. Schulz told of the Christmas program and talked about the class which started last June and is believed to be the first such effort in the city.

At the program, the band kept time to a portion of Tshaikovsky's "Nutcracker Suite" delighting themselves and their audience "The children for the first time were a part of church activities," Mrs. Schulz said.

During the year, the children used their instruments, which they made themselves, to keep time to action songs and games put to music, the teacher said.

There has been just one problem, she said, laughing. "Everybody wants to direct. At Christmas we had to play the same record twice because there were two directors."

Making the instruments was an awesome task, one we couldn't have done without Tom and Mary. Frequently they missed their own classes, without complaining, to help. Ms. Battle's article omitted my favorite soundmaker: coconut shells, designed for Danny to use as percussion instruments. He learned to use them at appropriate times, cued by the start of the music. Although he had made progress, his behavior was still erratic and unpredictable and I was nervous about his performance before an entire congregation.

The night of the program, Danny was so agitated that I held him in my lap, wondering if we were doing the right thing. Was this an ego trip for me, or was it really about giving the children a worthwhile opportunity? Was I putting Danny in a situation that was so unfamiliar that it was frightening? (I frequently face this type of question when I put Billy in somewhat stressful situations.)

The other children gathered at the front of the church, the record player in place, Billy facing the group as band director. I still had Danny, quiet and trembling, in my lap, not knowing what he would do. The music began. Danny jumped down from my lap with his coconut shells, marched to the front of the church, and joined the group. He and the other children were wonderful! They all returned to their seats near me, beaming with pride. It was a moment to remember and to cherish.

Billy's idol was his brother Tom, who had been an acolyte in the church for some time. When Billy, at age 11, expressed his wish to be an acolyte too, Tom said, "Well, if you're going to do it, you're going to do it right."

They began their Saturday afternoon training sessions, with Tom a tough taskmaster. The Sunday finally came when Billy was to be the acolyte. Although Tom assisted with the offering plates, Billy handled the candles alone. Bill and I were a little nervous, but Billy was confident and calm. The next week he received a letter from the minister, stating, "This note comes to tell you again of how proud we are to have you serving in our Acolyte Guild. You did a very fine job Sunday and we want to thank you for helping make our worship service more meaningful."

Several times Billy's frustrations and lack of ability interfered with his intentions. At one time he wanted to sing in the choir. Neither of us is blessed with a fine singing voice, but at Billy's insistence, the choir director agreed to let him try. As I sat in the congregation the following Sunday I saw him becoming obsessed with his shoestring which had come untied; he fretted with it to the point of distracting the worshippers, and we all agreed that the choir could manage better without Billy. Similarly, when we had moved to North Carolina and were members of the Episcopal Church, Billy was supposed to sit near the minister after lighting the

candles as acolyte. He became frustrated because he couldn't find the appropriate pages in the hymnal and I could see him fuming, almost to the point of talking out loud. Thereafter we marked the pages before the service and things went more smoothly.

Depending on where we lived and the availability of our chosen church, we went from the Lutheran church (where Bill was raised) to the Episcopal church (where there was a minister whose daughter was a good friend of Mary's) to the Methodist church (as in my childhood), where we have belonged ever since. Billy has seemingly had no difficulty in adapting to the different services. He simply observes and does what everyone else is doing. In singing, praying, and following the service ritual, he remains slightly behind everyone else, receiving his cues as he hears. When we moved to Tennessee, he informed me that he needed a new Bible. I said, "But Billy, you have a nice Bible." With some impatience he insisted, "Mom, I need a Tennessee Bible."

I think his attitude and service have influenced many people in the church body. While his appearance surprised many members of our various congregations, they have accepted him as a contributing and valuable church member. One memorable comment came from a friend of mine whose niece brought her young son, newly diagnosed with Down syndrome, to church. When she saw Billy ushering, she was impressed and encouraged about her son's possibilities.

Sometimes I envy the purity and simplicity of Billy's faith and his morals. There are no shades of gray in his life; his beliefs are black and white. Things are either right or wrong.

One example of his trust touched me so deeply. The night before his esophagus dilation, I heard Billy talking in his bedroom, which is just below mine. I crept halfway down the stairs, not wanting to intrude but wanting to help if he was in a panic. I couldn't distinguish his words, but after he stopped speaking, I heard him singing in that sweet, wonderful voice, "Jesus loves me..." all the way through and at the end, "Amen." It was the sweetest thing I have ever heard. I crept back upstairs, crying from his spiritual beauty.

Billy's faith is simple, trusting, and complete. When asked to contribute a prayer to our Lenten Meditations book, he dictated the following:

> I like the choir an' the beautiful music.
> I like communion.
> I like my Sunday school class.
> Joe has good sermons.
> I love my church.
> God is good to me.
> *Amen*

This my store an I work there six years

ABOUT ONCE A WEEK we drove by the construction site of the new Food City. Billy got out of the car, looked around, and climbed back in. "See Mom, it's so big, it's gonna have a elevator an' everything."

When we came to Kingsport we thought Billy would work in a library. With his excellent reference letter in hand, we went to the city library and asked to see the head librarian. She informed us that the work Billy had done, putting security strips in the books and maga-

zines, was being done by volunteers; she was not interested in exploring other alternatives with us. I said to Billy, "There are lots of nursing homes here. Let's try one of them."

His immediate response was, "No, Mom, I not want to work in a nursing home." I didn't blame him; both of us had experienced enough sadness there. We gathered together his last psychological report and reference letters and went to the vocational rehabilitation office. He was referred to Goodwill Industries for evaluation and possible employment. From there Billy was assigned a job coach, went through an evaluation process, and was introduced to Food City.

Six years ago, the old store seemed big enough!

After a brief orientation and training in the proper way to bag groceries, Billy was on his own. He confided to me recently that he was scared: so many people, everyone busy, traffic in and out. I realized how different this would be for him, different from the protected atmosphere at the library, even the cloistered feeling at the nursing home. At a food store he would interact with people from all walks of life; he would be expected to perform in rush-hour traffic and in slower stretches of time. No wonder he was scared.

I had hoped that Billy could use public transportation for this job, but since we live outside the city limits the city bus did not serve us. I talked with taxi drivers, hoping to enlist a driver whom I could trust and who would be dependable. When this didn't work out, I realized that I would need to provide his transportation. Fortunately, the store is only about fifteen minutes from our house and often Jos gives Billy a ride on his way home from Eastman.

Shortly after Billy began his new job, Jos brought him home one evening. As soon as I opened the door I could tell from his hang-dog expression that something was wrong.

"What's wrong, Billy?"

"I got farred."

"You got fired?"

"Yes, Mom."

"What happened?"

"I said bad word to the customer."

Billy doesn't usually swear; he has a disdain for "bad words." I knew there was more to this episode than a rude comment. Later, as both of us calmed down, the scenario developed.

Picture the "I Love Lucy" episode in the candy factory, with chocolates zooming past Lucy on the assembly line. Apparently the groceries were coming at Billy so rapidly that he could not get them into the plastic bags quickly enough. In utter frustration, he stopped working, looked at the customer, and declared, "I tired of this shit."

Unable to reach the job coach, I attempted to contact the assistant manager who had fired Billy. He had left for the evening, so I made an appointment for the next morning with Ed Moore, the manager whom we would learn to admire and respect. After hearing the story, Ed fixed the problem with one sentence: "Billy, you can ask for help." The realization that he could ask the cashier to assist him and soon afterwards finding a friend in Jonathan made all the difference in Billy's attitude and performance.

In general, three groups of people work as baggers at Food City: people who have retired and work at part-time jobs, high-school students who work after school hours and during holidays, and people who have disabilities. Jonathan had worked at Food City for a number of years, adding other duties to his primary job as a bagger. He became Billy's informal coach, sharing tips ranging from, "Don't eat onions for lunch," to "Pitch in when someone else needs help." Although younger than Billy, Jonathan stepped up as a big brother to him. They frequently bring in buggies from the parking lot together, laughing and joking in the process. There is a camaraderie among the cashiers and baggers that I have never seen before. Over time, as Billy entered the store to begin work, I could hear greetings of "Hi, Billy!" and even from cashiers, "Hey, Billy, work with me today!"

In addition to friendships with the employees, Billy has developed relationships with some of the customers. A number of friends from our church also frequent the store, usually choosing to go through Billy's line. He is polite to the customers and careful in the way he bags the groceries. Occasionally, however, he has encountered a customer who did not return the courtesy. One evening as Billy and I were eating supper, he told me about such an event.

"Mom, a lady call me a bad name."

"What happened, Billy?"

"Well, I did NOT break the eggs. I put them in the bag very carefully."

"Did she think you broke them?"

"Yes, but I did not."

"What happened then?"

"She tole me to get out and call me a bad name."

"What did she call you?"

"I can't say it."

"You can tell me anything."

"She said damn."

"Then what happened?"

"I start to cry, tears run down here," pointing to his cheeks. "Sally tell me to go outside."

"Did you go outside?"

"Yes, and then come back. I not like that lady yell at me. Danny tole me forget it. But I not like it."

Most people are kind and appreciative. Now when we are at the mall, or other places, his customers recognize and greet Billy. Again, I am Billy's mom; he knows more people than I do. Recently we were at a restaurant where the waitress recognized Billy and praised his good work; she received a good tip.

Some of the action in this large, downtown store was totally foreign to Billy. He had a taste of the real world as revealed in a conversation with Mary:

"Today in my store, is fighting. Is a bad peoples. Said bad words. Alan is call the police. An' bad peoples in handcuffs. An' it's shoplifting. An' it scared me to…it scared me. And everybody got scared. An' I saw that fighting. With fists."

There were other events, such as a mother hitting her child, that were shocking to him. He was distressed that people could be so angry and mean.

As Billy developed skills and confidence plus knowledge of the contents of the store, his tendency to shop in excess emerged. The combination of a checkbook, a familiar store, and a fifteen-minute break created an outstanding opportunity to spend money. While I cautioned him about spending too much money, I also felt that he was entitled to use the money he earned. In addition to groceries, he purchased items for our home, such as laundry soap and toilet articles. On special occasions he brought candy or flowers to me and to Mary.

The shopping became problematic when Billy's supervisor phoned me that he was using extended break time to shop; this practice was not acceptable. He

and I had a long talk about the possibility of losing his job and we decided he could shop after work. Since he still wanted to do his shopping by himself, another problem occurred. He was spending more money than he had in the bank.

We had a big lesson (frequently repeated) about bank accounts and the necessity to have enough money in the bank to cover the checks he wrote. I pointed out that if his checks were returned to Food City, his job would be in jeopardy; this fact hit home. Although I had set up an account to cover any returned checks, he still got a notice from the bank when this happened. He began looking through the mail each day to see if there was a letter from the bank—several of these notices caused him to pay attention to his balance. Now he checks with me frequently to see how much money he has and is far more careful with his spending.

Understanding and counting money is still an elusive concept for Billy. He buys a drink, a snack, or both during his break and doesn't know how to count the amount he needs. He began writing $5.00 checks, which had to be cashed at the office each day. He admitted that he was embarrassed to have someone count it for him, so he began the practice of taking a five-dollar bill with him each day to buy his snack. Now, when he banks his check, he retains enough five-dollar

The following Associates NeeD to Be
At sStore 605 on sunDay NovemBer
4th at 2:00pm for a ManDay
Meeting IT iS Extremly Impotant
Ihat you AT you AttenD

bills to last for the week. It works; periodically we count and sort the change he has collected and exchange it for bills.

In addition to his checkbook, Billy carries his cell phone to work. It's not that he needs a cell phone, but that it is what other people have—his claim to normalcy. For the same reason, or at least partially, he wants a girlfriend. He was attracted to one of the cashiers, Sara, and came home one day saying that he had a date with her. Sara, a lovely girl, phoned me to say she wanted to take him to a movie. He was so excited. I drove him to the theater and dropped him off; Sara brought him home. She made it clear to him that it was a one-time event, but still he could say he had a date. Now he claims Billie, who works in the pharmacy, for his girlfriend. Billie is a beautiful, mature woman who hugs Billy when he comes to work and tells him that she is his girlfriend. There is no mention of a date, and it seems enough for him to be able to call her his girlfriend.

Last fall one of Billy's supervisors, Sue, was transferred to the Colonial Heights Food City. She indicated to me that she would like to have Billy join her. Since it would be far closer to our home, I suggested it to him and he said he would think about it. I put no pressure on him; I had him leave his friends once and didn't want to do that again. A few weeks after I mentioned it to him, he said, "Mom, I did think about it. I will transfer to Colonial Heights."

When I talked to Sue about Billy's decision she said the transfer would have to be initiated by Ed, Billy's boss. Billy and I made an appointment with Ed, stating Billy's request for a transfer. Ed was very nice but told Billy, "You would have to work nights, and you would miss your friends from this store and your friends from the church." In spite of his objections, I asked Ed to call the manager at the Colonial Heights store. Weeks went by and we didn't hear anything; Sue said she hadn't heard anything either. Finally Billy, at my request, asked Ed if he had called the other manager. Ed said, "No, Billy, I need you here until after Christmas." With that indication of need and appreciation, we gladly dropped the request.

Ironically, Billy did work at the Colonial Heights store for a few months. Last spring the announcement was made that the old store would be replaced with a larger, more comprehensive one. As plans for demolition were made, all employees were assigned to stores in the Food City chain according to their choices. Not one employee was dismissed. Billy is so fortunate to work in a store with that kind of management. When the employees from the old store came to Colonial Heights, the atmosphere was a little tense, because the store became overcrowded and busier than usual. Before long, however, I began to hear "Hi, Billy!" again.

Part of me had hoped that Billy would choose to stay at the Colonial Heights store, close to our home. However, when the grand opening arrived, there was no contest. Billy chose to work in the Kingsport store with Jonathan and his other friends. Now he points with pride to "my new store" and is again bagging groceries, pushing buggies, and greeting people with a big smile.

An I got a good life.

BILLY'S BIRTHDAYS have always been causes for celebration, but his 50th birthday was one to be remembered. It became a family reunion, with children, grandchildren, uncles, cousins and special friends; they came from Georgia, North Carolina, New York, Pennsylvania, Maryland, and even Japan. The major event was dinner at a Mexican restaurant, requested by Billy, followed by a Marilyn Monroe birthday cake designed by Mary and of course, a barrage of gifts. Lynn sat by

Billy, recording the presents; he exclaimed and hugged the giver as he opened each one. One gift brought tears to my eyes—a gold ring from his brothers and sister, inscribed "Wonderful Brother." More than a celebration of his birthday, this event was a celebration of Billy.

Billy and I have carried the theme of "celebrating differences" into our current presentations. Because of the visibility of Down syndrome, it provides a vehicle for discussing all diverse groups and exploring tolerance. One of our favorite opportunities is speaking to SHOUT (Students Helping Others Understand Tomorrow). A group of selected high-school students, SHOUT is sponsored by the Kingsport Chamber of Commerce, designed to inform future leaders of possibilities for service in the area. For several years, Billy and I have been asked to meet with the group on Diversity Day, one of the five categories in the program. One of the stated goals for this session is: "To initiate, foster, and promote an understanding and appreciation for all people and their unique perspectives and contributions to the world."

My thrust is the development of attitudes from tolerance to acceptance to celebration of diversity. Billy shows his slides, illustrating the normalcy of his life and the importance of his family. His real message, however, takes place during his interaction with the students during lunch and after the program. Initially reticent, they find that he is easy to talk with and fun to be around. Evaluations referred to it as "an eye-opening day," stating, "Billy was awesome; it was definitely an amazing experience." In planning their graduation ceremony, the students asked that Billy hand out their certificates. On the appropriate night Billy, dressed in suit and tie, shook hands and gave out certificates to all the students. At the end of the session, students write letters to thank the program leaders. One letter addressed to me read:

We were very privileged to have you speak to us on Diversity Day. Your presentation was a touching and heartwarming experience. Not only did you show us that you should not be ashamed of or try to hide your differences, but you urged everyone to CELEBRATE what makes them special. I think nearly everyone can agree with you that Billy has a way of teaching people that no one else is capable of. He has an extraordinary gift and that is something to celebrate. On behalf of everyone in the SHOUT program, thank you. We were blessed to have you!

It is a joyful opportunity to be involved with this group—future parents, professionals, and employers.

Another program that we have regularly participated in is the North Carolina Center for the Advancement of Teaching in Cullowhee, North Carolina. A center of the University of North Carolina, NCCAT was designed to attract and retain good teachers by offering seminars geared to their needs and interests. For a number of years I have participated in a seminar called "Finding My Place: Inclusive Classrooms." There are usually about thirty teachers from all over North Carolina who participate in this seminar which lasts for five days. Other presenters and I discuss with the teachers topics such as the nature of inclusion and strategies for implementing it. On one day of the week Mary drives Billy to the Center so he can do his presentation and interact with the teachers. He is always a highlight of the week and is particularly motivated by the opportunity to visit with his friends at the library.

It is such a privilege for me to work with teachers who are so concerned about their students and who are searching for ways to accommodate all students in their classrooms. This model allows us to interact during the days and evenings in a beautiful setting, providing informal discussions and activities. One teacher wrote a note to me indicating her appreciation:

> I'm taking home a new outlook on many issues. Thank you for being you and for sharing Billy.

These programs are examples of the progress we have made in the education and acceptance of children who have disabilities. Just as we—family, friends and acquaintances—have come to recognize Billy's unique character-

istics and to celebrate him, we celebrate the differences in all people. The increasing inclusion of people with disabilities into the mainstream of society makes that celebration possible for everyone.

I hope that, in sharing my stories and my life, people will realize that persons with disabilities can make huge contributions to their families and their communities. It is important that we give them opportunities to be givers as well as receivers and to value their efforts and their accomplishments.

I share with Billy the sentiment that "I got a good life." He refers to our present home life as "peace an' quiet" and is a happy man. We particularly enjoy our quiet mornings, when he comes upstairs, greets me, brings me a cup of coffee and joins me in watching our morning television show. Our favorite times are with family members who visit us and in celebrating family events.

Sometimes I feel as if I am at a picnic when rain has been predicted. I don't know how long the picnic will last, but I plan to enjoy every minute of it. However, like all parents who have children with disabilities, I am wary of the future.

Long ago, I used to wish that Billy would precede me in death, but I don't feel that way anymore. I hope he will enjoy his "good life" for a long time. When I first raised the question of my death, I said to him, "You know, Billy, I will probably die before you do." Quick as a flash, he asked "Can I have your car?"

Since that time, Billy has experienced the death of his father and of his grandmother. I know that he thinks of them. Recently we were at Wal-Mart, where all the Halloween costumes were displayed. Billy commented, "That 'minds me of my dad." I didn't get that until he explained how his dad hated all the Halloween decorations at his nursing home. One Sunday as we were driving home from church, Billy said, "That was Memi's favorite song."

"What song was that?"

"You know, Gladanit."

"Hmm, oh, you mean, 'Rejoice and be glad in it.'"

"Thas what I said, Gladanit."

Still, when I talk about the eventuality of my death, he exclaims, "Don't talk 'bout dying, Mom. I not like to talk 'bout it."

But we must.

In Chapter 10 of this book, a reference was made to Dan Boyd's three stages of acceptance of a child who has mental retardation. On this, the other end of the continuum, I have defined three stages of letting go.

Stage One. I acknowledge that I am not the only person who can provide Billy with the services and support that he needs. Although my entire family and many others have helped raise Billy and give him the self-esteem that he has, I am the one responsible for him in his adult life. I have been the one to advocate for him, to secure services for him and, yes, to push him to become a productive, secure man. When I am no longer in the position to assist him, there are other people who can and will step in.

Stage Two. I have made every effort to ensure that if a transition must take place, there are options available for Billy's welfare and security. When he was placed on the Division of Mental Retardation Services waiting list, he was assigned a case manager—a person who would advise us of Billy's available services and of additional services that might be needed in the future

Billy's case manager has met with us in our home periodically and has provided us with a great deal of information. She gave us *The Family Handbook*, which describes the services provided by the Division and other agencies. The last time the case manager met with us, I asked Mary and Billy to join us. At this point, our questions revolved around options for residential living, chiefly supported living. With this provision we could picture Billy living in an apartment with assistance in daily living skills. There are other options depending on the skill level of the individual with mental retardation. Our next step is to visit some of the apartments; Billy is eager to do that. Although he doesn't like to discuss the possibility of my death, he was excited about the prospect of being on his own. Our case manager has a tremendous load, but she is always willing to spend as much time with us as we need, and to either answer our questions or refer us to other sources.

There are other options available for semi-independent living. The children and I have talked about the possibility of Billy's staying here in our home, with someone to share the space or someone to oversee his living alone, providing transportation and other needs. This might work as a transition measure until other situations would be available.

In addressing Billy's financial situation, we have made several provisions. I understand that if he were to inherit anything from my estate, his government benefits would be at risk. Therefore, in making my will, I omitted his name as a beneficiary. While this seems heartless, it protects him from losing Social Security Disability benefits and Medicare or Medicaid. In order to provide for his needs beyond those entitlements at my death, we have established a Special Needs Trust. With Mary as trustee, distributions from this trust could be used for specific purposes without jeopardizing his entitlement to receive governmental assistance.

Stage Three. This is my faith journey. Today I heard that faith is more like courage than belief. I pray for the faith, the courage, to relinquish my responsibility when the time comes. In writing this memoir, I clearly see the pattern of my life—the plan that God had for me: the sequence of events that sent me to college, to my career, to this place in my life. Billy has been in the center of this plan, and the plan is still at work.

Billy's brothers and Jos will be there for Billy in any way possible, and Mary has agreed to succeed me as his caregiver, his adviser, his advocate. I know that she will always act in his best interest; I trust her completely. I have done my best; I am ready to let go. *But not quite yet!*

Billy has his own plan.

During a recent visit from Tom, he, Billy and I were sitting on the front porch. Billy had brought his *Dr. Who* books to show Tom; they got into one of their fourth-dimensional, time-travel conversations. Tom asked, "Billy, where do you think Dad is?"

"Heaven."

"And where do you think you will go?"

"I go with my Mom."

❋

Acknowledgments

FREQUENTLY, PEOPLE TELL ME, "You have done a wonderful job in raising Billy." I hasten to tell them that Billy's development into such a fine man has resulted from the influence of a host of people. In addition to his loving and supportive family, we have had encouragement and affirmation from teachers, friends, employers, and sometimes from strangers who interact with him. I am deeply grateful to all the sensitive people who have contributed to his growth and to mine.

In writing this book I have also relied on input from family members and from friends. I appreciate those who have read the pre-publication copy and have made sensitive and validating suggestions and comments. They include Lisa Bloom, Embry Burrus, Beth Calvert, Gurney Chambers, Jos de Wit, Michael Dougherty, Michelle Estes, Beverly Jackson, Ann Overton, David Shapiro, Ann Turnbull, Nan Watkins, and David Westling. Thank you for your time and for your insight. I am also grateful to my editor, Betsy White, for her in-depth and enthusiastic appraisal of my work.

My children have made this book possible. John, while writing his own book, carefully read each of my chapters, provided immediate feedback, and explored publication issues for me. Tom gave me early and valuable advice, urged me to include my "gravel roads" and made succinct comments all along the way. Mary brought her dynamic writing, editing, and design skills to the task of bringing my mission to the public.

Billy was the inspiration for the book, my teaching, and much of my life.

1. Given Billy's distinctive characteristics, why was his diagnosis of Down syndrome delayed until he was 18 months old? What impact did the late diagnosis have on the family? On Billy?

2. The presence of a child with a disability changes the dynamics of a family. How did Billy's siblings react to his birth and early childhood? How did their relationships change as they became older? What effect did he have on their development?

3. In describing her birth family, the author reveals the relationships she had with her parents. How did each of these relationships affect her later decisions, e.g. marriage and career choices?

4. The author writes about traumatic events occurring in her childhood. How do these types of events affect the way we learn to deal with people?

5. What were the warning signs that trouble was brewing in the relationship of Jane and Bill? If this marriage took place today instead of in the 1940s, how would societal changes influence the way Jane and Bill might have dealt with problems?

6. Many mothers work outside the home today. How do parents balance the desire to raise their children themselves and to provide for them financially?

7. The author states that she loved teaching kindergarten. Was her decision to leave that position and go to college a good choice for the family? For her?

8. The decision to remove Billy from the special school and to enter him into an all black school was in variance with the norm at the time. How does personal need relate to societal change? How would you have responded to the teacher's asking, "Would you give me permission to spank Billy if he needs it?"

9. The move to the mountains appeared to draw the family together. What went wrong? Why was Jane surprised to discover their financial situation? How could she have avoided it? Could she have been more supportive of Bill?

10. Bill is the tragic figure in the story. What factors influenced Jane's decision to stay in the marriage?

11. How did Billy's role in the family change as he became an adult?

12. What role did Jane's mother play in her adult life? How could this have been a more positive relationship?

13. What coping strategies did Jane develop during her life? Do you have strategies of your own creation, or that you have adapted from others?

14. Can you relate to the frustration and exhaustion that Jane experienced as a care-giver? How do you cope with your responsibilities?

15. Is the struggle for inclusion of Billy in the mainstream of life worth the effort and anxiety his family encounters? Could they have followed a simpler path? What choices are acceptable and available in our society now? How are these choices changed in relationship to the severity of a family member's disability and the resources of the family?

16. You may be a family member of a person with a disability or someone to whom this is an unknown experience. Given your situation, how did you react to this book?

17. It is now recommended by professional organizations representing obstetricians and gynecologists in the United States and Canada that all pregnant women be offered prenatal screening for Down syndrome. When Down syndrome is diag-nosed prenatally, about 90 percent of the time the pregnancies are terminated. After reading this book, has your view about making this choice changed in either direction?